T0365219

Geoffrey Tristram

A VERY BRITISH ORGANIST

"I am He"

David Baker

authorHOUSE

AuthorHouse™ UK
1663 Liberty Drive
Bloomington, IN 47403 USA
www.authorhouse.co.uk
Phone: UK TFN: 0800 0148641 (Toll Free inside the UK)
*   UK Local: (02) 0369 56322 (+44 20 3695 6322 from outside the UK)*

© 2022 David Baker. All rights reserved.

No part of this book may be reproduced, stored in a retrieval system, or transmitted by any means without the written permission of the author.

Published by AuthorHouse 07/08/2022

ISBN: 978-1-6655-9982-5 (sc)
ISBN: 978-1-7283-7419-2 (hc)
ISBN: 978-1-6655-9981-8 (e)

Print information available on the last page.

Any people depicted in stock imagery provided by Getty Images are models, and such images are being used for illustrative purposes only.
Certain stock imagery © Getty Images.

This book is printed on acid-free paper.

Because of the dynamic nature of the Internet, any web addresses or links contained in this book may have changed since publication and may no longer be valid. The views expressed in this work are solely those of the author and do not necessarily reflect the views of the publisher, and the publisher hereby disclaims any responsibility for them.

This work is dedicated to Geoffrey Oliver Tristram, 1917-1979,
Organist and Master of the Choristers, Christchurch Priory, 1949-1979,
and William Baker, 1916-1973, the author's father.

Michael and Carolyn Tristram would also like
to dedicate this book to their Mum,
Rene Tristram (1922-1994),
without whom GOT would never have achieved
all the wondrous things that he did.
Despite a debilitating illness (Parkinson's disease -
eventually diagnosed in about 1975),
she kept strong for him and us and kept the cogs
and the heart of 'Church Hatch' ticking,
especially in the kitchen!

Note

Profits from the sale of this book will go appropriately in support of
the music and choir at Christchurch Priory, with particular emphasis on
supporting those talented members of the Priory's music community with
lessons which they otherwise would be unable to afford.

CONTENTS

Foreword.. xi

Preface xiii

Acknowledgements...xvii

A Note on the Sources for the Biography.............................xxi

List of Illustrations xxiii

About the Author..xxvii

1. **Early Life and Career**... 1

   Forebears and Early Life in Stourbridge 1

   Move to Reading and Reading School 4

   Studying the Organ, RCO Examinations, Thalben-Ball, and
   Cunningham 6

   Early Career and Marriage.. 14

2. **Move to the South Coast** 25

   All Saints' Church... 25

   Teacher 30

      Southbourne High School 30

      Ringwood Grammar School...................................... 32

      Poole Grammar School and Twynham County
      Secondary School.. 33

      St Peter's School, Bournemouth 39

   Bournemouth Gilbert and Sullivan Society....................... 52

3. **Organist and Master of the Choristers, Christchurch Priory**.... 55

   Application, Appointment, Initial Strategy....................... 55

   Developing the Music...61

   'The Best Parish Church Choir in England'....................... 65

Workload 68

'Magnificent Acts of Worship' 70

Maintaining High Standards and Celebrating Success as Mr.
Music 76

Reminiscences, Anecdotes and More 84

4. The Priory Organ 117

The Instrument in 1949 117

The Compton Rebuild of 1951 120

Rushworth & Dreaper, Degens & Rippin, and the 'Nave'
division 124

Compton becomes Compton Makin, then Nicholson 130

5. Recitalist 139

First Love of a 'Magnificent Organist' 139

A National Reputation 139

Broadcasts and Recordings 143

Technique and Performance 'Twitches' 145

Repertoire 147

Other Performers and the Summer Recital Series 149

Tributes 152

6. Life at 'Church Hatch' 155

An 'Elegant Mansion' as House and Home 155

Family and Visitors from Far and Wide 158

Railways and Other Enthusiasms 164

Michael and Carolyn Remember 169

End Note Geoffrey Tristram: a very British Organist 181

Death and Funeral 181

Tributes 183

Memorials 186

Legacy 189

Appendices

A: GOT's application for the post at Christchurch 195

B: Specification of the Organ at Christchurch Priory prior to
the 1951 Rebuild.. 201

C: Specification of the Organ at Christchurch Priory after the
1951 Rebuild, with additions to 1968... 203

D: Specification of the Compton Organ at St Peter's School,
Bournemouth... 207

E: Specification of the Makin Organ at Christchurch Priory............211

F: List of Recitals given by GOT, compiled from surviving
programmes..215

G: Sample List of Visiting Recitalists' Programmes (1963-1979) 277

H: Analysis of GOT'S Collection of Recital Programmes by
G.D. Cunningham 315

I: List of Broadcasts by Geoffrey Tristram on the BBC
according to BBC Genome Website; compiled by Michael
Tristram 329

J: Discography.. 337

K: List of pieces on the CD or SoundCloud Compiled by
Michael Tristram 339

Index.. 343

FOREWORD

I feel very honoured to be writing a few words as a Foreword to this biography of my old friend Geoffrey Tristram. As a musician he had all the attributes of the old-fashioned versatile all-rounder as he maintained the choir and music at Christchurch Priory at a very high level and I recall his choir's periodic broadcasts of Choral Evensong for the BBC as being first class. Like many another organist of his generation he taught in a school to earn his daily bread but managed to maintain his organ playing at the very highest professional level and became one of the outstanding recitalists of his generation. He was also a splendid fellow who was great company and a very good friend. For some years I was on his list of summer recitalists at the Priory and my wife and I always thoroughly enjoyed staying with him and his family at Church Hatch where we were made very welcome indeed. They were great days to which my wife and I look back with very great affection.

Dr Roy Massey, MBE

PREFACE

Back in the 1960s, my parents and I always had our summer holidays in Bournemouth. There was a fantastic series of Wednesday evening organ recitals at Christchurch Priory. My father and I (among many others) would enjoy the (silent) trolley bus journey from Bournemouth to go and hear the great Geoffrey Tristram, or some other giant of the profession. Tristram himself was a brilliant player: how I longed to be like him! What a role model! What a giant! Even his name sounded heroic!

At the end of each recital – which always included some of the most difficult parts of the organ repertoire – audience members (including my father and me) would cluster round the strange 'cage' or 'chantry chapel' on the north side of the nave that enclosed the organ console. Having waited expectantly for several minutes, a tall handsome man, casually dressed in sports jacket, trousers, and cricket sweater would appear, to be mobbed by the admiring crowd. That must be the great Geoffrey Tristram! As we walked away with the recitalist's other admirers, my father and I would always notice a short, stocky, balding man emerge and lock the door to the chantry chapel and then disappear. We decided that this must be the page turner.

Before our annual holiday in Bournemouth, I would write (enclosing a stamped addressed envelope, of course) each year to organists in the area, asking if I could 'have a go' on their instruments when we were next on vacation. I became confident enough as a player to write to the great Geoffrey Tristram himself, never expecting him to reply. Remarkably, he did, and gave me a date and time to report to his fine Georgian house near the Priory. I could not wait until the great day arrived. My father and I stood at the entrance to 'Church Hatch'. The Priory clock struck the appointed hour. I pressed the bell. The door opened. The short, stocky, balding man stood there.

'We have an appointment to see Geoffrey Tristram. Is he available?' my father said.

'I am he', came the modest, self-effacing reply.

The page turner was no such thing; rather he was the brilliant recitalist that I had longed to meet. It was the handsome, cricket-sweater-wearing man who turned out to be the page turner![1] I was taken into the Priory and allowed two hours on the instrument. Geoffrey Tristram returned at the end of the evening, just as I was finishing Bach's well-known Toccata and Fugue in D minor. As I came to the final chords, my great hero leaned over and added the Tubas! He then said, 'have you heard of The Sound of Music?' I looked at my father, who shrugged. I said that I had. 'Well,' he continued, 'you'll be sick of the sound of music by the time you have finished!' Geoffrey Tristram then laughed and walked us out of the Priory. We parted company at 'Church Hatch'. He wished me well in my future career. I walked on air for the rest of the holiday. My father and I would chuckle periodically at our wrong assumption as to who was the player and who the page turner!

That would have been the end of the story, were it not for the fact that I published a short reminiscence on my Halifax Organ Academy website as part of a longer piece called Deceptive Appearances. The blog talked about how performers look is not always the way they perform. I thought nothing more of the post until I was contacted by Carolyn Tristram, Geoffrey's daughter, who had seen the reminiscence. She also introduced me to Michael, her brother. Thus began an enriching relationship that led to an article in Organists' Review, a new edition of his beautiful Mass in A flat, a reissue of some of his magnificent organ recordings, and this book.

I feel immensely proud and privileged to have been allowed to write this biography of Geoffrey Tristram. That he was a profound influence on me – and so many others – is something of an understatement. The least I could do was to capture his life and achievements for future generations while still possible to engage with many who knew and were inspired by him and his music.

Professor David Baker
Mytholmroyd, West Yorkshire,
June 2022

---

[1] Don Gittins (1923-2014), a clerk at the local Lloyds Bank for much of his working life, not wanting or needing promotion because it would take him away from Christchurch and the Priory, as Michael Tristram recounts.

William Baker (1916-1973) was born in Bradford, West Yorkshire, the year before Geoffrey Tristram. He died suddenly of a heart attack, aged 57. He served in the King's Own Yorkshire Light Infantry in World War II. His first career was as a sign writer, but in 1948 set up Binbak Models with his friend and colleague Jack Binns. They went on to be famed for the supply of high-quality toys, including a scale model of Windsor Castle for the Royal Family. He was a lifelong enthusiast for church and choral music, and a fine bass singer.

ACKNOWLEDGEMENTS

My thanks must go to the many people who assisted in the compilation of this book, without whom it would not have been written. First and foremost, I am grateful to Carolyn and Michael, Geoffrey Tristram's daughter and son, who provided reminiscences, material, contacts, and much else, along with their blessings on the project and innumerable valued suggestions as to how the biography should be put together.

Dr Roy Massey, MBE, has provided not only his memories of Geoffrey Tristram, but also the excellent foreword to this book. To him go my thanks.

I am grateful to Sarah Beedle, former Editor of Organists' Review, who published my 'letter to the editor' (as did local newspapers in the Christchurch area) which elicited much material. Sarah then published an article by me about Geoffrey Tristram's life and work.[2]

Much of the research work for this book, along with the new edition of the Mass in A flat and the SoundCloud folder, was carried out by Ted O'Hare, one of my advanced organ students. He was assisted by another advanced student, Dr Rebekah Okpoti.

Special thanks go to Richard Hands for his research into his Father's extensive negative catalogues and for remastering those many pre 1950s photos so happily chosen to be included in this book.

To all those who provided written or verbal reminiscences (or both) and sent me material for possible inclusion in the book, my heartfelt thanks. Their names are listed below.

Brother Bernard FSC (St Peter's School)

Jeremy Blandford

John Broad

Ken Brown - Archivist of Reading School

---

2   Baker, David, 'Geoffrey Tristram'. *Organists' Review*, September 2021, pp.33–7.

Daniel Campbell

Marian Chapman (Geoffrey Tristram's sister-in-law)

Christchurch History Society (and especially Janet Burn and John Ward)

John Coffin

Columba Cook

David Cordell

Andy Denison

Fred Dinenage

Joe Gallagher

Christine Gerveshi

Richard Hands

Geoffrey Howell

Clifford Jones (Christ's Hospital)

Nicolas Kynaston

Kevin Lawton-Barrett

Dr Simon Lindley

Nick Lipscombe

Geoffrey Morgan

Gillian Morgan

Natula Publications[3]

Tim Norris

[3] The author and the Tristram family have made every effort to contact any copyright holders of the archival material used in this publication attempting to gain permissions and acknowledge that Natula Publications has granted permission for the photos and quotations from Peter Jones's work to be used in the present publication. The author and Tristram family will happily acknowledge any copyright in subsequent editions of this book if requested.

Ray O'Luby

Ian Orbell

Oxford Duplicating Service

Terry Powell

Priory Archivist

The Very Reverend David Shearlock, Dean Emeritus of Truro [Assistant Curate of Christchurch Priory, 1960-64]

Rayner Skeet

Reverend Canon Peter Strange

Oliver Tristram-Bishop (GOT's grandson)

Jonathan Wearn

Pam Willetts (Geoffrey Tristram's cousin)

Dennis Robert Wright

Pamela Young (neè Pantlin)

A NOTE ON THE SOURCES
FOR THE BIOGRAPHY

Much of the material for this book has come from Irene Tristram's scrapbooks of press cuttings, recital programmes, orders of services, correspondence, and other related primary sources. This has been sorted, de-duplicated and tabulated. The period 1948-67 is well covered in terms of performances; not all programmes are available thereafter, but there is enough to give a clear indication of GOT's repertoire and range of venues during his life. Similarly, the programmes of visiting recitalists at the Priory for 1963 – 1979 are complete enough to give a good picture of the repertoire that was being played during the second fifteen years of GOT's tenure of office. Correspondence is similarly more comprehensive in the early years than from the 1960s onwards. Quotations from this material – and from the many interviews carried out during the research – has been only minimally edited, as indicated. Much personal information is taken from a handwritten talk that GOT gave in the mid-1970s to a local women's group. This is referred to as 'GOT speech' in the references.

LIST OF ILLUSTRATIONS

Publicity portrait of Geoffrey Tristram .... Front Cover

William Baker xv

Professor David Baker xxviii

Baby Geoffrey, with parents Oliver and Elsie Tristram xxix

Cotton weaver's shuttle 1

A dapper young Geoffrey Tristram 2

GOT on the Compton Organ at Stourbridge's local Odeon Cinema 3

A Teenage Geoffrey Tristram 5

GOT graffito, 1934 5

ARCO Results 9

FRCO Results 12

GOT proudly wearing his FRCO hood and gown 13

First page of Articles of Agreement 15

GOT at the console of the organ of St Mary's, Reading 16

GOT and friend on the tower roof, St Mary's, Reading 19

GOT and lifelong friend Gordon Hands 20

GOT and Irene (Rene) Wellstead 20

Wedding Day, 30 March 1948, Christ Church, Reading 21

GOT, rarely without a cigarette, by the Thames 23

Undated, handwritten letter of commendation for GOT from
G.D. Cunningham 26

Reference for GOT from Rural Dean Reverend Anthony
Williams, 21 May 1949 28

Rare photograph of GOT relaxing on holiday, late 1940s? 29

Letter from the Headmaster, Ringwood Grammar School, 27
October 1948 31

Letter dated 21 June 1957 from Kenneth Savidge, Head of
Religious Broadcasting, B.B.C. Western Region 36

Letter of Appointment dated 9 August 1957 38

St Peter's School Production of The Mikado in the early 1960s.......... 39

GOT as judge on a competition.. 45

Press cutting about GOT's production of Oliver! at St Peter's in
July 1971.. 48

GOT and Rene at a Bournemouth G & S Society dinner, along
with Don Gittins and his wife Barbara 54

First page of GOT's application for the post of Organist and
Choirmaster, Christchurch Priory...................................... 58

Priory choirboys rehearsing for a Christmas Carol Service............61

Letter of Recommendation for GOT from the Vicar, Canon
R.P. Price, 15 January 1951 65

Congratulatory letter from Jimmy Taylor.............................. 66

Letter of recommendation from Reverend Canon Robin Price,
22 October 1958... 69

Photograph of the Priory Choir, 1960/61.............................. 70

Letter of appreciation from Douglas Fox, 18 January 1968............. 71

BBC flyer advertising 'Songs of Praise' from Christchurch
Priory, recorded 3 October 1967.......................................74

Priory choristers' cartoon about pay 77

Priory Choir recital programme, 29 September 1976................... 78

Various greetings to GOT from the Gentlemen of the Choir 81

Christchurch Priory Choir, 1973...................................... 98

Mass in A Flat.. 99

The Priory Organ in the South Transept circa 1910 118

The Priory Organ Console, circa 1910 119

Front page of the organ-builder's leaflet describing the 1951 rebuild...121

The 1951 Console 123

The Priory Choir and Sanctuary, showing the 'Chantry Chapel',
'Cage', or 'Barbershop Poles' housing the console on the left
(north) side of the choir stalls 124

The 'Plumber's Backyard': Christchurch Priory Pipe Organ as it
looked from 1951 to 1999 129

Makin's leaflet describing the 1973 Organ 134

The Nave console of the 1999 Organ 136

Pictures of the 1999 rebuild by Nicholson of Worcester:
mechanical action console, pipework detail and case (finally!),
taken by Oliver Tristram-Bishop, GOT's grandson 138

Reading Festival 141

Screenshots of one of GOT's (black and white) broadcasts from
the Priory 144

GOT's Recordings (see Discography for details) 145

GOT at the Makin Organ shortly after its installation 149

Raymond Mosley (violin), accompanied by GOT on the Makin
Organ 150

Royal Festival Hall 16 February 1964 151

GOT at the Royal Festival Hall Organ 152

GOT's York Minster Recital Programme, 12 August 1978 153

Christchurch Priory 156

Two Pictures of 'Church Hatch' 157

The young Tristram family in the 'snug' 158

GOT, assisted by Sue (from Iran) hosting one of many 'Church
Hatch' parties 161

GOT and family with a group of foreign students 162

GOT and family in the back garden at 'Church Hatch' 163

Picnic with relatives from Reading, late 1950s 164

The Beeson 'Duchess' 165

The Britannia, made (with help) by GOT 166

GOT and Gordon Hands were regular visitors around steam
engine sheds in the days before Health & Safety! 167

On the beach with Rene, Kay Hands (Gordon's wife) and their
son Richard, 1949 167

One of GOT's Rovers 168

'WOO' – the family mini 169

Rene, with golden retriever Patsy 175

Swiss N Gauge Landscape Railway – a 60th birthday present for
GOT. 178

GOT playing the Makin organ, with Carolyn as page turner............179

First page of a letter to Carolyn Tristram, 29 August 1965............... 180

GOT and Rene at Glyndebourne just weeks before he collapsed
and died...181

Details of the Geoffrey Tristram Memorial Prize
at Reading School 188

Memorial Plaque, 1981...191

GOT at the Makin Organ 191

ABOUT THE AUTHOR

Professor David Baker

David Baker was born in Bradford, West Yorkshire, in 1952. After several library posts at Nottingham, Leicester, and Hull Universities, he became Chief Librarian of the University of East Anglia, Norwich, in 1985. He was promoted to Director of Information Strategy and Services in 1995, and Pro-Vice-Chancellor in 1997. He was Principal and Chief Executive of Plymouth Marjon University 2003-2009 (where he holds an Emeritus Professorship) and Deputy Chair of JISC 2007-2012. He has written widely in the field of library and information management with 20 monographs and over 100 articles to his credit, alongside international consultancy work, training and development, and conference presentation over thirty years.

David's first love was the church organ, which he began playing at the age of 12. By the time he was 16, he was an Associate of the Royal College of Organists. He gained his Fellowship the following year. In 1970 he was elected Organ Scholar of Sidney Sussex College, Cambridge, graduating with a First-Class Honours degree in Music three years' later. He took an MMus degree from King's College, London in 1974. He has remained active as musician and musicologist, with the first edition of his book The Organ (Shire Publications, 1991) selling over 10,000 copies. A second edition was published in 2003 and a second revised edition in 2010.

He has undertaken recital tours to Germany, Italy, and Scandinavia and when organist of Wymondham Abbey, Norfolk, performed the entire organ works of J S Bach in 26 recitals. He still performs regularly as recitalist and accompanist. He is a regular writer and reviewer of organ and choral music and recordings (especially for Organists' Review) and was Deputy Editor and then Editor (until December 2008) of The Organ magazine and has twice edited the Journal of the British Institute of Organ Studies. David is Chair of the Board of Directors of the Institute for Contemporary Music Performance.

He now focuses on teaching the organ and in 2011 he founded the Halifax Organ Academy, which aims to offer high quality tuition and support to organists of all ages and backgrounds within West Yorkshire. He is also an accredited tutor for the Royal College of Organists.

David is writing a book (having already published several articles and papers) on the great Victorian Organist and Choirmaster, John Varley Roberts, whose organ music he has now edited and published, alongside that of Roberts's 18th century predecessor, William Herschel. His interest in Herschel and Roberts began many years ago when he undertook research for his undergraduate dissertation at Cambridge, his topic being the music of Halifax Parish Church in the 18th and 19th centuries.

David also writes fiction for fun, with an interest in detective stories and late Roman Britain. His latest novel, set in Victorian Yorkshire, is The Organ Loft Murders. He also tries his hand at poetry from time to time.

David Baker

Baby Geoffrey, born 2 August 1917, with parents Oliver and Elsie Tristram

CHAPTER ONE

Early Life and Career

Forebears and Early Life in Stourbridge

Geoffrey Oliver Tristram (GOT for short) was born in Stourbridge, Worcestershire, on 2 August 1917, the only child of Oliver and Elsie Tristram. He supposed that he was 'cut out to be a musician', for when only a few months old, he 'used to play on the linoleum'.[4] Research shows that his Tristram forbears were in Sefton, Lancashire in the 1570s. GOT's great, great, great grandfather Thomas was born in Salford, near Manchester, in 1792, his parents William and Margaret having moved from Sefton, Lancashire, to work in the mills there. The family still possesses a 'shuttle' from the days when Tristrams worked in the mills.

Cotton weaver's shuttle used by GOT's forbears in the Lancashire mill. Known as the 'Flying Shuttle' but nicknamed the 'bullet' as it flew across the loom at great speed and had iron tips on either end to stop the wood from splitting. When the weavers replaced the cotton 'reel', they had to thread the end through a tiny hole at the top - just like threading a needle. The only way to get the end through was by sucking it; this was known as 'kissing the shuttle'. Sadly, by doing this, as well as breathing in the fine cotton fibres in the mill, tuberculosis was a very common illness and a deadly one at that.

---

[4] GOT speech.

GOT's great, great grandfather, also called Thomas, was born in Salford in 1819. By the time of the 1851 Census, Thomas had married Jane Dodd (born in Ireland) and moved to Derby, working there as a power loom weaver.[5] James Tristram (GOT's great grandfather, 1843-1881) initially worked as a cotton weaver but, towards the end of his life, became the landlord of the Noah's Ark public house in Derby. James's son, and GOT's grandfather, Oliver Tristram (1864-1949) became a master tailor, living in Hove, West Sussex. GOT's father, also called Oliver (1885-1959) became a banker after serving as a Private in the Royal Marine Light Infantry Regiment.

A dapper young Geoffrey Tristram

GOT was proud of being born on the edge of the Black Country. It was 'his everlasting delight to be in Worcestershire – about 100 yards inside Worcestershire on the Worcestershire - Staffordshire border' and was always glad to have any excuse to go back to the Midlands. He remembered 'the old women in their widows' weeds with their shawls and bonnets, sitting on the doorsteps of their cottages smoking their clay pipes [and]

---

[5]   Information provided by Carolyn Tristram from her research into the Tristram family through census records.

watching their children in rags and tatters playing in the streets ... the furnaces of the steel works lighting up the night skies with their lurid glow, the steel workers clad in their moleskin trousers – no shirts, sweat rags round their necks, drinking cold tea and pouring off this white hot liquid into ingots of many tons in weight, and eventually, after it had become more solid, pushing and prodding it by means of huge calipers through the many processes of the rolling mills where one false move or a slip, could mean certain death'.[6]

He later commented that the place of his birth and early years was much changed when he went back: 'it is different now, so many of the endless rows of slum property and ribbon development, dating back to the times of the Industrial Revolution, have been bulldozed down and high-rise flats have taken their place ... I would be sorry to see the end of the Black Country customs; the only thing I have lost is my Midlands accent, but [I] can soon fall into it again – it comes naturally to me'.[7]

GOT would return to Stourbridge periodically as a teenager, sometimes playing the two-manual, ten-rank Compton organ in the local Odeon Cinema. One of GOT's cousins, Mrs Pam Willetts, well remembers him playing between the films with all the popular tunes of the day such as Nelson Eddy's Sweethearts'.

GOT on the Compton Organ at Stourbridge's local Odeon Cinema

---

6 GOT speech.

7 GOT speech

Move to Reading and Reading School

GOT did not 'play in the streets … like all the other little boys and girls of the Black Country' because, in 1925, when he was eight years old, the family moved to 52, Highmoor Road, Caversham, Reading. He had already 'started music under Miss Burford of Alexandra House, Stourbridge' aged seven, and had passed two Trinity College examinations, in each case with honours, by the age of nine. That year, it was said his ambitions were changed when he heard the four-manual Willis organ in Reading Town Hall.[8] He had perfect pitch.

GOT was educated at Reading School from 1926 to 1934. He studied music, learning violin and viola with Miss A.G. Pantling, L.R.A.M., as well as piano and theory with Dr E.O. Daughtry (1877-1943), Music Master there. The school was not much to his liking. He recalled in later life: 'the problem [was that] I hated school; the school masters were monsters; it was not so much education rather intimidation. School days were the longest of my life'. GOT was made to play percussion in the local orchestra. 'Counting bars and rests … affected [his] concert going [making him] break out in a cold sweat every time the orchestra comes onto the platform [ever since]'.[9] Daughtry was 'a martinet', though an early recital programme at St Mary's, Reading, has GOT playing a piece by Daughtry, 'Jesu Thou Joy'. Daughtry held Doctorates in Music from both Trinity College, Dublin, and Cambridge University, where he had been Assistant Organist at King's College and house master at the Leys School. He was also Organist at St Mary's, Reading, a Lecturer at Reading University, and Conductor of the Berkshire Symphony Orchestra.[10]

---

[8] Newspaper cutting, dated 1971, from a Reading newspaper, reviewing a recital given by GOT on the Town Hall organ as part of the Reading Festival of that year.

[9] GOT speech.

[10] Information taken from Daughtry's entry in Biographical Dictionary of the Organ | Dr Edmund Osmund Daughtry (organ-biography.info).

A Teenage Geoffrey Tristram

GOT graffito, 1934

GOT was involved in occasional mischief: on one occasion, he and lifelong friend Gordon Hands were charged with pumping the school organ's bellows and amused themselves by planting stink bombs, 'secretly concocted in the school chemistry lab'. The effects permeated the entire hall and 'kicked up quite a stink in all ways'.[11] GOT's graffito on a pipe in the school organ also survives, along with similar markings by Douglas Guest, late Organist and Master of the Choristers at Westminster Cathedral, and Gordon Hands.[12] Hands, a lifelong friend of GOT, played for boarders' services for many years. 'His running repairs on the organ during sermon time were a regular feature'.[13] GOT is reputed to have said that of all the organs he had played, the one in the school chapel was by far the worst.[14] While at Reading School he composed and orchestrated a march for the annual concert. The composition was played by the school orchestra and GOT conducted the performance himself. Dr Daughtry was known to GOT and his fellow pupils as 'Draughty'. Students would sing off key to avoid being in the music master's choir in big school; Daughtry's response to this was to say: 'you are so bad, boy, you will go into the choir and learn how to sing'.[15]

Studying the Organ, RCO Examinations, Thalben-Ball, and Cunningham

GOT's original ambition was to be a concert pianist (a school concert programme lists his playing one of Liszt's Liebesträume). He decided that his hands were 'too small' (he could only stretch one octave on the

---

[11] GOT speech.
[12] *Reading School Magazine*, September 1993, p.29. The organ was originally built by Nicholson of Worcester and rebuilt (with electric blowing) in 1935. It is interesting to note that this instrument was overhauled by the John Compton Organ company in 1950-1, the same time as they were rebuilding the organ in Christchurch Priory. *Reading School Magazine*, September 1993, p.10.
[13] *Reading School Magazine*, September 1993, p.12.
[14] *Reading School Magazine*, September 1993, p.18. The instrument was replaced in 1993. *Reading School Magazine*, September 1993, p.22.
[15] *Reading School Magazine*, September 1993, p.12.

keyboard),[16] so he 'gave it up in favour of the organ', though he was often complimented on his piano accompaniments. He was 'introduced to the organ by an older boy who became County Music Advisor', despite making the 'clarinet [sound] like trams going round tight corners [and having] size fourteen boots'.[17] He was allowed to play the chapel organ at Reading School. 'Even though it was not a very good one',[18] thus began his lifelong love of the organ.[19]

GOT's first attempt at becoming an Associate of the Royal College of Organists (ARCO) in January 1934 resulted in a good 'pass' on the paperwork side, including exercises in both 'strict' and 'free' counterpoint and 'piano accompaniment', with full marks on the ear tests. There was, sadly, a requirement to retake the playing element, GOT's registration coming in for especial criticism. By the end of that academic year, however, the headmaster of Reading School was congratulating him for gaining the diploma, 'a fine performance for one of his age', and 'an uncommon distinction for a boy to win while still at school'.[20]

---

16 *Christchurch Times*, December 1970.
17 GOT speech.
18 *Christchurch Times*, December 1971.
19 *Christchurch Times*, 1 January 1971; GOT speech.
20 Speech Day Programme, Reading School, 18 October 1934.

THE ROYAL COLLEGE OF ORGANISTS

KENSINGTON GORE, LONDON, S.W.7.

Candidate's Number _154_

JAN 1934 19

Name _E O Fairbairn G._

To be inserted **after** the Examination.

The following are the marks awarded to you at the recent Examination for Associateship, with the Examiners' notes upon the Organ playing.

In order to pass in the Organ work a Candidate must obtain not less than 66 marks, and to pass in the Paper work he must obtain not less than 66 marks and a pass in the Essay, for which, however, no marks are awarded. The Essays of those Candidates who fail to obtain 66 marks in the Paper work are not considered by the Examiners.

FREDK. G. SHINN,

Hon. Secretary.

	Strict Counterpoint (15)	Free Counterpoint (15)	Piano Accompaniment (15)	Ear Test (12)	Melody (6) Bass (6)	Melody or Bass (4 part) (18)	Questions (12)	Total (99)
Paper Work ...	12	11	11	12	11	11	3	71

	PREPARED PIECES					TRANSPOSITION		
	Accuracy of Notes and Rests (21)	Time and Pace (9)	Phrasing (9)	Change and Management of Stops (9)	Vocal Score (12)	Accuracy of Notes (18)	Observance of Indicated Tempo (9)	Accompaniment (12)	Total (99)
Organ Playing ...	11	5	4	4	8	12	7	8	59

EXAMINERS' REMARKS

Pieces
Group 1

(a) Mechanical registering, making for balance between manuals. Untidy part playing.

(b) Phrasing of melody too broken; + a general lack of movement. Registering weak.

Vocal Score ... Hands not together

Transposition ... Fair

Accompaniment

N.B.—This Report is final, and no questions upon it will be entertained or answered, neither may any of the above particulars appear in a printed announcement.

8

The Royal College of Organists

ASSOCIATESHIP PAPER WORK

This is to certify that *G. O. Tristram Esq*
passed in the PAPER WORK SECTION, but failed to satisfy the
Examiners in the Organ Playing Section at the Examination held in
January, 1934, for ASSOCIATESHIP.

This paper will exempt the Candidate above-named from further
Examination in Paper Work for Associateship, and the holder is required
to produce it in the Examination Room for inspection.

FREDK G. SHINN,

Hon. Secretary.

KENSINGTON GORE, S.W. 7

N.B.—The information contained in this Certificate may not appear in any
printed announcement.

ARCO Results

9

Similarly, in July 1935, GOT passed the paperwork for Fellowship of the Royal College of Organists (FRCO) but frustratingly (one assumes), failed the practical examination by a mere three marks, largely because some of the keyboard tests were 'not quite up to standard'. This deficiency was remedied the following year when he passed comfortably. His FRCO mark sheet survives. The examiners' comments give hints of things to come: 'good all-round playing, well-varied without exaggeration, steady without stiffness; excellent control and good style'.

THE ROYAL COLLEGE OF ORGANISTS
KENSINGTON GORE, LONDON, S.W. 7.

Candidate's Number 72

Jan 17 19 35

Name _G. O. Goodman_
To be inserted after the Examination.

The following are the marks awarded to you at the recent Examination for Fellowship, with the Examiners' notes upon the Organ playing.

In order to pass in either Organ playing or Paper work a Candidate must obtain not less than 66 marks in that particular part of the Examination.

FREDERICK G. SHINN,
Hon. Secretary.

	Counterpoint (15)	Fugue (15)	Questions (12)	Test (12)	Orchestration (12)	String Quartet (18)	Composition (15)	Total (99)
per cent	73·33	80	16·66	33·33	58·33	66·66	53·33	62·62
Paper Work	11	12	2	10	7	12	8	62

		PREPARED PIECES								
	Accuracy of Notes and Reus. (18)	Time and Pace (12)	Phrasing (12)	Choice and Management of Stops (9)	Vocal Score (9)	Transposition (9)	Sight Reading (12)	Extemporisation (9)	Bass and Melody (9)	Total (99)
Organ Playing	12	8	8	6	3	6	7	6	5	63

EXAMINERS' REMARKS

Pieces		
	(a)	A good steady pace — fluent and fairly clean.
	(b)	Slight rhythmic blemishes but generally well managed.
	(c)	Some evidence of feeling for melodic shape — not always quite rhythmic.
Vocal Score		Too many inaccuracies.
Transposition		Adequate
Sight Reading		Without control & often inaccurate.
Extemporisation		Adequate
Bass and Melody		Bass not played in time — some inappropriate harmony.

N.B.—This Report is final, and no questions upon it will be entertained or answered, neither may any of the above particulars appear in a printed announcement.

11

THE ROYAL COLLEGE OF ORGANISTS

KENSINGTON GORE, LONDON, S.W. 7.

Candidate's Number... 40

July 24 1935

Name... E. A. *Jacobson* ...
To be inserted after the Examination.

The following are the marks awarded to you at the recent Examination for Fellowship, with the Examiners' notes upon the Organ playing.

In order to pass in either Organ playing or Paper work a Candidate must obtain not less than 66 marks in that particular part of the Examination.

FREDERICK G. SHINN,
Hon. Secretary.

	Counterpoint (15)	Fugue (15)	Questions (12)	Ear Test (12)	Orchestration (12)	String Quartet (18)	Composition (15)	Total (99)
Paper Work ...	10	11	7	11	7	11	11	68

	PREPARED PIECES									
	Accuracy of Notes and Rests (18)	Time and Pace (12)	Phrasing (12)	Choice and Management of Stops (9)	Vocal Score (9)	Transposition (9)	Sight Reading (12)	Extemporisation (9)	Bass and Melody (9)	Total (99)
Organ Playing ...	12	8	8	5	5	5	8	5	7	63

EXAMINERS' REMARKS

Pieces ...
(a) Accurate but needed more dignity of style showed little resource in use of Organ
(b) Rather disjointed in touch — Again limited use of Organ
(c) Generally showed more enterprise

Vocal Score ... } Not quite up to standard
Transposition ... }

Sight Reading ... Time a little erratic — otherwise good

Extemporisation ... Mechanical & too sequential

Bass and Melody ... Very good

N.B.—This Report is final, and no questions upon it will be entertained or answered, neither may any of the above particulars appear in a printed announcement.

FRCO Results

12

GOT proudly wearing his FRCO hood and gown following a successful result

GOT gained a scholarship via the Royal Academy of Music to study with Dr. G.D. Cunningham (1878-1948), the famed Organist of Birmingham Town Hall, and Professor at the Royal Academy of Music. The regime was a hard one. Tristram later wrote: '4am paper train from Reading to Birmingham, Breakfast at New Street, Practice at 8am, back home about 4pm'.[21] Cunningham thought much of Geoffrey Tristram. In later testimonials, the Town Hall Organist thought GOT 'an extremely gifted musician', a 'splendidly musical player with a fine technique and admirable taste ... carrying out any work he undertook with thoroughness and enthusiasm'. He said that Tristram had 'the highest ideals ', being 'untiring' in his commitment to 'all that is best in music ... not only [as]

---

[21]   GOT speech.

a fine organist but an all-round musician'.[22] GOT also studied under
Dr. George Thalben-Ball (1896-1987), Organist of the Temple Church,
London, and Cunningham's successor at Birmingham Town Hall.
Thalben-Ball reputedly said that Tristram was the best student he ever
had. Like GOT, Thalben-Ball had a stupendous technique based on his
abilities as a pianist as much as an organist. [23]

Early Career and Marriage

In 1935, GOT was articled to a firm of estate agents, following in his
uncle's footsteps, having been advised against taking up a career in music.
'In those days, music was not taught in school ... and church organists
were lucky if they were paid as much as £100 a year'.[24] The articles of
agreement between Geoffrey Tristram, his father Oliver, and Mr Cecil
Bernard Richards, of the firm of Ayres & Richards, were signed on 2
November of that year. GOT was 'placed and bound' as a pupil clerk
for three years, being required to 'faithfully and diligently' serve in the
'profession of auctioneer, surveyor, valuer and estate agent'.[25] Owing to
Richards's death in 1936, GOT had to finish his clerkship with Messrs
Martin & Pole.

---

[22] Undated testimonial letters from G.D. Cunningham, presumed to be late 1930s/
early 1940s.
[23] Rennert, Jonathan, *George Thalben-Ball*. Newton Abbot: David & Charles,
1979.
[24] *Christchurch Times*, December 1970.
[25] Articles of Agreement, 2 November 1935.

[copy]

A R T I C L E S
Memorandum of Agreement

made this ~~second~~ day of
~~November~~ One Thousand Nine Hundred and Thirty Five
BETWEEN OLIVER TRISTRAM of 52 Highmoor Road Caversham
Reading in the County of Berks Bank Official of the first
part GEOFFREY OLIVER TRISTRAM (the Son of the said
Oliver Tristram) of the second part AND CECIL BERNARD
RICHARDS of 23 Market Place Reading in the County of
Berks Auctioneer and Estate Agent carrying on practice
under the style or Firm of "Ayres & Richards" (hereinafter called "the Principal" which expression where the
context so requires or admits shall include the executors
and administrators of the said Cecil Bernard Richards and
so far as possible the partner or partners for the time
being in the said partnership Firm of Ayres & Richards)
of the third part WHEREAS the said Oliver Tristram has
applied to the Principal to accept his Son the said
Geoffrey Oliver Tristram as an Articled Pupil which the
Principal has agreed to do in manner and on the terms
hereinafter appearing - - - - - - - - -
NOW THESE ARTICLES W I T N E S S E T H as follows -
1. In pursuance of the said agreement the said Geoffrey
Oliver Tristram of his own free will and with the consent
of his Father the said Oliver Tristram hereby places and
binds himself as a Pupil Clerk to the Principal to serve
him for the term of THREE YEARS from the ~~fourth~~
day of ~~November~~ One Thousand Nine Hundred and Thirty
Five - - - - - - - - - - -
2. The said Oliver Tristram for himself and on behalf of
his Son the said Geoffrey Oliver Tristram covenants with

*First page of Articles of Agreement, dated 2 November 1935, 'placing and binding'
GOT to being a pupil clerk in the profession of 'auctioneer, valuer and estate agent'*

At the same time, he was gaining a reputation as a fine organ recitalist. GOT was described by the Vicar in St Mary's Reading parish magazine as, 'this brilliant young organist', often acting as deputy during Daughtry's final illness in 1943.[26] The organ at St Mary's was a fine four-manual by 'Father' Henry Willis. Originally built for the Industrial and Fine Arts Exhibition of 1862, the instrument won the 'prize medal for general excellence of tone and for several novel inventions', having a 'purity of tone, prodigious power and grandeur'. The swell shutters were 'operated by pneumatic action, which was initiated by blowing into a mouthpiece, thereby freeing the right foot completely from the swell pedal'.[27] When the Exhibition closed in 1864, part of the organ was installed in St Mary's. It was enlarged in 1873, rebuilt in 1926 by Bishop and again in 1936 by Henry Willis III, as a comprehensive and versatile instrument incorporating all the latest fashions, gadgets, and tonal innovations.[28] [29]

GOT at the console of the organ of St Mary's, Reading

[26]   *St Mary the Virgin, Reading, Parish Magazine,* June 1943, p.39.
[27]   National Pipe Organ Register, R02014
[28]   National Pipe Organ Register, A00123
[29]   Clutton, Cecil. 'The Organ at St. Mary's Parish Church, Reading'. *The Organ* XVII:11-20, 1937/8. This article describes the Willis rebuild of 1936. The specification from 1926-1936 is given on page 123 of the same volume.

It was on this organ that GOT, 'a very brilliant organist', according to the local newspapers, gave one of the opening recitals, aged 19. The programme included chorale preludes by Bach, Karg-Elert and Harold Darke, as well as works by César Franck, Guilmant and Saint-Saëns. A newspaper cutting about this recital in GOT's scrapbook reads as follows:

> One must regard Mr. Tristram as one of the most promising organists in Berkshire. There was something refreshing in his playing of Bach, particularly the Fantasia in G, which he kept at a uniform time, and his interpretation of the chorale prelude, 'Valet will ich dir geben', was good. Another ambitious choice was the well-known 'Choral in A minor' (Franck). Mr. Tristram surmounted the great technical difficulties of this composition in such a masterly manner that, except perhaps for those with personal experience of organ playing, it was only too easy not to realise his skill and cleverness.
>
> The 'Fantasie in E flat' (Saint-Saëns), with its attractive introduction, was well managed, and from a listener's viewpoint was delightful. In the robust chorale prelude, 'Ein feste Burg' (Karg-Elert), Mr. Tristram gave good examples of climax building. As a contrast, the chorale prelude, 'St. Peter' (Dr Harold Darke), elaborated on a simple theme, proved the acid test for phrasing. Mr. Tristram provided a comparison between the ancient and modern in his treatment of Wall's arrangement of 'Organ Solo' from Thomas Arne's Third Organ Concerto, written about 250 years ago. He certainly compiled a programme which would appeal to the varied tastes of the hearers. Mr. Tristram should be an inspiration to the younger school of organists in Berkshire.

A further recital at St Mary's elicited another effusive review (also from GOT's scrapbook) from a second Reading critic.

At his recital on Saturday at St Mary's, Reading, Mr. G.O. Tristram, F.R.C.O., gave an example of wise programme planning. In a performance by a single artiste two points can be borne in mind; to demonstrate his own versatility, and to please an audience drawn from all sources. This can only be done if he has a large repertoire, and an open mind! Possessing both, this gifted player can be relied upon to give a programme sufficiently varied to show his musicianship and virtuosity alike, and to interest the discriminating as well as the ordinary listener. His performance gave proof of clear part-playing, expressive phrasing, interesting registration, and, most important, knowledge of the right moments for simplicity and for grandiose treatment. Works performed were the G major prelude and fugue of Bach, four chorale preludes of Brahms, Mendelssohn's sixth sonata, Liszt's Prelude and Fugue on B.A.C.H., and pieces by Karg-Elert, Morandi, Whitlock and Lemmens.

Other reviews of GOT's recitals in the area at the time talk of the 'virility and expressiveness' of his playing, 'characterised by a high level of technical skill', the 'brilliant accuracy of his technique' and 'the artistry of his registration', including in such virtuosic works as Liszt's Introduction and Fugue on 'Ad nos, ad salutarem undam', and Elgar's Organ Sonata (especially the first movement). Works by Bach (the Toccata in F seems to have been a favourite), Brahms, Hollins, Mendelssohn, Schumann, and Vaughan Williams, among others, figure in these performances, along with the occasional transcription, as for example of Saint-Saëns's 'The Swan', perhaps a reference to his occasional forays into the world of the cinema organ, though G.D. Cunningham also played the piece in an organ arrangement by Guilmant from time to time.[30] 'Reading is fortunate in possessing such an outstanding player as Mr. Tristram, and best wishes will be extended to him for the prosperous career which he so well deserves', wrote one reviewer, while another summarised GOT's early achievements as follows.

---

[30] As for example at a recital at Birmingham Town Hall, 23 April 1947.

An Accomplished Young Organist

One of the most notable careers of local musicians must be that of Mr. Geoffrey O. Tristram, the versatile young Reading organist, who is rapidly climbing the ladder to well-deserved fame. The other day I sat at the organ stool of the magnificent Willis organ in the church of St Mary the Virgin and saw him juggle with the various pistons and stops. He is a wizard of the organ, and compositions beyond the reach of moderate players seem just 'child's play' to him. I happened to mention a piece often heard on the wireless, and Mr. Tristram played it without music... At the present time Mr. Tristram is studying under Dr. G. Thalben-Ball, Organist at the Temple Church, London. With this experience, coupled with the excellent tuition received from Dr. E.O. Daughtry, some church will be very fortunate at a future date in having this brilliant young organist at the head of its music. Mr. Tristram is an inspiration to budding young musicians, and his attainments up to his present age (19) will, I hope, be amplified in the future.[31]

GOT and friend on the tower roof, St Mary's, Reading

---

[31] Unattributed newspaper cutting, presumably from a Reading newspaper, 1936.

GOT and lifelong friend Gordon Hands

GOT later won a scholarship to Oxford, but World War II intervened and instead, he ended up working for the Post Office Telephone Exchange, where he met Irene (known to all as Rene) Grace Wellstead, whom he married at Christ Church, Reading, on 30 March 1946. He was 28 and she 24.

GOT and Irene (Rene) Wellstead (soon to be Mrs G.O. Tristram)

Wedding Day, 30 March 1948, Christ Church, Reading

The choir sang Bach's 'On my Shepherd I rely' and chanted Psalm 67, while the couple left the church to the Wedding March from Mendelsohn's Midsummer Night's Dream. GOT must have had a hand in the organ music before the service:

Pastorale on Psalm XXIII	Percy Whitlock
Fidelis	Percy Whitlock
Prelude on 'St Columba'	Robin Milford
Andante Cantabile (Symphony IV)	Widor

GOT was then also Organist and Choirmaster of Whitchurch Parish Church, where there was a modest two-manual by Walker, dated 1901.[32] He conducted choirs, too, as for example the Reading Allied Postal Choir during World War II in performances of works such as Edward German's *Merrie England*.[33] As well as being 'an organ player of brilliant attainment with quite outstanding gifts as a recitalist', the Bishop of Reading, Arthur Parham, regarded Geoffrey Tristram as 'an accompanist of taste and distinction [who handled] a choir in rehearsal and controls his choir boys with remarkable success'.[34]

These last comments appeared in the bishop's various references for GOT as he applied for major organ posts, including (August 1945) the post of Organist and Choirmaster of Wakefield Cathedral. While the referee was effusive in his praise of Tristram as organist, and though commending him as a candidate for the job, the reference commented on GOT's limited experience of choir training. Probably as a result, he was unsuccessful, the post going to Dr Percy Saunders, Organist of Doncaster Parish Church. GOT applied for similar posts over the next few years but felt that jobs only went to 'old men' in those days,[35] being put off after one especially difficult interview with the Dean of a certain cathedral. 'Not since he was a very young man' did he 'aspire to be a cathedral organist'.[36] He was quoted as saying that 'apart from anything else, the salary is abysmally low, and, in any event, in the days of radio and television, one doesn't need such a position to gain acclaim',[37] though it was later reputed that he turned down at least one cathedral role because of the high regard in which he was held at the Priory, having read the Vicar's testimonial on GOT's behalf.[38]

[32] National Pipe Organ Register, D02131

[33] Various undated newspaper cuttings from the scrapbooks refer to his conductorship.

[34] Letter from Arthur Parham, Bishop of Reading [also Vicar of St Mary's Reading and Archdeacon of Berkshire] 19 October 1944. Bishop Parham had previously been Precentor of Christ Church Cathedral, Oxford.

[35] GOT speech.

[36] GOT speech.

[37] *Christchurch Times*, 1 January 1971.

[38] Information from Richard Hands, Gordon Hands' son.

GOT, rarely without a cigarette, by the Thames, probably at Caversham

CHAPTER TWO

Move to the South Coast

All Saints' Church

Moving to the south coast in 1946, still working as an estate agent, GOT quickly made his mark on the local music scene. In March, he was leading the singing at a festival at the Southbourne Methodist Church[39], and by the end of the year, he had been appointed Organist of All Saints Church, Castlemain Avenue, Southbourne, where there was a fine three-manual organ by Hill, Norman & Beard, built in 1926.[40] Geoffrey and Rene Tristram were then living at 'Withycroft', Tuckton Road.

GOT was soon broadcasting recitals for the B.B.C. from All Saints. 'Broadcasting in those days was not the easy recording session of today. Everything went out live then. It was nothing to get up at one in the morning for some programme on the overseas network. And at Southbourne, there was no 'phone. The BBC had to borrow a line from a neighbour to transmit the programme'.[41] The programmes for GOT's broadcast recitals from Southbourne show his ability. That for 24 September 1948, for example, lists him playing Bach's Toccata in F, Bossi's Scherzo in G minor and Franck's Choral in A minor, while that for 21 December 1949 included Percy Whitlock's Carol, Mulet's Noël and Mozart's Fantasia in F minor. All were to become firm favourites in his recital repertoire.

As later at Christchurch Priory, GOT arranged recitals at All Saints, performing many of the major standard works from the organ repertoire, including the whole of Elgar's Sonata in G major (11 September 1948).

---

39 Southbourne Methodist Church Sunday School Festival, 26 May 1946, Programme. Irene Tristram distributed the prizes.
40 National Pipe Organ Register, R01240
41 *Christchurch Times*, 1 January 1971.

25

Jongen's Sonata Eroica was by now a regular, too, as for example at a recital given by GOT at Salisbury Cathedral on 21 May 1948. On a return visit the following year (9 July 1949) he finished his recital at Salisbury with the demanding Toccata, from the Suite opus 5 by Duruflé. Visiting recitalists also came and played at Southbourne. On 28 June 1947, G.D. Cunningham was the guest recitalist.

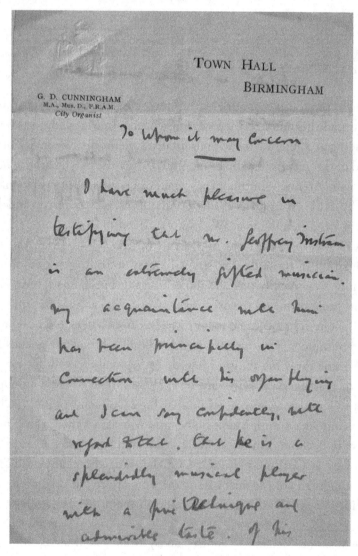

Undated, handwritten letter of commendation for GOT from G.D. Cunningham

GOT began to teach the organ while at Southbourne, continuing to do so after his move to Christchurch Priory. One such was Lilian Pantlin, who became one of his students in the late 1940s, and, like some of his other pupils, occasionally deputised for weddings. However, throughout GOT's career, the bride and groom often insisted on Geoffrey Tristram playing for them! Geoffrey Howell (who believes he may have been named after GOT) remembers that:

> My mother told me that my grandfather [H.W.S. Osborne][42] had known Geoffrey Tristram quite well. During the late 1940s he got to know him at All Saints' Southbourne and used to go and sit with him at the console during Sunday services. Tristram moved to Christchurch Priory ... the year before my parents were married. My grandfather was determined that the wedding would be at Christchurch Priory and my father had to take lodgings in Christchurch to allow this to happen. They were married on 10 June 1950, and I can only presume that Tristram was at the organ.

An article in the Southbourne parish magazine[43] summarises GOT's time at the church.

> His first service at All Saints was the accompaniment of the midnight celebration at Christmas, 1946. He had the very difficult task, for a young man, of succeeding Mr. Croucher, who had over nearly 40 years, built up a fine tradition of music at the Church. The new Organist, however, immediately gained the respect and affection of his Choir, and building upon the excellent foundation of

---

[42] Howell, Geoffrey (Ed.) *H.W.S. Osborne: An Armchair and the Pipe of Peace— Some Reminiscences after Forty Years' Service with the National Provincial Bank (1898-1938.* Chesterfield: Bannister Publications, 2017. Osborne had been Organist of St. Matthew's, Skegness, before moving to Southbourne. In retirement, he wrote up his reminiscences, later edited and published by his grandson. H.W.S. Osborne died in 1957.

[43] All Saints Southbourne Parish Magazine, November 1949.

his predecessor, raised the musical standards of All Saints'
to ever fresh heights. Particular mention must be made of
the two Christmas Carol services, so greatly appreciated
by all of us, and so beautifully rendered by both Choir and
Organist. Mr. Tristram, as is well known, is in the very
front rank of the organists of this country, and his recitals
on the magnificent instrument in the Church, have been
appreciated by an ever-growing company, through the
medium of the B.B.C. He will be sadly missed at All
Saints', by his Choir, who have worked so hard for him,
and by all who appreciated good music. We wish him
every happiness and success in his new appointment.

Reference for GOT from Rural Dean Reverend Anthony Williams, 21 May 1949

GOT was ambitious for advancement within the organ world, and in
1949 he applied unsuccessfully for the prestigious post of Organist at St
Mary Redcliffe Bristol in succession to Ralph T. Morgan. The post went
to Kenneth R. Long, who left in 1952. Garth Benson, a lifelong friend

of Geoffrey's, was appointed in 1953. Tristram's references for the Bristol post came from Geoffrey Milroy, Curate of All Saints, Southbourne (later Priest Vicar and Succentor of Exeter Cathedral) and the Vicar, Anthony Williams. The two men were effusive in their praise of GOT, both in terms of his choral training and direction, while the Rural Dean commented that Geoffrey Tristram was 'an exceptionally able performer [and] a young and vigorous man [who] should make a name for himself'.[44] At the time, as did many other church organists of his generation, GOT was studying for the Bachelor of Music degree from Trinity College, Dublin as an external candidate.[45]

Rare photograph of GOT relaxing on holiday, late 1940s?

---

44   Letter from Reverend Anthony L. Williams, 21 May 1949.
45   Letter from Reverend Geoffrey Milroy, 23 May 1949.

Teacher

While still working as an estate agent, he began to look for teaching roles. Because of his own schoolboy experiences,[46] he determined that he would treat his pupils better than he had been treated himself. He was also a gifted and painstaking organ teacher, whose surviving students still hold him in great affection, as reflected later in this book.

Southbourne High School

A letter of 8 March 1946 from Miss V.E. Hicks, Principal of Southbourne High School[47] said that while the 'staff on the music side' was complete, GOT was encouraged to send information about his 'lessons both for private pupils and class singing'. GOT had been enquiring about becoming a 'visiting music master' at the school. He was able to boast that while in Reading, he had built up a 'choral society of over 70 members' and a large teaching practice. He also became a 'Teacher of Pianoforte', having become 'very fond of teaching'. In particular, he 'coached young people successfully for the pianoforte examinations of the Associated Board of the Royal Schools of Music and adults for the well-known Diplomas'.[48] He consistently showed his 'keen enthusiasm' for his subject, always taking the opportunity to 'pass on his own love of music to others'.[49]

---

[46]   GOT speech.

[47]   Miss Hicks was the speaker at the Southbourne Methodist Church Sunday School Festival where GOT led the music in 1946.

[48]   Letter from GOT, 3 December 1948.

[49]   Letter from J.D. Lovelock, County Music Adviser for Hampshire, 9 January 1951.

TELEPHONE No. 4352

Headmaster:
L. J. LING, M.A., B.Litt.;
F.V.C.M. (Lond.)

Interviews Wednesdays 2-4 p.m.
or by appointment

(Founded 1577)
PERSEVERE

RINGWOOD GRAMMAR SCHOOL
WEST HILL ROAD
BOURNEMOUTH
HANTS

LJL/PJW

27th October, 1948.

Geoffrey Tristram Esq., F.R.C.O.,
Withycroft,
Tuckton Road,
SOUTHBOURNE.

Dear Mr. Tristram,

        Thank you for your letter accepting the
post here as Music Master from the commencement of
next term which is on January13th and I presume you
would like to come on Tuesdays, Wednesdays and Fridays
as arranged, and therefore we shall look forward to
seeing you on Friday 14th January. No doubt you will
come to see me before that date to arrange how you
would like your lessons and how the music pupils can
be worked in on the various days.

        Mrs. Key informs me that you have already
contacted her and I am sure you will get every
co-operation from her for when I mentioned that you
were taking it over, she seemed very relieved and very
pleased that the music could be left in such capable
hands. She does however make the point that you might
look for another school for 3 days a week and come to
us for 2 days a week, leaving her assistant Miss
Briginshaw to cope with the piano pupils and perhaps
some work in Form 1 & 11. Personally I am not very
pleased with this idea for although I have nothing
against Miss Briginshaw I do feel that a Master is
necessary particularly from the discipline point of
view. Also that if she is going to be responsible for
all piano lessons it means that the boys are being
taught by somebody without any qualification, and
whereas we realise that this is only a very minor

Contd....

*Letter from the Headmaster, Ringwood Grammar School, 27 October
1948, following GOT's appointment as Music Master*

31

David Baker

Ringwood Grammar School

From January 1949 to July 1952, GOT was Music Master at Ringwood Grammar School (a private school for boys), then located in West Hill Road, Bournemouth. Initially, he taught for three days a week, but increased his hours and responsibilities as more students took music. GOT 'showed from the start that he meant business and quickly pulled up the teaching of music and singing to a high level'. He also taught music as a class subject, gave piano lessons, and trained the school choir for services and other major events in the school year. He was regarded as a 'thoroughly loyal and devoted colleague, popular in the Staff Room and easy to get on with'.[50]

Ian Orbell, a student at Ringwood for four years from 1949, writes of Geoffrey Tristram as his music teacher there:

> I have to own up to not being a great lover of school in any form or place but took more interest in music. From the age of approximately eight, I started to learn cornet with the Poole town brass band, 'scratching' out a basic noise at eleven. This was a time when Mr. T was the part time music teacher at the school. I only really knew him as the organist from Christchurch Priory.
>
> An annual concert was being put together and a request was put out for students with ability to perform in any way on stage. My name and ability reached Mr. T and I then spent a number of lessons, with him on piano, when we rehearsed [The Lost Chord, by Arthur Sullivan]. We made it to the concert, held in Bournemouth Town Hall and I blew my way through my first ever solo performance with knees knocking!!
>
> My recollection of that spell in his company was memorable, as he was a lovely chap and, aside from other schoolwork, I did learn a few pointers from him to take

---

[50]   Testimonial from Laurence J. Ling, Head Teacher, 27 July 1952.

me forward with my music interests. In my teens, with National Service looming, I went into the Royal Tank Regiment band for three years, and on demob spent three years with the Royal Artillery territorial band. This took me on to a new course playing in small dance groups and traditional jazz bands plus an 18-piece big band and the Westbourne student orchestra, run by Alfie Jupp, lead violin with the Bournemouth Symphony Orchestra,[51] all on a hobby basis, while forming and running a company with my son.

Geoffrey was a creative element to my beginnings, far more than my schooling, the lack of which does not seem to have had too much impact on my life, as my son continues with a very successful company. Now 82, I 'hung' up my trumpet about 18 years back and entered retirement when I was 73.

Poole Grammar School and Twynham County Secondary School

On the resignation of the then Head at Ringwood, Laurence J. Ling, GOT determined not to renew his own contract because of 'certain changes' that were being made by Ling's successor with which GOT 'could not and would not' associate himself.[52] As a result, he moved to Poole Grammar School (where there were some 650 boys) as Director of Music, succeeding Norman Charleton-Burden (who went to Norfolk and was twice Organist of Wymondham Abbey in the 1950s[53]). GOT stayed for six years, until July 1957. During that time, he taught up to third-year sixth form level, including General Certificate of Education (G.C.E) to 'A' level. Unaccompanied four-part singing became a speciality, along with musical notation, score reading, and the theory of music. Daniel Campbell remembers his time there as a student:

---

[51] Jupp and GOT performed together in recitals at the Priory.
[52] Letter from Laurence J. Ling, 27 July 1952 for all the quotations in this paragraph.
[53] Wymondham Abbey - Wikipedia

My memories of Geoffrey begin at Poole Grammar School in the autumn of 1956. Alas, in those days, music seemed to count for nothing, not even the opportunity to take an 'O' level in that subject. The headmaster of the day was only interested if you could be outstanding on the sports field or were a genius at maths! In the so called 'music room' was an enormous radiogram beneath a fitted green baize cover, normally only switched on by Geoffrey to hear the Test Match scores. It's no wonder that he went to St. Peter's School at Southbourne where they appreciated his skills and, seemingly, money was no object.

'In addition to the normal timetable' at Poole, GOT trained the school choir for the annual school concerts and recitals and the operatic society (which he founded), together with the orchestra, for all-male performances of Gilbert and Sullivan operas, including Pirates of Penzance, Mikado, and The Gondoliers. The reviews were always glowing, as for example that for GOT's Mikado, performed in 1953:

> The brilliance and immaculate presentation of Poole Grammar School Operatic Society's production ... left me lost for words. And if it is the duty of a critic to find fault, then I have failed in my duty: I could find nothing whatsoever lacking in this most remarkable show.

> Rich words of praise, but richly deserved. More than 2,000 people saw this production in Parkstone Great Hall from last Wednesday to Saturday last week, and I am sure they will all agree that it would be difficult to flatter the results of months of patient work by producer Edna Tice and musical director Mr. Geoffrey Tristram. For this production had one thing that professionals and G and S societies of many years standing would find it hard to improve upon – enthusiasm. Mr. Tristram tells me that this was the most difficult of the three shows he has so far attempted.[54]

---

[54] *Poole and Dorset Herald*, 2 February 1953.

And for The Gondoliers, two years' later:

> Not even the most skilful hand of Man can make a superb wine when Nature does not bestow a vintage year, with all its implications. And similarly, not even the expert guidance of a producer like Edna Tice and a musical director as accomplished as Geoffrey Tristram can create a good comic opera from an all-male cast without Nature lending a hand.
>
> That is, of course, when they are dealing with the youthful members of Poole Grammar School Operatic Society, whose fourth Gilbert and Sullivan production ... was presented in Parkstone Great Hall last week. It rests in the hands of Nature as to whether they will be able to cast the show with unbroken treble voices of the necessary clarity for the 'female' roles in an all-male presentation, and whether the older voices will have settled sufficiently to cope with the male parts ... Even so ... they soared well above the standard one would expect from a school operatic society.[55]

Choral singing at Poole was of 'a sufficiently high standard to warrant a broadcast by the B.B.C.',[56] including an anthology of words and music for Trinity Sunday, 1957, devised by Cecil Mitchell and produced by Kenneth Savidge.[57] The Corporation staff in charge of the broadcast were full of praise for 'such fine music', not least because 'the words were particularly clear, and the general style of singing admirably fitted the mood and character of the programme as a whole'.[58]

---

[55] *Poole and Dorset Herald*, 28 March 1955.

[56] Letter from GOT to the Head Teacher, Brockenhurst County High School, 22 October 1958. He was applying for the post of Director of Music there. He was unsuccessful.

[57] Details of the programme (a cutting presumed to be from either the local newspaper or *The Radio Times*) gives the title of the programme as 'The Glory of the Eternal Trinity'. The broadcast took place at 10.00 am on 16 June 1957.

[58] Letter from Kenneth Savidge, Head of Religious Broadcasting for the Western Region, to GOT, 21 June 1957.

THE BRITISH BROADCASTING CORPORATION

Head Office: Broadcasting House, London, W.1

Broadcasting House, Whiteladies Road, Bristol, 8

TELEPHONE AND TELEGRAMS: BRISTOL 33052

21st June 1957

Dear Geoffrey,

Thank you and your choir of Poole Grammar School for giving us such an excellent performance of the music for the Trinity Sunday Anthology. I hope you were able to hear the programme and were yourself pleased with the result.

Cecil Mitchell who compiled the programme asked me to send you his best thanks and appreciation for producing us such fine music. The words were particularly clear, and the general style of singing admirably fitted the mood and character of the programme as a whole.

Just to put it in writing that you will be doing Choral Evensong for us on the afternoon of Wednesday, September 4th, from 4.00-4.45pm. Would you, in consultation with Canon Price, be so kind as to send us as soon as may be a complete Order of Service, including your final Organ Voluntary. As I mentioned when I saw you last weekend, we would like to have a choice of music in the case of the Canticles and the Anthem to avoid unnecessary duplication with previous Choral Evensong broadcasts. Perhaps it might not be a bad idea if we could arrange provisionally for rehearsal on that day at 2.30 p.m.

Every good wish,

Yours,

Kenneth

(Kenneth Savidge)
Religious Broadcasting, West Region

Geoffrey Tristram, Esq.,
Church Hatch,
Christchurch,
Hants.

PJ

*Letter dated 21 June 1957 from Kenneth Savidge, Head of
Religious Broadcasting, B.B.C. Western Region*

36

Because his F.R.C.O was recognised 'as being of equivalent graduate status under … the Burnham Report', GOT was paid £326.5.0d per annum on appointment at Poole, rising to £356.5.0 from July 1952.[59] He was recognised as a qualified teacher by 1953,[60] completing his probation in June 1954.[61] The fact that he was 'entirely responsible for [the school']s music …was latterly recognised by his post being graded as one of Special Responsibility'.[62]

The two Heads of Poole Grammar School during GOT's time there recognised that 'in addition to possessing musical gifts of the highest order, [Geoffrey Tristram had] a natural ability as a teacher of boys'. His control was excellent, his exposition clear, his understanding of pupils complete, while his sense of humour was 'individual and compelling'.[63] The school 'owed [Geoffrey] Tristram a big debt of gratitude for his enthusiastic and selfless work … [not least] the amount of time which he … put in outside school hours … even the unmusical are given more than the rudiments of musical appreciation for no one could help being captivated by Mr. Tristram's enthusiasm, his skilful presentation and his brilliant performance on the piano'.[64] John Coffin, a student at the Grammar School from 1952 until 1957, sang as a soprano in both HMS Pinafore and The Mikado and then, after his voice broke, in The Gondoliers. He recalls how GOT led the Morning Assembly from the school's grand piano as well as teaching class music to him. GOT gave John a lifelong love of music as well as model railways! GOT was 'a brilliant man much loved by the boys he taught'.

In July 1957, GOT relinquished his post at Poole to become Music Master at Twynham County Secondary School, Christchurch,[65] 'to gain further experience in a mixed secondary modern school'.[66] In addition, the

---

[59] Letter from the Borough Education Officer to GOT, 17 February 1953.

[60] Letter from the Ministry of Education, 17 August 1953.

[61] Correspondence from the Ministry of Education, 21 June 1954.

[62] Letter from N.J. Cleave, Head Teacher, Poole Grammar School, 1 July 1957.

[63] Letter from N.J. Cleave, Head Teacher, Poole Grammar School, 1 July 1957.

[64] Letter from F.H. Stevens, Head Teacher, Poole Grammar School, 16 July 1954.

[65] Correspondence from Hampshire Education Committee, 4 June and 9 August 1957. Carolyn Tristram has been a teaching assistant there since 2006.

[66] Letter from GOT to the Head Teacher, Brockenhurst County High School, 22 October 1958

David Baker

Suez Crisis of 1956 was making it difficult to get petrol (a 24-mile round trip from home) and GOT's attempts to travel to the school by moped did not last long, especially when, as Carolyn Tristram recollects, he attempted to enjoy his creature comforts, smoking a cigarette while clinging onto the handlebars of the bike. While at Twynham (a short walk from his home), GOT introduced part singing and choral work, along with G.C.E. studies.

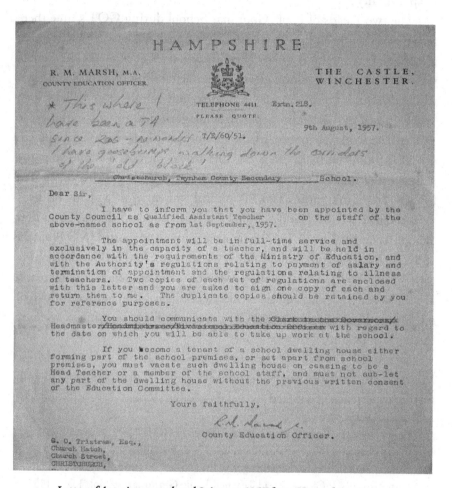

Letter of Appointment dated 9 August 1957 from Hampshire County Council to GOT as 'Qualified Assistant Teacher' at Twynham County Secondary School with daughter Carolyn's written comments as she has been a Teaching Assistant at the same school since 2006

St Peter's School, Bournemouth

In 1960, GOT was invited to join the de la Salle Brothers[67] at St Peter's School in Bournemouth as Head of Music, also teaching English. He was instrumental in starting annual week-long performances of Gilbert & Sullivan operettas and, later, other shows. GOT expended 'tremendous efforts ... over nearly two decades in introducing so many pupils to G & S and giving immeasurable pleasure to them and to the audiences who ... supported their productions.[68] Boys sang the female parts until the girls of St Mary's Convent joined in the performances. GOT's son Michael, a pupil at the school, was Peep-Bo, one of the three little maids in Mikado. He was also in the chorus of Ruddigore and Pirates of Penzance, and then Walter Wilkins in Edward German's Merrie England. In a later production of The Mikado, daughter Carolyn, one of the few girls in the sixth form at that early stage when female students were admitted, was Peep-Bo.

St Peter's School Production of The Mikado in the early 1960s; one of GOT's first productions at the school after more than a decade of G&S experience with Poole Grammar School and Bournemouth Gilbert & Sullivan Society

---

[67]   For further information, see https://en.wikipedia.org/wiki/De La Salle Brothers

[68]   *The Rock*, 1979.

Michael Tristram writes:

> St Peter's was a rugby playing school, but that was too
> rough for Dad and so he insisted that I didn't play (I
> had asthma as a child). In due course I was allowed to go
> sailing on games afternoons (sailing became my hobby
> and sport once my voice broke) Dad having got me to
> try, very unsuccessfully, horse riding (frightening), rowing
> (not strong enough), fishing (too boring), fencing (too
> dangerous)!

GOT was heavily involved in the design of the theatre at St Peter's
and the acquisition of a superior three-manual electronic organ, whose
specification GOT is reputed to have drawn up. The school also enjoyed
having their carol service in the Priory (quite an ecumenical innovation in
those days!). GOT accompanied the operetta performances, sometimes on
the school organ to avoid the extra cost of an orchestra. Joe Gallagher, a
student at the school, remembers that GOT also conducted the productions
from the console. This feat amazed the community and audiences alike
(although it was suspected that GOT was happier being in control of the
whole of the music rather than relying on instrumentalists playing on cue!).
Tim Norris, a pupil at St Peter's from 1967 until 1976[69] remembers these
performances:

> Other moments, especially at school, were the Gilbert
> and Sullivan theatrical performances in the newly built St
> Peter's School Hall with orchestra pit and more. I would
> be invited back to play percussion in the pit for all the
> G&S productions with rehearsals and performances.
> GOT conducted and/or sometimes played the school

---

[69] Tim was also a boy chorister at Christchurch Priory (1969 - 1978). He writes:
'I had joined the Army as a Junior Musician in the Band of The Royal Signals
initially based at Junior Musicians Troop, Royal Artillery, Woolwich, SE London
(1976-1978) and then after initial training I joined the senior band based at
Blandford Camp in Dorset (1978-1980). While in the Army as a musician I
would continue to sing in the Priory Choir when home at weekends and on
leave; happy days'.

Makin organ, which was lowered into the orchestra pit. The one I particularly recall was The Sorcerer. The second half of the show opens with a ghostly figure entranced with a tea-trolley apparently moving unaided across the stage. Dry ice and smoke were blown across the stage to cover-up the thin cord pulling the trolley from the wings and back. Sadly, on one performance somebody had left the side door open and the dry ice and smoke flowed into the orchestra pit and the whole band except me, as I was stood up playing percussion, could not see and had to stop playing. GOT was not best pleased but kept conducting regardless. I don't think the audience knew any the wiser: the joy of live performances; GOT ever the professional.

Columba Cook adds to the story:

[My brother] Aidan played the Sorcerer and my older brother, Gus, did the pyrotechnics. I am not sure how that happened as Gus never went to the school at all. I just remember that each night of the performance Gus used increasing amounts of flash-powder which smoked-out the auditorium a little more each evening – no wonder the orchestra had problems in the pit! Fortunately, Geoffrey never complained - he had a great sense of humour and always saw the amusing side of everything. Geoffrey never seemed to be fazed by anything although, looking back, some things must have been quite a trial for him.

Aidan was at St Peter's from the age of 13 and had much more interaction with Geoffrey. Aidan went on into a career in show biz – and is still at it. He pretty much started off in West End shows. Aidan took part in quite a few of St Peter's G+S operettas, and it was this that sparked his interest in the performing arts. Apparently, at one point, Geoffrey offered to put Aidan in touch with people he knew at the Sadlers' Wells. Obviously, Geoffrey was very well connected, and I think Aidan regretted not taking him up on the offer. The family encouraged 'more sober' pursuits, so Aidan went on to do a degree in English and French at Strawberry Hill before following his heart into the theatre.

When there was an orchestra, GOT, who devoted much of his free time to ensuring that the productions were the very best that they could be, conducted from the pit below the stage. The orchestra was made up of school pupils, supplemented by other professional musicians known to GOT, who also involved singers from the D'Oyly Carte living in the area. The Priory choir came into the school from time to time, and day pupils were often also members of the church choir. The School Madrigal Society performed at the Priory on one occasion in the summer recital series, as for example on 23 June 1965. GOT also took the school choir on tours, memorably to Notre Dame in Paris, where his Mass in A flat was performed. GOT was reputed to have said that 'the roof beams rattled during the 'Sanctus' on that occasion; but then he had also instructed his choir to 'praise God loudly, otherwise he'll never hear us!'

Peter Strange, a close family friend and 'unofficial brother' to Michael and Carolyn Tristram, started at St Peter's in 1962. He recalls that GOT was 'a quirky teacher, but very much loved'. Ray O'Luby, a student there at much the same time, writes:

> Though I was not particularly into serious classical music before attending Geoffrey Tristram's lessons, a lot of us back then at least were familiar with a few popular standards [such as] the 1812 and William Tell Overtures, which were often played on radio request programmes - pre the dominance of television - and which we nearly all listened to. Ironically, compartmental choice nowadays has probably meant that the early introduction to a broad range of music is much less.
>
> G.T., as I remember, had a dry sense of humour in his role of educating us 'uncultured lot' - as I think he would

call us - to really listen to, not just hear, the power of great music. Rimsky-Korsakov's Scheherezade, with its dramatic storm section, was a particularly effective hook in his teaching programme.

Geoffrey Tristram was indeed an inspirational teacher, and I've remained a devotee of orchestral music ever since. I can't say I was ever inspired to take up his own choice of instrument though - my other influences at the time being the Shadows and the Beatles - but I think he might have been impressed with my sing-along guitar version of 'If I had words', based on the last movement from Saint-Saëns's great Organ Symphony, as featured in the Hollywood film Babe, about a talking pig. Then again, perhaps not.

Tim Norris remembers:

While at St. Peter's ... I sang in the main school choir (there was a Chapel choir which was run by one of the older De La Salle Brothers) which sang for school termly masses and special events which included the Southern Independent Television series 'Carols for Christmas' which was a Christmas carols competition broadcast over six programmes shown on a Sunday evening, on consecutive weekends. The school choir rehearsed for about six weeks before we all travelled to the Southern Television studios by coach. The studios were then at Northam in Southampton. It was a real adventure for the choir as we left Southbourne early mid-week in the morning to go and sound-record the newly composed Christmas carols in a sound studio with four session musicians. Each session would last about four hours with breaks; we would be treated to lunch and tea before returning to St. Peter's at about 4.30pm. We would then return a few days later to the television studios to mime to the earlier made sound recordings in front of a live audience, which was always funny, as things invariably would go wrong - but this was a wonderful experience for young and senior student musicians. I do particularly remember GOT taking his shoes off on more than one occasion and, standing behind a working TV camera, he would wave the shoes at us to make us laugh and smile more. Presumably his feet were clean as I don't remember him having smelly feet. Once the series had been put 'in-the-can', as they say, the shows were broadcast nearer Christmas. I think it was in 1974; it may have been 1975. Funny thing I do recall is that the first new composed carol we ever sang was called 'Carol, Carol, Gaily'. I'm not sure who composed it, but this was the carol that won the whole competition. As GOT said at the time, 'and we have just spent weeks preparing, rehearsing, and recording all those other entries and the very first one we ever sang wins. That's showbiz!' Once the tv series had been aired and over the school choir were taken on a trip, by train (GOT loved trains and all things to do with model-railways), to Brighton via London Victoria. That was a fun day out. We went on the pier, went to the fun-fair and we had fish and chips and stayed out till late, before returning to Christchurch rail station and back up to school. If you could have seen GOT in a dodgem car on the pier you would have laughed. I know we did. Happy days.

About two years later a similar TV series and music competition was recorded at Christchurch Priory entitled 'Hymns for All Occasions'. We choristers and the gentlemen of the choir together with local choral societies and youth choirs came together over many weeks to record the series. My two younger brothers Simon and Adam were in the choir at this time and the three of us had great fun. Simon caused some chaos in one of the recording sessions: he had obviously become bored with all the stops and starts and had placed a copy of The Beano comic in his music folio and this had been spotted by the producer via the camera shots from above. 'CUT, CUT, CUT' was heard loudly over the outside broadcast tannoy system. GOT was persuaded to retrieve the offending comic from my brother's music folio. He was not best pleased but saw the funny side of things and nicknamed my brother Gnasher from this moment on*!*

GOT as judge on a Southern Television hymn or carol competition

The experiences at Southern Television were just as rewarding for Fred Dinenage, the TV presenter:

> In the 'sixties and early 'seventies [it] was just the happiest place to be. And one of my happiest memories was presenting a programme called 'Carols for Children'. Geoffrey Tristram was our senior judge in this competition for carols written and sung by young people. My musical knowledge was somewhat suspect - my speciality at the time was presenting sports programmes! I remember saying to Geoffrey: 'I'm not too clued-up on music and musical terms!' 'Don't worry about it, Fred', I remember him saying. 'Anything you need to know, just ask me'. And I did - on more than one occasion. A lovely, gentle,

and wonderfully knowledgeable man. It was a privilege to have known him - and worked alongside him. And the programme, I'm pleased to say, was a huge success. More due to Geoffrey and our young singers than me. Sadly, little or no footage still exists of those Southern Television programmes - but the memories linger on.

Tim Norris has especially fond memories of GOT's support for instrumentalists at the school:

At Saint Peter's ... I played in the school concert band and sang in the choir ... Geoffrey encouraged as many pupils as possible to play in the school band under the direction of Mr Fred Payne (brass) and assisted by Mr Tibby Turner (woodwind). After Mr Payne's death, Geoffrey asked the boys what they wanted to do and we decided that those left should form a swing band. Geoffrey telephoned the Bournemouth Symphony Orchestra and they contacted and agreed to send Paul Ringham, then second trumpet player in the BSO, to run the swing band. We had an agent, we called the band the Smiley Glenn Miller Band and under Paul's direction we played out all over the town and at the Pavilion Ballroom, the Winter Gardens for tea dances, hotels, and ... and many other venues. Brilliant, and such a thrill for all those in the band. Five saxophone players, five trumpet players and drums, bass (provided by me on tubs) and singers. Geoffrey's legacy of good community-music making was being carried forward. One of the school's trumpet players Joseph Atkins now plays in the BBC Symphony and Concert Orchestras, having played in the BSO with Paul Ringham at the age of sixteen whilst still at St Peter's doing A levels. He went to the Royal Academy of Music in London. Many of those boys from St Peter's went on to play in conservatoire bands and orchestras and three of us joined the Army and became military musicians. One pupil, John Reidy, trained as a teacher and came back to the school and joined the staff and continued to play his saxophone in the new music department as it morphed over the years.

In time, many of the players in the St Peter's bands, swing band and G&S orchestras for shows would occasionally get together and we formed the Taverners Big Band, and we would, 33 years later, create 'Stompin on the Quomps',[70] a cool annual jazz festival held on the Quay at Christchurch. The Taverners were always and will continue to be the main act, but at least five or six other jazz band swing bands and groups now play as part of this annual first weekend in August event in partnership with the Regent Centre for the Arts in the High Street in Christchurch. The Taverners Big Band[71] included many players from the St Peter's Jazz Band. We called ourselves the Taverners, after the Castle Tavern Pub three doors down from 'Church Hatch' ... Links within links within links and all stemming from the late, great G&T, as we boys used to call him at school.

This incredible side to Geoffrey's musical educational qualities was amazing. He would do so much to encourage all the instrumentalists and singers at St Peter's, and his infectious energy has lasted with me for years. Although now semi-retired, I have built upon this legacy with all the groups, bands, ensembles and of course the school, which worked in partnership with Foundation Music at the University of Winchester. When I came out of the Army I worked for the President of the UK Music Trade, Eddie Moors, who ran and owned ... a huge business situated at 679 Christchurch Road, Boscombe Bournemouth

70 https://stompin.org/ https://www.facebook.com/StompinontheQuomps
71 https://www.facebook.com/watch/?ref=search&v=10156593537057516& external_log_id=b4f077a5-fc9c-4859-8f3b-0a5c64a6efcd&q=Taverners%20 Big%20band

[and] supplying the UK and Europe with instruments, sheet music, electronics and much more. Eddie Moors Junior was educated at St Peter's and played the clarinet in the school concert band but not in the swing band. Eddie took me under his wing and another strand of my musical education started. He often spoke of G&T, and we would over the next six years work closely with the Bournemouth Music Centre at King Park Junior School with five orchestras and bands. The Christchurch Music Centre[72] at Twynham School is still going [and] is a part legacy of G&T's influence. I occasionally play and help the current students out and we have performed annually in the Priory; amazing community music-making and makers.

Press cutting about GOT's production of Oliver! at St Peter's in July 1971 (daughter Carolyn is second on the right)

72   https://www.facebook.com/ChristchurchMusicCentre

Christine Gerveshi, a student at St Peter's from 1970-1972, remembers:

He was a unique character, very much loved by the pupils. He taught the 'music appreciation' class, which meant that we all got to relax and listen to some of the great English composers. He encouraged us to go to the BSO concerts [GOT had close links with the Bournemouth Symphony Orchestra at the time], which I certainly did. He directed us in Oliver in 1971; we had great fun and put on a wonderful show thanks to him. We must have endeared ourselves to him because thereafter we were 'his choir'.

One unforgettable memory is that he arranged that 'his choir' should give a concert of Christmas carols at the Priory in December 1971. We were all awed by the experience of performing in that glorious space; the connection with centuries of Christmases past was tangible.

In the spring of 1972, he decided to take 'his choir' to Paris for a weekend; I have no idea where the idea came from. We made the trip by ferry and train; I had never left England before and was thrilled! He deposited us in a B&B then left us to our own devices for the rest of the trip! Amazingly, we all came back unscathed, with so many stories to tell, having walked endless miles through that beautiful city.

I took my Grade 8 piano exams while at St Peter's. With the pressure of A levels, things weren't going well. Mr. T. caught me practising on the piano in the auditorium a couple of times. He scooped me up and took me to his house to play on his infinitely better piano instead. He kindly gave me some pointers which, I am sure, enabled me to just squeak a Pass in the exam. Just one example of his gruff kindness.

David Cordell also remembers GOT with affection:

> I was at St. Peter's from 1972-1979. What I most remember
> was he gave me a love of The Planets composed by Holst,
> having played us a recording during class. Don't know
> why but that particular recording has stuck with me for
> over 40 years. I also remember with fondness attending
> a performance of the Mikado which I seem to remember
> [GOT] loved and which I still like to watch to this day. I
> do remember being a little frightened by him when I was
> 11. He seemed a little gruff, but I think underneath it all
> there was an affable person, who loved music and tried
> to convey it to boys who weren't always so interested.
> He definitely is one of the teachers I remember by name
> even though I'm not the most musically talented. It's
> nice to have you collect these memories …[they] help us
> remember where we have come from.

Giving students a love of music was clearly a major element of GOT's
legacy as a teacher. Terry Powell writes:

> I attended St Peter's School in Southbourne from 1959-
> 1964 and this was where I met Mr Tristram who took
> us for music. He was so passionate about music that you
> couldn't help responding with similar enthusiasm. One
> of his small moments it seemed in most lessons was to
> improvise on 'Three Blind Mice' as light relief to what
> went before. It was he who encouraged us to attend musical
> performances and he encouraged the class to watch the
> BSO in action and so I attended my first symphony
> concert at the Winter Gardens in Bournemouth for a
> performance which included the 1812 Overture and I sat
> behind the orchestra on the uncomfortable seats but ones
> which allowed you to watch at close quarters.
>
> I took part in two Gilbert & Sullivan operettas. In
> both, Mr. Tristram led the musical rehearsals and the

performances, in The Mikado he conducted a small group of musicians and the Gondoliers he accompanied and conducted from an organ. These performances lasted a full week. How great it is to enjoy music and when inspired to do so by the likes of Geoffrey Tristram.

GOT was renowned at St Peter's for his wicked sense of humour. During one mass in the school hall, he was playing a great accompaniment to the final hymn when one of the brothers thought he heard the tune of 'Three blind mice' in the bass part. When asked afterwards if this was the case, GOT simply grinned. Joe Gallagher, also a pupil at St Peter's, recollects how teachers would be greeted on entrance to the hall with a 'suitable musical leitmotif'. Columba Cook also remembers GOT's musical humour:

> I initially auditioned for G+S because [my brother] Aidan told me they were such fun. I believe it is fair to say that it was Geoffrey who made them so rewarding and enjoyable to be part of. I clearly remember singing scales for him at the audition. He sometimes played the scales, and even whole pieces of music, slightly out of tune to great comedic effect. The great comedian, Les Dawson, used to do something similar as part of his act. It always reminded me of Geoffrey; it was highly amusing and, of course, very skilful.

He could also be a disciplinarian. Some of his former pupils can still recall vividly his requirement to write out fifty lines (or so) as punishment: 'I must always endeavour to remember that I will receive long (or laborious, depending upon source) and arduous punishments if I fail to [insert example of broken rule here] ...' Kevin Lawton-Barrett, for one, remembers this 'line'. He writes:

> There's no doubt [GOT] was a wordsmith, somewhat strict too, but I always found him to be a warm, slightly comic man, but then I came from a prep school with a terror of a headmaster, so Geoffrey was more approachable.

Nick Lipscombe comments:

> I was a pupil at St Peter's RC School at Southbourne and
> Geoffrey was our music teacher. I left in 1978 and had no
> idea he had passed away the following year. To be clear, I
> am not musically gifted in any shape or form and much of
> what Geoffrey treated us to by way of organ recitals and
> explanations of the theory of music went way over my head.
> But I remember him with great fondness. He was a kind
> and considerate man and he was willing to talk to you if you
> were willing to listen. The most enduring memory I have of
> Geoffrey, and one which I follow to this day, is that he could
> not abide people who chewed their nails. He used to single
> out the culprits, myself included at that time, and show the
> rather bulbous nature of one's fingers as a result of this habit.
> Hands were an extension of one's personality, he would say.
> I also recall another rather amusing story. One day he was
> in conversation with one of the Franciscan brothers and
> he recoiled and said in a rather loud voice 'you have not
> cleaned your teeth this morning!' I have, throughout my
> life, thought about Mr Tristram. He left a lasting impression
> on me. He was a delightful man and a wonderful organist.

The St Peter's community realised how fortunate they were to have
GOT as their Director of Music for almost 20 years. He delighted in
sharing his consummate skill as a musician with those who were interested,
though he had little patience with those who were not. His humour, his
sharp wit, his discipline, and above all, his musicality, are still remembered
by staff and students alike, many of whom acquired their love of music
through GOT, some going on to careers as professionals, including in
music production and stage direction.

Bournemouth Gilbert and Sullivan Society

GOT was Musical Director of the Bournemouth Gilbert and Sullivan
Society in succession to Herbert Parrish, the 'founding' conductor for the

first production in 1947. Between 1948 and 1959, GOT was responsible for some ten productions at the Palace Court Theatre, though in 1953 and 1954 Cyril Knight, of St Peter's Church, Bournemouth, was Musical Director. At the time, GOT must have been too busy directing Poole Grammar School Operatic Society in their equivalent performances.

Members of the Society still remember GOT's work with affection. 'Over three decades Geoffrey proved to be a good friend … always living up to the superlatives used about him; "perfectionist" and "professional" were [words] often quoted, as were "a great character", "full of good humour", "terrific ability", "the best". His response to late attendees at rehearsals was a dry 'how good of you to come'. This generally ensured that the offending member would not repeat the offence. During a bad practice, he was known to put on his hat and coat, walk out, and then promptly come back in again! Once, while performing The Mikado the chorus poked fun at him as they sang 'the Priory Organist, he never will be missed!'

Other reminiscences of GOT's time with the Society include the following:

> He had an 'alarming habit' of walking through the chorus, listening to individuals. Strange unexplained fits of coughing heralded his approach on many occasions. Another of his bêtes noirs were the 'knitting Nellies'. Woe betide any member of the chorus who sought to knit in his presence, for the 'clitter clatter' disturbed him mightily.

> 'Can we have that in English?' was a favourite. As the men's chorus in Ruddigore reached lower and lower depths, [GOT] commented that it was 'like an air-raid siren running down'. Taking his place at the piano during rehearsals, he would weave threads of other songs into the accompaniments and introductions. To everyone's delight and amazement a snippet of 'I do like to be beside the seaside' would float across the hall.

Reviews in the local newspapers of performances by the Society during Geoffrey Tristram's time as Musical Director consistently pay tribute to the high standards reached.

GOT and Rene at a Bournemouth G & S Society dinner, along with Don Gittins and his wife Barbara. Don was the dapper cricket-sweater-wearing page turner for GOT. He recorded many of GOT's performances on tape reels. Some of these now in the family's possession have very thankfully enabled the publication of a selection of hitherto unheard live recordings of GOT's recitals at the Priory.

CHAPTER THREE

Organist and Master
of the Choristers,
Christchurch Priory

Application, Appointment, Initial Strategy

Geoffrey Tristram applied for the post of Choirmaster and Organist[73] at Christchurch Priory in August 1949. The previous Organist, Vivian Stuart, had resigned on 31 July of that year.[74] Keen to make 'the music offered in Christchurch Priory worthy of the highest tradition', he submitted a 'short report' (Appendix A) as part of his application. This 'embodied a few [practical] suggestions … regarding the possibilities respecting … future musical policy'. The 'major points of the issue' were organised into three groups: congregation; choir; organ. GOT recommended 'a happy balance between the amount of music performed by the Choir … and the Congregation'. Congregational practices were proposed as part of a policy of encouraging people 'to sing and play their part in the Services of the Church'. 'Radical changes' were to be avoided, with any alterations being 'so gently and carefully introduced over a long term … to cause the

---

[73]   The job title varied over the years, sometimes being 'Organist and Master of the Choir' rather than 'Organist and Choirmaster'. However, the description most often used seems to have been 'Organist and Master of the Choristers', so this has been the title adopted throughout the book.

[74]   Quoted in Tutte, Harold, *The Organs, Organists and Masters of the Choristers and Gentlemen of Christchurch Priory Church*. Christchurch: privately printed, [1980], p.16.

minimum amount of inconvenience and upset'. The 'report' emphasises the 'prime object of the Choir, as indeed all the music of the Church' was to:

a) lead all the music in which the Congregation take an active part in such a manner as to be conducive to good congregational singing.
b) perform anthems as a fit and worthy offering to Almighty God and the edification of the Congregation as listeners.

Music 'performed by the Choir alone' was to be 'carefully and sincerely interpreted … to convey to the listeners the message of the words and the beauty of the work'. Steps were to be taken 'immediately to increase the working strength of the singing boys to 16 with the possibility of a further increase to 18 with anything up to 6 probationers … at all times upon which to draw and dismiss any who, after a period of anything up to six months' probation did not prove to be intelligently interested in the music and satisfactory from a point of view of discipline'.

GOT was already well acquainted with the 'various methods of recruiting boys' by the time he applied for the Priory post, and recommended:

a) Making friends with headmasters of schools in the district and gaining permission to visit and talk to the boys in the schools and then, if necessary, call and see the parents of any concerned.
b) Direct appeal to the members of the congregation to encourage their sons to join the Choir.
c) Making the life of the existing Choirboys so interesting and attractive that they themselves will bring in their friends.

The report continued by stressing that, while 'the happiest choirboys are invariably not paid … a sum of money [should be] earmarked for the provision of regular activities for the boys in sports and equipment, visits to places of interest and general enjoyment. It will be easily understood that money spent in this way will do far more to encourage the boys in their sense of fellowship and loyalty to the Church'. GOT stressed that he would be focussing on this aspect of recruitment in the first instance, on the grounds that any choir 'is as good as, and no better than, its trebles'. He continued:

> Regarding the gentlemen of the choir, it is my experience that if the standard of work is high and of an interesting nature, I am confident that there will be nothing but enthusiasm and loyalty on the part of those who so freely give of their time and without whom little or nothing could be done.

GOT's perfectionism was evident in the next section of the report, concerning 'choice of music':

> I would strongly emphasise the need ... to perform music which is ... well within the limits of the technical capabilities of the choir, giving adequate time and rehearsal to each ... work to be performed and leaving no part, however small, to chance ... I should persevere with the task of laying the foundations for good choral technique - proper breathing, tone, production of vowel sounds, enunciation of words, clearness of diction and the many other necessary details to secure this end ... Having built a basis upon which to work, the whole character of the choral music can be gradually uplifted into a thing of beauty and joy.

GOT felt that 'Organ playing in the Services of the Church' could be 'a definite asset or [a] hindrance to devotion'. As such 'all accompaniments ... should be sufficiently artistic in suggesting rather than imitating the character of the sung words in order to make the music live in the minds of those who attend the Services. In the same way, carefully chosen voluntaries can do much to help and assist the worshipper'. Similarly, 'by playing the hymns in a rhythmic manner with a certain flexibility of registration, transposed, if necessary, into such a key as to be within the compass of the singers in the congregation, encouragement is given, and more enjoyment will result'.

Finally, and prophetically, he stressed that he would 'be happy to arrange and give a series of weekly organ recitals throughout the summer months, the entire proceeds of which could be devoted to organ or choir funds. In the course of time when the choir had become so proficient, then choral recitals and other musical Services could be introduced'.

First page of GOT's application for the post of Organist and Choirmaster, Christchurch Priory

GOT was successful in his application. The Vicar of Christchurch, the Reverend R.P. Price, wrote to him on 13 September 1949 offering him the post.

> Dear Mr Tristram,
>
> I am very glad to be able to write and formally offer you the post of Choirmaster & Organist here at a stipend of £200 per annum[75], in addition to which there would be the fees from weddings, funerals etc. There are just one or two points I would like to mention.
>
> 1. We do not normally expect our organist to play on Sunday afternoons. But occasionally in a church such as this, there are youth parades, civic services etc. I take it you would not expect a fee for such occasions nor, if none of our voluntary organists were unable to play, for children's services at the great Festivals?
> 2. We have very few choral services on weekdays apart from such days as Christmas, Easter & Whitsun Eves, Good Friday, Dedication Festival, Lady Day (for Mothers' Union). I presume you would be willing to consider these as part of your normal work.
> 3. It has been the custom here for the organist to offer his services free at the marriages or funerals of prominent church workers.
>
> I have put all this rather crudely but it is best for everyone's sake to be clear on such matters so perhaps you would let me know your views on these points. Without entering into any binding agreement perhaps you would also confirm – as you have already told us – your willingness to remain with us for a reasonable time. About the house ['Church Hatch'] – this is managed by a special committee and I

---

[75] Equivalent to £7,530 at 2022 prices. Value of 1949 British pounds today | UK Inflation Calculator (in2013dollars.com)

think the best plan would be for you to get in touch with the Secretary, Mr Stanley White...

I don't know how long notice you would wish to give to your present Vicar but we need not hurry you as Mr. Head is quite willing to continue as deputy organist for the time being.

I am sure you are going to do great things for our music – I only wish you had come three years ago - & I look forward to a very happy time.

Yours sincerely,

R.P. Price

PS I should be grateful if you would refrain from making the appointment public – especially in the press - until I send an acknowledgement of your reply to this letter which I will do by return.

The Christchurch Times for 21 October 1949 announced Geoffrey Tristram's appointment as Organist and Choirmaster at the Priory. The article commented that he was 'already well known in Bournemouth through his broadcasts and recitals of church music'. GOT was quoted as being 'happy to have been chosen ... as he feels that with such a beautiful church, the scope for music is practically limitless ... and intends to take full advantage of the resources offered'. He was 'grateful for the kindness ... shown to him by the Vicar, churchwardens, members of the choir, and other officers of the church, and [looked] forward to a period of happy cooperation for the benefit of the music of the church'.[76]

---

[76]   *Christchurch Times*, 21 October 1949.

Press cutting from the early 1950s about the Priory choirboys rehearsing for a Christmas Carol Service

Developing the Music

In 1949, 'numerically, the choir was strong, but musically the standard was very poor – it left very much to be desired'.[77] GOT found the choir 'disjointed': the singing stood out as being 'every man for himself'; the music was 'three parts junk'.[78] The Vicar agreed, confirming that at the time 'the standard both of singing and discipline left much to be desired'.[79]

---

[77] *Christchurch Times,* December 1970.

[78] *Christchurch Times,* 1 January 1971.

[79] Letter from Reverend Canon R.P. Price, 22 October 1958.

Canon Price's reference in the appointment letter wishing that GOT 'had come three years ago' no doubt related to the fact that the previous postholder, Vivian Stuart, 'though a musician of great experience and wide ability', was unable to deal with the choristers, resulting in 'a lack of harmony between the Organist and the Choir'.[80]

GOT soon 'brought about an immense improvement both in the singing of the choir and the discipline of the boys'. He was quickly held in 'great regard' by all within the church community, 'both as a musician and teacher of music', having 'gifts of a very high order'.[81] Such was the allure of the organ and choral music after GOT's appointment that the queues of people waiting to attend major services at the Priory would regularly stretch down Church Street!

The Priory soon had 'the privilege of being one of the very few, apart from College Chapels and Cathedrals, to provide Choral Evensong broadcasts for the B.B.C.'[82] The Priory organ, choir and organist were renowned throughout the country.[83] As early as 19 November 1950, the Priory choir was broadcasting choral mattins.[84] A newspaper article dating from the early days of GOT's time at the Priory reads as follows:

> The British Broadcasting Corporation, apparently, is very much pleased with the Christchurch Priory Church. The Reverend Martin Wilson was greatly impressed with the service broadcast last Sunday evening [20 April 1952], and I should think that any who may have felt that broadcasting had interfered with the orthodox routine of services must be grateful that the opportunity of enjoying the service was shared by many hundreds of thousands. Some of these might be completely deprived of any form of

---

[80] Quoted in Tutte, Harold, *The Organs, Organists and Masters of the Choristers and Gentlemen of Christchurch Priory Church*. Christchurch: privately printed, [1980], p.16.

[81] Letter from Reverend Canon R.P. Price, 15 January 1951.

[82] Letter from GOT to the Head Teacher, Brockenhurst Count High School, 22 October 1958.

[83] *Christchurch Times*, 27 February 1957.

[84] Cutting, presumed to be from *Radio Times*, dated 19 November 1950, listing the music for the service.

participation in public worship but for the radio. And the frequency with which the B.B.C. uses the Priory either for direct broadcasts or recordings by Geoffrey Tristram gives good proof that they think a lot of its acoustic qualities. [85]

The same newspaper article included a section headed 'Organ Broadcasts':

Music from the organ of the Priory Church is included in the fifteen-minute programmes of organ music being broadcast to at least twenty-five different countries or states spread over the four quarters of the globe during the coming summer and autumn months.

Part of what the B.B.C. calls its Transcription Service, the programmes have been recorded in cathedrals and abbeys throughout the country. In the West Region, the resident organists of Christchurch (Geoffrey Tristram), Salisbury, Winchester and Bath have been chosen for the recordings.

In addition to being broadcast to so many places abroad, the programmes are also to be heard by the Forces in Egypt, Germany, Benghazi, Cyprus, Trieste, Japan, Tripoli, and East Africa.[86]

The choir boys all came from local schools and were 'subject to intensive training in their work'.[87] GOT was seen as being 'especially gifted as a trainer of voices – so much so that the [choirboys'] singing [was the] standard of a Cathedral choir'.[88] GOT's personality and leadership meant that he had 'no trouble as regards discipline', having 'the great gift of being able to communicate enthusiasm for music to his pupils'. There were 'none of the difficulties experienced in many parishes of obtaining

---

[85] *Christchurch Times*, 20 April 1952.
[86] *Christchurch Times*, 20 April 1952.
[87] Letter from Reverend Canon R.P. Price, 15 January 1951.
[88] Letter from Reverend Canon R.P. Price, 22 October 1958.

recruits ... and of holding them'. Both the boys and the men showed 'the utmost keenness for their work'. [89] Jeremy Blandford writes:

> I recall [GOT's] views on the recruitment of choirboys. Several prominent churches at that time were trying to lure boys into their choirs by offering subsidised organ, pianoforte or other instrumental lessons. Geoffrey would have none of it, proclaiming that such measures missed the point and appealed to parents and not to the boys. In his reckoning boys would apply themselves unstintingly if given a simple reward - a packet of chips - after a long and demanding rehearsal.

The music lists for the choral services – and most notably the evensongs broadcast on radio or television over the years – certainly demonstrate an ability to perform the full range of settings and anthems expected of a cathedral choir. This was evident on the many occasions when the Priory singers were invited to perform services at various cathedrals when the resident choirs were on holiday. One such example was Winchester Cathedral, where 'only selected choirs [were] being invited to sing ... and the Priory choir was the first to be selected'. GOT accompanied at all the services.[90] Indeed, it was said that 'if Winchester diocese were ever split and the Priory became a cathedral, the choir is already there – a well-deserved compliment to Mr. Tristram and his voluntary choir of men and boys'.[91] The choristers also began to have regular opportunities to show off their skills and repertoire in the summer recital series at the Priory. GOT was willing to perform less well-known compositions alongside the traditional cathedral choir repertoire, as for example at a special service for Rogationtide, when the choir sang 'a little-known Litany by 17th century composer Henry Loosemore, who was organist at King's College, Cambridge. Photographic copies of the score [were] especially prepared for the occasion by the B.B.C. ... The 30-voice choir [rehearsed] ... for the [previous] six weeks'.[92]

[89] Letter from Reverend Canon R.P. Price, 22 October 1958.
[90] Undated and unattributed press cutting from GOT's scrapbooks.
[91] Undated and unattributed press cutting from GOT's scrapbooks, but presumed to be the *Christchurch Times*, October 1970.
[92] Unattributed newspaper cutting, 23 May 1954.

'The Best Parish Church Choir in England'

The Vicar, Canon Price, considered that 'due to the genius of the organist and choirmaster, Mr Geoffrey Tristram ... the Priory ... had the best parish church choir in England'.[93] All this came from amateurs: the senior male alto, for example, was the local fishmonger![94] The accolades certainly flowed in thick and fast, starting in the 1950s. J.I. ('Jimmy' Taylor), a director of the John Compton Organ Company, wrote of:

> the fine show which came from the Priory ... The singing was quite first class and the organ sounded really magnificent, especially in the two and a half minutes or so in which you were allowed to play part of the Franck 'Pièce Heroïque'. I wish I had been there to hear the remainder. I hope the BBC have duly noted the splendid effect of the organ on the air and that this will be only one of many times that we shall hear the organ on the radio in your expert hands.[95]

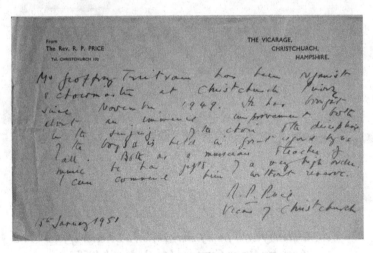

Letter of Recommendation for GOT from the Vicar,
Canon R.P. Price, 15 January 1951

---

[93]   *Christchurch Times*, 22 April 1955.

[94]   Information from Richard Hands.

[95]   Letter to GOT from J.I. Taylor, 23 March 1953. Compton's had rebuilt the organ two years earlier. No doubt the organ-builders were especially pleased that 'their' instrument sounded so good on the radio!

TELEPHONE & TELEGRAPHIC ADDRESS:
ELGAR 6666-7-8.

RAILWAY STATIONS:
PASSENGER: NORTH ACTON (CENTRAL LONDON RLY.)
GOODS: PARK ROYAL (G.W.R.)
WILLESDEN JUNCTION (L.M.S.)

THE JOHN COMPTON
ORGAN COMPANY, LTD.

DIRECTORS:
JOHN COMPTON.
J. I. TAYLOR.
J. W. BYRON F.C.I.S.
E. JAMIESON.
J. F. BROAD.
LOUIS MORRIS.
C. HAWTIN.

Minerva Road,
North Acton,
London, N.W.10.

JIT/BH/C - 23rd March 1953.

Geoffrey Tristram, Esq.,
Church Hatch,
Christchurch,
Hants.

Dear Mr. Tristram,

Just a line to most heartily congratulate you on the
fine show which came from the Priory last evening. The
singing was quite first-class and the organ sounded really
magnificent, especially in the two and a half minutes or
so in which you were allowed to play part of the Franck
Piece 'Heroique'. I wish I had been there to hear the
remainder.

I hope the BBC have duly noted the splendid effect of
the organ on the air and that this will be only one of
many times that we shall hear the organ on the radio in
your expert hands.

With kindest regards and all good wishes,

Yours very sincerely,

J. I. Taylor

J. I. TAYLOR.

Congratulatory letter from Jimmy Taylor, a Director of John
Compton Organ Company Ltd, 23 March 1953

Harold Helman wrote an especially glowing review of one broadcast service:

> There are times when we never know how we stand when we hear a broadcast church service. At times we suffer rather a muddle of psalm singing (which of course may be due on occasion to the varied acoustics of a building, or perhaps a general misunderstanding of their poetry) and of course, we do hear many fine efforts which have been worth both the listening and the time.
>
> On January 4th, [1956] many heard a very fine service broadcast from Christchurch Priory, Hampshire. I regard it as one of the finest musical efforts we have heard over the air for a very long time; and most listeners seem to agree on this point. While this service was progressing one seemed to venture into a land that was radiant with sunshine; and when we realise that quite a lot of today's music is mechanised, this would seem to be quite a lot to say.
>
> The Priory Church is Norman and Gothic ... and is a magnificent building ... A wonderful stone screen separates the nave and the choir ... The singing of both men and boys was excellent and most reverent and will be remembered with gratitude by all who were privileged to hear it. All through, this service was a fine lesson in musical appreciation. It had a definite personality. There seems to be much live talent here, and given good music to work at, backed up by a superb organ, I look forward to many more broadcasts from this noble and ancient church.[96]

Small wonder, then, that in the Parish Newsletter celebrating the 10th anniversary of GOT's appointment to the Priory, Canon Price was able to write that the Priory owed him 'a very big debt of gratitude for having brought the music at the Priory to a standard which excels that of many

---

[96] *Music Teacher and Piano Student*, February 1956.

cathedrals, for the enthusiasm which he inspired in the members of the Choir and for the inspiration which Sunday by Sunday we derived from the musical part of the services'.[97] In 1961, 'at his farewell presentation on leaving to become Dean of Hereford, Canon Price again expressed his appreciation and said he had experienced some of the most glorious services at the Priory. They had a wonderful standard of music and the services had always been offered with great joy. The glory of the worship at the Priory was something which would always remain with him'.[98]

Workload

All this resulted in a heavy workload for the Organist and Master of the Choristers at Christchurch Priory, not forgetting GOT's role as schoolteacher on top of being a famous recitalist. Daughter Carolyn remembers how 'very often after a day of teaching, Dad would drive the length and breadth of the country playing recitals in cathedrals and major parish churches'. An item in the parish magazine for early 1956 described a typical 'busy week' for GOT:

> The first week of the New Year has been a very busy one for Priory Church organist, Mr. Geoffrey Tristram. On Sunday, Mr. Tristram broadcast an organ recital on the West of England Home service. On Wednesday a national broadcast was made of choral evensong from the Priory Church and followed by a recording of carols to be relayed in an Epiphany Anthology tonight. Then yesterday Mr. Tristram travelled to All Saints' Church, Cardiff, for a recital on a new organ.[99]

---

[97]   Quoted in Tutte, Harold, *The Organs, Organists and Masters of the Choristers and Gentlemen of Christchurch Priory Church*. Christchurch: privately printed, [1980], p.17.

[98]   Quoted in Tutte, Harold, *The Organs, Organists and Masters of the Choristers and Gentlemen of Christchurch Priory Church*. Christchurch: privately printed, [1980], p.17.

[99]   Clipping presumed to be from the Parish magazine, early 1956. It is not clear which of the three Cardiff churches dedicated to All Saints was being referred to here. All Saints Church, Cyn-Coed Road, Cardiff (National Pipe Organ Register entry V00534) had a new organ in circa 1961 which would not fit with the presumed date of GOT's opening recital.

GOT accompanied other choirs, often also playing organ solos, especially when they performed or broadcast at the Priory, as for example the Southampton Singers, conducted by Arnold Williams, on 4 July 1956, and again on 18 October 1957,[100] or the Christchurch Harmonic Choir, New Zealand, who performed under their conductor William Hawkey at the Priory on 29 September 1965. GOT also contributed regular 'interludes' between other regional radio programmes and was the organist on a radio 'magazine programme' entitled 'The Faith in the West'.[101]

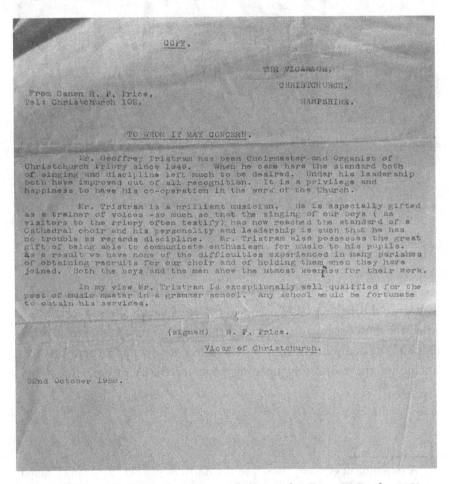

Letter of recommendation from Reverend Canon Robin Price, 22 October 1958

---

[100] *Radio Times*, 22 March 1957.

[101] Various clippings from the mid-1950s, presumed to be from *Radio Times*.

Photograph of the Priory Choir, 1960/61. Reverend Canon
Price was about to leave to be Dean of Hereford

'Magnificent Acts of Worship'

Praise for the Priory Choir, its services, performances, and broadcasts[102] continued throughout GOT's tenure of office. One such was in early 1968, when the eminent organist and teacher Douglas Fox was moved to write to GOT to compliment him on the effectiveness of the performance, 'including the tantalising opening pages of the A minor Choral [by Franck]'.[103]

---

[102] A recording of evensong, broadcast live on 16 September 1970, can be found at (28) BBC Choral Evensong: Christchurch Priory 1970 (Geoffrey Tristram) - YouTube. The introit is Pitoni's 'Cantate Domini'; canticles are Murrill in E; the anthem is Harwood's 'O how glorious'; the final voluntary is Mulet's *Tu es petra*.

[103] Letter to GOT from Douglas Fox, 18 January 1968.

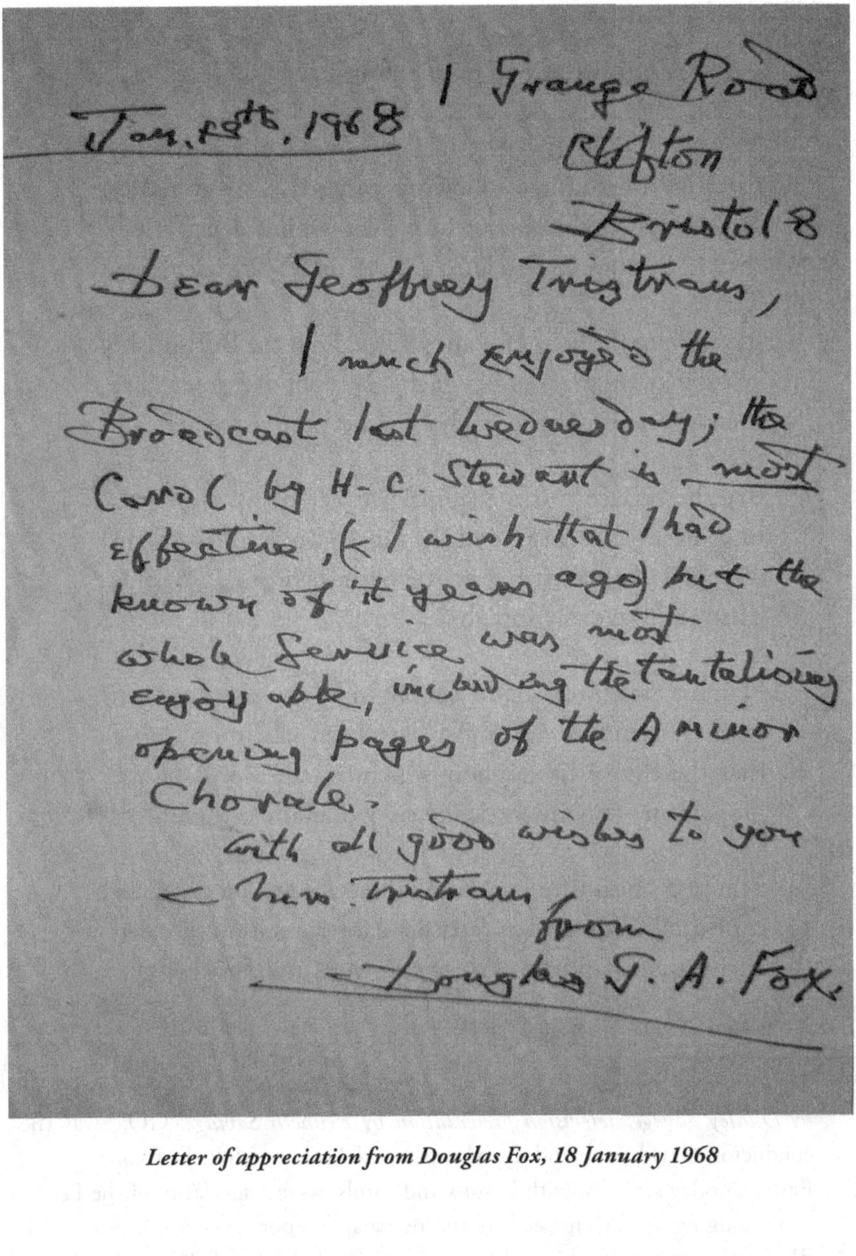

Jan. 18th, 1968   1 Grange Road

Clifton

Bristol 8

Dear Geoffrey Tristram,

I much enjoyed the Broadcast last Wednesday; the Carol by H-C. Stewart is _most_ effective, (& I wish that I had known of it years ago) but the whole Service was most enjoyable, including the tantalising opening pages of the A minor Chorale.

With all good wishes to you & Mrs. Tristram

from

Douglas G. A. Fox.

Letter of appreciation from Douglas Fox, 18 January 1968

The choir also appeared on television, as for example at a 'Songs of Praise' recorded in Christchurch Priory on 3 October 1967 and shown on 12 November that same year on BBC 1[104] and another one on Easter Sunday, 1971.[105]

Congratulations pour in on Priory service

Messages of congratulation have poured in from many parts of the country following yesterday's great Easter service of Sung Eucharist which went out in colour[106] from the 11th century Christchurch Priory on BBC-1 television.

It went into millions of homes throughout the British Isles and the joyful manner in which it was put over must have been a great lift to those who watched and listened.

For the service was a magnificent act of worship in a most beautiful setting and the music, under the brilliant direction of organist and master of the choristers Geoffrey Tristram, was truly superb.

Hours of hard work had been put in by choirmaster, men and boys, and viewers must have been left in no doubt that the Priory has a choir which, in the words of the programme announcer, is the envy of many cathedrals.

Schubert's beautiful communion service was an excellent choice and the choir's sympathetic interpretation revealed a true understanding of this great work and its message.

---

[104] *Songs of Praise, recorded in Christchurch Priory, Hampshire ... Hymns introduced by Dudley Savage; television presentation by Kenneth Savidge.* GOT was the conductor, David Stickland the organist, and Anthony Holt the soloist.

[105] Easter Sunday services, with lessons and carols, were a speciality of the Priory choir, judging by both music lists and newspaper reports.

[106] BBC 1 first transmitted in colour on 15 November 1969. BBC Blogs - About the BBC - 46 years of colour TV on BBC One

Bruckner's majestic Ecce sacerdos provided a magnificent introit, and the communion hymns, O Saving Victim (Sydney H. Nicholson) and Now the Green Blade Riseth illustrated the choir's devotion and deep understanding of religious music.

Later, at Evensong, the Vicar, Canon Leslie Yorke, paid a special tribute to Mr. Tristram and the choir for their part in the service. Celebrant at Sung Eucharist was the Vicar and an Easter message was given by the Bishop of Winchester ... [who] said ... that those who worshipped at the Priory were, under the leadership of the Vicar and with the help of many friends in England, America and elsewhere, making valiant efforts to raise thousands of pounds year by year to preserve 'this wonderful part of our national heritage'.[107]

---

[107] *Christchurch Times*, 11 April 1971.

Songs of Praise

Recorded in

Christchurch Priory, Hampshire

on

Tuesday, 3rd October, 1967, at 7.30 p.m.

to be shown on

Sunday, 12th November, 1967, 6.50—7.20 p.m.

B B C — 1

★　★　★

Hymns introduced by Dudley Savage

★　★　★

Conductor : **Geoffrey Tristram**

Organist : **David Stickland**

Soloist : **Anthony Holt**

★　★　★

Television presentation by Kenneth Savidge

BBC flyer advertising 'Songs of Praise' from Christchurch Priory, recorded 3 October 1967

Music at Christchurch Priory was also much appreciated by local people. Gillian Morgan writes:

> Aaah, Geoffrey Tristram, such wonderful memories of Christchurch Priory in a golden period of its history! Apart from Geoffrey being a legendary organist and choral director, the Priory was also fortunate to have the most incredibly charismatic vicar, Canon Leslie Yorke. Between these two gifted individuals, the music and services were virtually the hub of Christchurch.
>
> I am 'a native' of Christchurch and grew up with the Priory being a very central point in my life. I probably have my father to thank for my interest in church music in general as he was a chorister at Christchurch, Oxford (oddly!) and he would always discuss and compare different choral pieces. Of course, it was the swinging sixties and I was a teenager at the time so some would think it unusual for someone of that age who was hooked on the Beatles or the Rolling Stones to also be a great fan of organ music... so much so, that I was a regular at the Wednesday organ recitals, and never missed one of them!
>
> Geoffrey's allure was so great that my memories of the Christian celebrations of Easter, Christmas, etc. are almost electric. The queue for Easter Sunday morning service used to stretch all the way down Church Street, all eager to eager to hear Canon Yorke's sermon, but most of all, to appreciate the magic of the Priory organ and the fabulous choir. I don't think I have felt that atmosphere quite like it again. Christmas too brought people from far and wide, and the building was always packed ready to listen to Geoffrey's versions of all the great pieces.

Maintaining High Standards and Celebrating Success as Mr. Music

The high standard of choral singing and organ accompaniment continued throughout GOT's 30 years as Organist and Master of the Choristers.

> Now there is nothing but praise for the efforts of the 14 men and 20 boys in the choir. The Priory Church has no difficulty in finding choirboys either, at a time when church choirs are dwindling through lack of interest. It's not as though they get paid much either — music costs the Priory Church £160 a year. Such success depends on the qualities and ability of the choirmaster. He must instil among his class an enthusiasm sufficient to defeat the competing demands of homework and entertainment. And when the demands of the choir include practice two or three times a week, as when preparing for special events, they need a great deal of enthusiasm and loyalty. Mr. Tristram has never found this lacking. 'They are wonderful youngsters', he said of the choirboys. 'I don't find the kids nowadays are no good. Their hearts are in the right place, in spite of the modern lack of parental control'.[108]

---

[108] *Christchurch Times*, 1 January 1971.

Priory choristers' cartoon about pay (undated)

ADMISSION BY PROGRAMME 30p

CHRISTCHURCH PRIORY CHURCH

A RECITAL

by

THE PRIORY CHOIR

on

Wednesday, 29th September 1976 at 8 p.m.

PROGRAMME

Motets

Cantate Domino	Giuseppe Pitoni, 1657-1743
O Bone Jesu	G.P.da Palestrina, 1525-1594
Ave Verum	William Byrd, 1542-1623
Exultate Justi	T.L.da Viadana, 1564-1627

Canticle

Te Deum in C	Benjamin Britten, b. 1913

Anthems

Rejoice in the Lord alway	Henry Purcell, 1659-1695
The Heavens are telling the glory of God (from 'Creation')	
	Joseph Haydn, 1732-1809
I was glad when they said unto me	C.Hubert H.Parry, 1848-1918

INTERVAL

Motets

Let all mortal flesh keep silence	Edward Bairstow, 1874-1946
Beati Quorum Via	Charles V.Stanford, 1852-1924
Justorum Animae	" "
The Russian Contakion for the departed	

Anthems

And I saw a new heaven	Edgar Bainton, 1880-1956
My beloved spake	Patrick Hadley, 1899-1972
Let all the world in every corner sing	Ralph Vaughan Williams, 1872-1958
Evening Hymn	Balfour Gardiner, 1877-1950

****

Priory Choir recital programme, 29 September 1976

In 1969, GOT celebrated 20 years at the Priory. 'Music lovers through the area' readily agreed that 'the local' was 'the richer for his presence'. Music at the church had been 'so upgraded through his efforts that the choir [had] earned the reputation of being one of the finest in the country ... The Priory had anxious moments when [GOT] was taken ill last Christmas [1968] with a severe heart attack [It was his second; the first was in 1965].[109] But he has been back on duty for some time now, as brilliant as ever, and the Priory hope to see him around for many more years to come'.[110]

---

109 Information from Peter Strange.
110 *Bournemouth Evening Echo*, 20 November 1969.

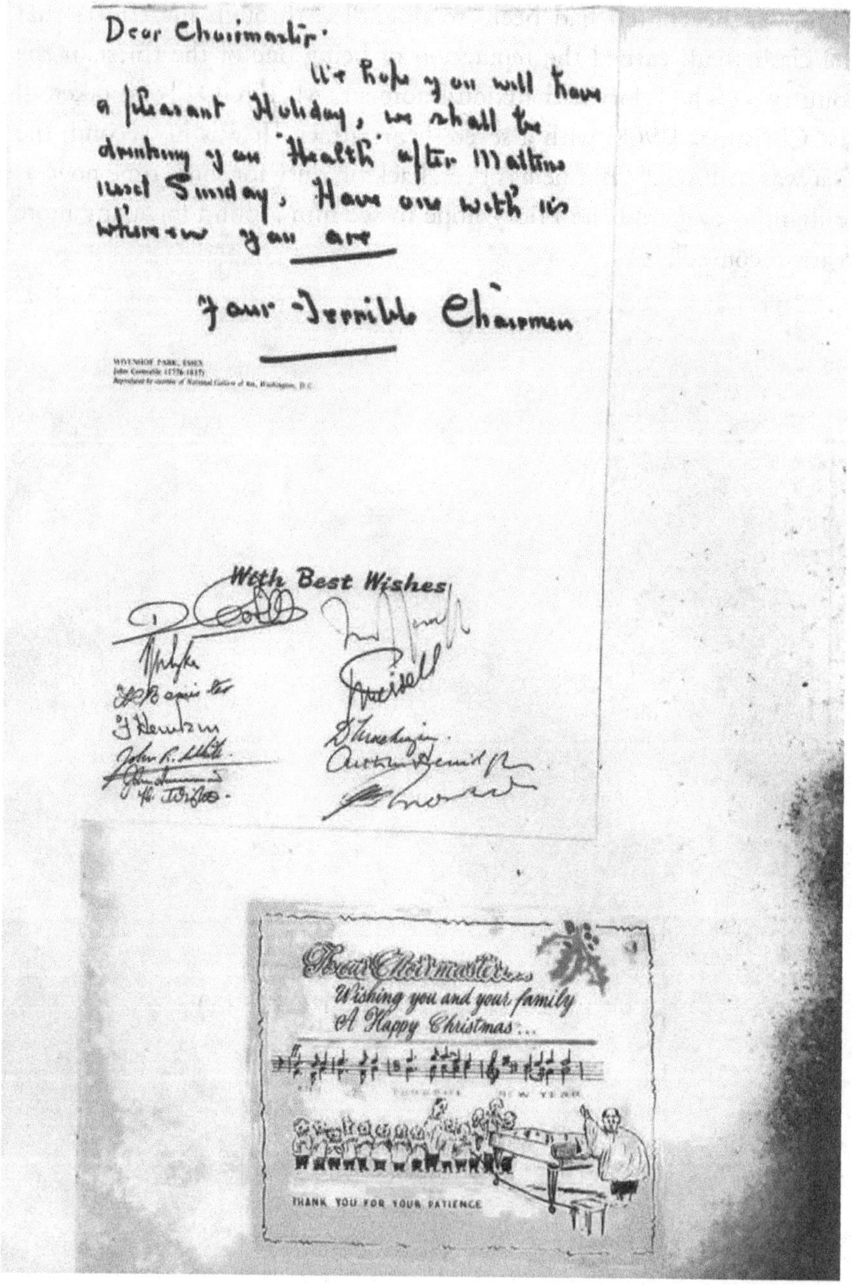

Dear Choirmaster.

We hope you will have a pleasant Holiday, we shall be drinking your "Health" after Mattins next Sunday. Have one with us wherever you are

Your Terrible Chairmen

With Best Wishes

Dear Choirmaster...
Wishing you and your family
A Happy Christmas...

THANK YOU FOR YOUR PATIENCE

Various greetings to GOT from the Gentlemen of the Choir

In late 1974, GOT celebrated his 25th anniversary as Organist and Master of the Choristers.

Tributes to Priory town's 'Mr. Music'

A wonderful record – that's how the Vicar of Christchurch, Canon Leslie Yorke, described Mr. Geoffrey Tristram's service to the 11th century Priory Church at the weekend. Mr. Tristram has just completed 25 years as organist and master of the choristers at the Priory. And at a special luncheon-party on Sunday the clergy, churchwardens, choirmen and their wives expressed a warm thank you to him. They presented him with a set of wine goblets and a cheque, and for Mrs. Tristram there was a large bouquet of flowers. The luncheon-party, provided by Mr. Tristram's family, was a surprise event – he returned home after Mattins to find the party arranged and all the well-wishers present.

Like all the Sundays since Mr. Tristram took over musical direction at the Priory 25 years ago, it was a day for lovely music. Only on this occasion there was something extra special. At the Eucharist service the choir proudly sang the maestro's own composition of mass, the beautiful Tristram in A flat. And this was repeated at Evensong.

At all services throughout the day Canon Yorke paid tribute to Mr. Tristram's long service. And at the party the Vicar thanked him sincerely for what he had done for the choir and music at the church over the years. 'I don't think the music has ever been better than at the moment, due to Geoffrey's efforts and continual concern', he said. The Priory's music was known far and wide and Geoffrey was known nationwide. 'He has a great reputation, and we are all very proud of him and grateful for what he has done,' added the Vicar.

Mr. Tristram thanked the choir and clergy for their support and for the presentation gifts. Working out statistics, he reckoned he had attended services on 1,300 Sundays at the Priory, listened to 3,900 sermons, played 16,900 hymns and heard 5,200 hours of bellringing. 'I enjoy working with you all, we have a splendid choir and who could ask for more,' added Mr. Tristram.

The music scene in Christchurch and throughout the area is the richer for Geoffrey Tristram's presence. Through his efforts and encouragement, the Priory have earned the reputation of being one of the finest in the country. They have sung on television and radio and their traditional Christmas Festival of Carols draws a 'standing room only' situation every year. A record made by the choir was a complete sell-out.

But Mr. Tristram hasn't confined his talents to the Priory. He has made a name for himself through organ recitals on the B.B.C., has travelled widely giving recitals, was a successful musical director of Bournemouth's Gilbert and Sullivan Society and is Director of Music at St. Peter's School, Southbourne. In the recording world he has 'cut' several discs on the Priory organ including LPs. One of them, for organ and violin and made exclusively for an America company, won an award ...

The Priory choir have a reputation for family associations and Mr. Tristram's son Michael has been a member since a boy.

Many people will join the Priory in congratulating Mr. Tristram on his service and in the wish that he will continue for many more years as the old Priory town's 'Mr. Music'.[111]

---

[111]   *Bournemouth Evening Echo*, 4 December 1974.

Apart from 'bits and pieces' such as the (presumed lost) Easter Responsory, GOT did not have much time for composing: 'I'm a slow, laborious writer and time is too short', he said.[112] The Responsory was perhaps first performed at the Priory's traditional Easter festival of lessons and carols in 1959 and repeated in subsequent years. Words were chosen from the scriptures by the then Vicar, Canon Robert Price. The service sheet listed 'Robert Jefrys' (GOT's pen name) as the composer. The choir had 'pre-recorded the part of the angel choir and on [the] Sunday this was replayed from the east end of the church while the response was made by the choir at the west end. This was followed by the processional hymn "Jesus Christ is risen today"'.[113]

The Mass in A flat, still regularly sung by Christchurch Priory choir, shows what might have been had GOT been able to devote more time to composition. The manuscript score still survives, signed, like the Easter Responsory, by one 'B[rothe]r Jefrys'. The work sets the Latin text of the Mass, omitting the Credo. It is a demanding composition, both for the singers and their accompanist, as one would expect, given the reputation of choir and composer! GOT writes in an eclectic style, fusing elements of the English cathedral tradition – as evinced in the works of Harwood, Jackson, Murrill, and others - with writing more akin (not surprisingly) to the French 20th century organ school. Witness the organ part in the Sanctus: shades of Henri Mulet are evident! GOT is well capable of writing both jubilant, expansive music (Gloria, Sanctus) and more contemplative sections (the penitent Kyrie; the simple, devotional Benedictus; the haunting Agnus Dei). The work has a great (and at times, restless) rhythmic drive and vitality. A facsimile of the Mass in A flat can be found between chapters three and four.

Reminiscences, Anecdotes and More

Michael Tristram writes:

> Even at that age, my sole aim was to join the Priory choir, which I was eventually allowed to do as soon as I reached my 7th birthday, even though I wasn't tall enough to see

---

112 *Christchurch Times*, 11 April 1971.
113 *Christchurch Times* 5 April 1959.

over the choir desk and had to stand on a wooden kneeler! Two practices a week, 3 choral services every Sunday, up to six weddings on a Saturday in the summer season earning 2/6d per wedding which paid for my shared love [with his father] of model railways.

Dennis Wright (known as 'Bob' when a boy) had similar experiences:

I joined the Priory Church choir when I was seven in 1952 and worked my way up to Head Boy until I was 15 years old, when my voice broke.

I was introduced to Geoffrey Tristram in 1952 by my father Harold Wright. He was a great friend of his and was a tenor chorister since he was a boy to when Mr. Tristram died, when my father became a verger.

I used to go round to Mr. Tristram's house 'Church Hatch' when I was a boy regularly to help and learn model railways. He had a very large room full of model railways, a fantastic layout. It was through Mr. Tristram that I have a big model railway collection myself, all from the 1950s to 2018.

Mr. Tristram used to take the choirboys on outings to where they made and repaired steam trains – Eastleigh sheds, York Museum, and many other places.

Then when I was 11 years old, I went to Twynham Secondary School, Christchurch. Geoffrey Tristram was my music teacher. I left in 1961, just after Mr. Tristram went to teach music at St Peter's School in Bournemouth. He was always a good friend and nice man to me and my family.

Talking about pipe organs, he could play it with his eyes shut, even without music books. He knew everything about the organ and was always getting it improved. I sat in the console next to him a few times. It was wonderful.

Dean Shearlock, Assistant Curate at the Priory in the early 1960s, writes:

> My appetite [for church music] was further strengthened by the very high standard of the choral tradition at the Priory in GOT's time there. Just as a matter of interest, I ended my ecclesiastical career as chairman of the group which was the official body concerned with cathedral music, consisting of five deans, five precentors, five cathedral organists and the respective chairmen of the RSCM and the Choir Schools' Association. Those four years with GOT were a tremendously important influence over the whole of my ministry since. He was a brilliant choirmaster, insisting on getting things right: examples are the importance of Ds and Ts, especially in the singing of the psalms, and in his total abhorrence of scooping upwards until you managed to hit the right note.

Towards the end of his time at the Priory, GOT said he 'had no desire to move. My choir of men and boys are marvellous people. To persuade youngsters to give up all their Sunday mornings and evenings and a few hours during the week in rehearsal is no mean feat nowadays. The choirmen's wives, bless 'em all, don't seem to mind their husbands' absences, though they probably have to peel the potatoes and take their wives breakfast in bed in order to square them.' He added 'We do our best to aid worship within the limits of a very tight budget.'[114]

Choristers' birthdays would be celebrated with the relevant tune woven into the improvisation! GOT adopted the same approach at weddings, on one occasion weaving the tune 'she's a lassie from Lancashire' into the music![115] Dean Shearlock, Assistant Curate at the Priory in the early 1960s comments: 'I asked [GOT] once what was the secret [of his prowess as an improviser]: "years of studying harmony", was his reply. On one occasion I was preaching about London's mighty waterway; needless to say, he played the choir out at the end of the service with a subtly disguised version of "Old

---

114 GOT speech.
115 Information from Richard Hands.

Father Thames".' Michael Tristram also remembers many an occasion at the Priory 'with Dad on the organ improvising as required and depending on the season or a particular birthday of a choir member, would entwine the appropriate tune into what he was playing, with most completely oblivious!'

One Sunday evening as the choir was warming up in the vestry prior to Evensong, the verger came in and said to them, 'sorry but the Vicar can't make it tonight as he's not feeling very well'. GOT replied in a stage whisper, 'nothing trivial I hope?' During the sermon, GOT would often retreat into the north transept for a quick smoke. A choirman would provide a little cough to cover the sound of the striking match! Interestingly the fact that he 'snuck' out of the east end door of the Priory for a quick smoke during the Sunday sermons was well known to the choir and was only ever caught out once by a shorter than expected homily! GOT would also play 'church cricket' during services, according to Columba Cook: 'the general idea was that every time the vicar said "I" during a sermon it counted as a run; and every time the vicar said the word "God" it counted as a wicket'.

There was also the memorable incident when a very stuck-up usher refused GOT entry into the Priory for a posh wedding even when he argued, saying that he should be allowed in. That same usher had to come cap in hand with great apologies to fetch him a few minutes later! Richard Hands tells of a similar occurrence involving GOT and his encounter with an unfortunate jobsworth:

> On one occasion when we were down in Christchurch there was a big Scout service in the Priory. There was a long queue to the door of the Priory stretching back more or less to Church Hatch. Just before the service [GOT] strolled over, past the queue to the door where he was greeted by a Scouting jobsworth who told him he couldn't just jump the queue. Instead of arguing [GOT] told him that they would be needing him very shortly, that he lived just over there and that he wouldn't come back until the man came to apologise. He returned home and about ten minutes later there was a ring at the door and a rather embarrassed jobsworth who had been dispatched to clear up the mess!

GOT could certainly be determined, ('he was his own man', recalls Richard Hands) and did not suffer fools (even amongst the police) gladly, as suggested by the following newspaper report:

Choir master calls the tune in row with police

Church organist Geoffrey Tristram is determined to make the police face the music for slapping a £6 parking ticket on his car. And unlike almost every other motorist in Britain, he looks like getting his own way. For he will be at the organ when Dorset police have their annual parade at Christchurch Priory on Sunday. And for the first time he has decided that his fortissimo performance will cost the police £6 – the cost of his parking ticket.

Last night at his Georgian home in Church Street, beside the ancient priory, stocky, balding Mr Tristram said:

'I am damned annoyed. Normally I wouldn't dream of charging for my services as an organist at a special police service like this. If they will eventually let me off the fine, I will pay my £6 fee into police funds. If not, I shall keep their money to pay for my fine.

Mr. Tristram, who is 54, explained: 'my car was only there for a matter of minutes. I left the side door open and went in to pick the garage keys up. The phone rang. It was an urgent call … one of my choirboys had been injured. I dealt with it quickly and walked out to find that darned ticket stuck on the windscreen … I feel very irritated. I have lived here 26 years, and this is my first offence'.

The police meanwhile were resigned about paying the £6. An officer said:

That's fair enough. It's up to him …Once a ticket has been issued it cannot be withdrawn by the issuing officer. If Mr. Tristram writes to the fixed penalty office at Poole, I am sure he will get a sympathetic hearing'.[116]

That was not the end of it, as the Daily Express and local newspapers related at the time:

Organist in tune for 'ticket' tax

Organist Geoffrey Tristram's bill for playing at the police service in Christchurch Priory next Sunday has gone up.

He was going to charge £6 to cover a parking ticket he was given for leaving his car outside his home in Church Street, Christchurch, while he fetched the garage key.

But the fee has gone up to £9.23 – to cover income tax! After last night's Echo story about Mr. Tristram's predicament, he received phone calls from two accountants.

'They advised me to charge £9.23 to take tax into account. So that's what I'm going to do', said Mr. Tristram.

His garage fronts directly on to the road where there is a parking ban.

Mr. Tristram is director of music at St. Peter's School, Southbourne, and from colleague Paul Collier comes the following variation on 'A Policeman's Lot', with apologies to Gilbert and Sullivan:

When the citizens of Christchurch are a-parking
Are a-parking
Upon these rather silly yellow lines
Yellow lines

---

[116] Unattributed newspaper cutting, presumed to be from the *Christchurch Times*, 1972.

Do not try to stop the football fans a-larking
Fans a-larking
But try to build the police force funds with fines
Funds with fines
The motorists must always have a ticket
Have a ticket
With constabulary duties to be done
To be done
And if upon his windscreen you can stick it
You can stick it
Then a policeman's lot can be a happy one
Happy one.

Sunday's service is the annual one of the Dorset Special Constabulary.[117]

Rayner Skeet, now a singer in the Priory choir, recalls his time as one of GOT's organ students and practising on the organ.

> I received organ lessons from [GOT] at Christchurch Priory sixty years ago! I am happy to share some memories from that time as he was such a good teacher and I learned so much from him. I began organ lessons at St Christopher's Church, Southbourne where I was boy chorister and had first felt I would like to play the organ. My piano teacher, Geoffrey Dufall, was the choirmaster and organist and encouraged me to take up the organ. I then trained as a schoolteacher at King Alfred's College, Winchester, now the University of Winchester. As part of the main music course, I received organ lessons from Alwyn Surplice on the Cathedral organ and even got to play for a Choral Evensong sung by the Voluntary Choir.

---

[117] Unattributed newspaper cutting, presumed to be from the *Christchurch Times*, 1972.

However, it was when I started my teaching career in Bournemouth that I began to receive organ lessons from [GOT]. This is when I discovered how painstaking he was as compared to Alwyn Surplice. Through him I got my first position as organist and choirmaster at St George's Church, Jumpers, daughter church of the Priory, where I also trained a choir of men and boys.

I used to practice on the Priory organ on Monday evenings when the bell ringers also rehearsed. I would collect a large bunch of keys from [GOT] at Church Hatch and then let myself in through the outside door where later the bell ringers entered. I would then practice for an hour or two with just the light by the organ console to save electricity. One Monday evening, when it had got dark, I made my way down to the swing doors leading from where the bell ringers assembled to find the doors had been locked! I had always found them unlocked previously. So, I was now locked in the Priory! I was living alone with my mother at the time and when I hadn't got home at 10.00pm she telephoned [GOT] concerned about me. As I had his keys, he had to contact a churchwarden, collect his keys and I was finally released ... around 10.30pm.

It was quite an eerie experience for me, and I have often related the story to my pupils. In fact, the key for the swing doors was on [GOT]'s bunch but it was dark so, although I tried to find the key among so many, I went back to the console and began to play SOS as loud as I could! All sorts of strange sounds occurred whilst was I locked in like footsteps that vanished away into nothingness. I always took a torch after that! A fellow student at KAC lived at Alton and asked me if [GOT] would be prepared to play the organ for a recital at his parish church. [GOT] readily agreed and took me there and back in his car and on our return, we had fish and chips from his favourite fish and chip shop at Tuckton. Organ pieces I associate with [GOT] and that I learned from him were Karg-Elert's 'Choral Improvisation on Nun Danket' and Cesar Franck's 'Prelude, Fugue and Variation, both of which he recorded.

This chapter ends with a reminiscence from John Broad who, when welcomed as a 'returnee' to the Priory Choir was greeted with strains of The Mikado interweaved with the organ voluntary at the end of Mattins.

My involvement with [GOT] began somewhere in the mid-fifties after I was taken to a service at the Priory by my parents. There was a part of the service when the choir processed up the south aisle and it produced a moment I've never forgotten. A server in a magnificent startling white costume with bright red panels, led the procession of singers carrying a shiny brass cross which, at each stained-glass window, caught the sunlight and reflected the vivid colours onto the surrounding pillars. The effect on this young child was electric: I just had to be the guy carrying that cross. 'Would you like to be one of those?' my dad whispered. 'Oh, yes', I answered, not having seen or taken notice of the swarm of youngsters in blue and white following my new hero.

The following week, with mounting excitement, I was presented at a gathering of very tall older boys who were standing in a semi-circle around what appeared to be a large rock (the font) at the back of the church. They were all holding books but there was no sign of the man in white with red panels. Maybe he would come along later to show me what to do with the cross. The kindly teacher asked me to stand beside the tallest boy and asked him to share his book with me. I didn't know why I had to do this but perhaps I had to read about how to carry crosses. It was difficult for the tall boy because he had to hold his half of the book at the height of his left trouser pocket so I could peer over the edge of the book. After a short speech from the teacher and without warning all these boys suddenly burst loudly into song. It was an astonishing moment. I saw the finger of the tall boy tracing the progress of the words they were singing but I could only stand and stare in amazement. I had never been that close to children singing in tune and it was wonderful, a revelation, a warm bath of sound. I was hooked: forget the guy in the white costume, this was what I wanted to do!

From that moment on, in his undemonstrative way, [GOT] was to have a profound effect on my life and both my careers. He taught me to sing properly, holding a lit candle in front of each boy to develop breath control, taught us how to pitch notes by not reaching up to them from below but by 'placing' them from above, nose down, eyes up, never over-singing. 'If you can't hear the boy next to you, you're singing too loudly', producing a consistent vocal line by 'stroking the cat' from the head to the tip of its tail. 'A choir is only as good as its top line', he used to say; and he produced a top line the best in the south, to the extent that the first ever live 'outside' TV broadcast from inside a church was performed at Christchurch Priory. The choir had to be good to qualify for that and it was achieved on just three hours rehearsal per week - 6pm-7pm, Mondays, followed by cricket on 'The Quomps'; 6.30 - 8.30pm on Fridays. Four or five weddings on a Saturday on a busy weekend in April, or two or three throughout the summer gave us performance experience, confidence, and a certain polish.

The other key aspect of the Priory's success in those years was the series of virtuoso recitals given by [GOT]. In fact, every service became, at least in part, a concert. He could play anything and always at an international standard, so it was frustrating for him when his set pieces at the end of a service were adversely affected by a noisy and unappreciative crowd at the back of the church. His complaints went unheeded by the churchwardens until on one occasion, mid-voluntary, both arms went down flat on the Great and Swell manuals simultaneously creating the most appallingly violent cacophony followed by the slamming of the organ loft door, and complete silence at the back of the church, punctuated only by the sound of [GOT's] angry footsteps receding up the north aisle. For those of us who appreciated how lucky we were to hear organ music of such outstanding quality, (while warming our hands between the wings of the enormous heaters), it was a moment of triumph. The garrulous gossipers were silenced.

I loved singing and insisted on being there to perform in this wonderful choir even when it conflicted with family events. My parents wearily gave in to my demands and cut short holidays in order that I could be there every Sunday for every service. Even so, it came as a great shock when, at a choir rehearsal, [GOT] announced that I was to become the new Head Boy and the others had better behave themselves. There was no notice of this, and I was stunned. Head chorister of the great Priory choir. Astonishing! Whatever next?

Well, all boys eventually run out of treble vocal cords and after more than eight years (he taught us well, how to look after our voices) the high notes were becoming difficult and the descants beyond reach. I knew the end of life as a treble had come when the top A at the end of a particular anthem simply refused to appear and I had to respond to Trissy's nodded signal for a descant in the final hymn with a headshake of my own.

But it wasn't the end. After a year or so to let my new deep voice settle and get tedious things like 'A' levels out of the way, Trissy invited me to join the men in the back row whenever I was home from university. It was during one of those sessions and a choir rehearsal that [GOT] did something quite uncharacteristic. He never sang in the choir himself for obvious reasons, but on this occasion, he came and stood next to me in the bass section. We sang whatever piece it was and after giving performance notes and during the general changeover to new music he turned to me and said, 'that voice of yours will earn you a pretty penny one day'. I didn't know what he meant until years later.

I was at university in Birmingham and fortunate to have a room in the main student accommodation. In my first year after a particularly well-oiled bar session with the Welsh contingent, who were great natural singers, I decided, on retiring, that a bath would be in order. Encouraged by the resonant acoustic of the bathroom, I treated the other residents to an approximate version of 'Guide Me O Thou Great Redeemer' or some such at maximum volume. The echo was still dying away when the door to the bathroom was thrown open and there stood the Rev. John Bateman, Chaplain, and the block tutor. 'Don't you know what time it is? It's nearly 2 am! Report to my rooms at 8am tomorrow'. Suffice it to say that meeting was very uncomfortable and resulted in compulsory membership of the college choir, a compulsory audition at the Birmingham School of Music (now the Birmingham Conservatoire) and two years of singing lessons which I had to attend on pain of death. The singing teacher, René Soames, a famous tenor in his day, was initially nonplussed. 'You sing beautifully. Who taught you?' I explained. 'Well, he did a great job. I really don't think I can improve on that. I can't teach you anything technical. We'll just have to concentrate on repertoire'. And that's exactly what we did for two years. Until I got bored and said I was off to get a teaching job. Whereupon he reached across the grand piano for the Birmingham Mail newspaper and said, 'we can't let the last two years and all those others go to waste. Let's see who's in town'. I didn't understand what he meant. 'ENO is here in a fortnight but that's not a good idea just yet. Look, here we are - the D'Oyly Carte are at the Alex. I'll get you an audition'. He did and I auditioned on the enormous stage of the Alexandra Theatre and was asked to join the world's most famous opera company just six weeks later. Of course, [GOT] never missed an opportunity for a little musical levity so when I pitched up for my holiday stint at the Priory, singing in the back row, I was puzzled then amused to hear the 'Three Little Maids' theme emerging from the introductory processional music as the choir entered the stalls. He gave me a cheeky wink from the 'barbers shop' as we knew it and bits of G&S kept appearing throughout the service. I think we recessed to the main themes in the overture from Iolanthe.

[GOT] was tickled pink to have one of his choristers as a member of the D'Oyly Carte Opera Company and when I met the lovely young soprano, Rosalind Griffiths, who joined the company a year or so after me, and who succumbed to my offer of marriage, it was to him that we turned to play for our wedding. That was going to happen at the Priory, but I hadn't reckoned with the power of convention and as Ros was born and bred in Oswestry, Shropshire, where her parents still lived, the opinion of the future mother-in-law had to be respected. The marriage was duly transferred to Oswestry Parish Church and all the troops at Christchurch Priory were stood down. All except [GOT] who generously offered to play for us at the ceremony. There was no choir to lead the hymns and I think I was the only one who knew the tunes selected by [him] - perhaps the AMR had not yet reached that far north - so an entire church full of opera singers was reduced to unfamiliar silence. I had specifically requested the Gigout Toccata because its length fitted the length of the Priory main aisle, so adjustments had to be made. I was determined there would be no repeat of the noisy scrum witnessed at the Priory after some services, but the aisle was only about half as long as the Priory's. Consequently, the bridal party recession was conducted at an arthritic snail's pace, a shuffle of a couple of inches at a time plus pauses at each row to smile and pose for in line photos. I don't think [GOT] realised this was going on behind him but we arrived at the main entrance porch at the moment of the final chord. Both the Opera Company and [GOT] finally got to perform together at the reception when I asked him if he would conduct them in ' Hail Poetry' from The Pirates of Penzance. Very loud it was, too.

[GOT's] death just a few years later was a terrible shock. We had by that time given up the 'glamour' of the merry-go-round of eight shows a week, 48 weeks a year, then the more rehearsals then start all over again regime and, after more than 2400 professional performances I was teaching in Leicestershire in a Choral Scheme. This was set up to train young boys at a single sex comprehensive to sing and to do so for the services at the local church in Loughborough. However, while they could sing well enough, the church attendance element did not fit with family life in this industrial town. In a curious way, the memory of [GOT], which was still very much present, carried influence and provided a solution. We set off with a group of twenty boys and taught them to sing G&S - the Pirates of Penzance, The Sorcerer, Trial by Jury, HMS Pinafore - all performed as full shows with boys playing the female parts as well. It gathered big audiences and wild applause each time and the boys were hooked. We could and did get them to sing anything. The anything in this case was the music for Choral Evensong - introits, responses, psalms, canticles, anthems. A limited repertoire of each and then we took them on tour - to Lichfield Cathedral, Coventry Cathedral, Southwell Minster and, as a grand finale, York Minster where they performed a specially commissioned setting of the Canticles.

Time moved on, that school became co-educational, and I moved to other schools where, as deputy head or headteacher I tried to keep the choral tradition alive for boys. 'Sing smoothly. Like stroking a cat from head to tail. If you can't hear your neighbour you're singing too loudly. If you make the flame on this candle flicker, you're using too much breath'.

More than six decades later I can still hear those words.

Christchurch Priory Choir, 1973. Photograph taken for the cover of the Schubert Mass LP

Geoffrey Tristram

MASS IN A FLAT

101

BENEDICTUS.

Agnus Dei.

CHAPTER FOUR

The Priory Organ

The Instrument in 1949

No account of Geoffrey Tristram's life and work would be complete without some reference to the instruments on which he presided during his tenure of office at the Priory. A rebuilding of the old pipe organ was already being considered when GOT started in 1949. The newspaper report of his appointment in October of that year commented that he was 'carefully studying the plans and [looked] forward to the completion of the work. During the summer months he [hoped] to arrange a series of recitals every week and ... to invite eminent organists to play'.[118] Another newspaper report of GOT's appointment to the Priory was headed 'Old Organ – New Organist'.[119] The instrument that GOT inherited had three manuals and pedals, and incorporated material from the original organ of 1788, though the bulk of the pipework and mechanism was by 'Father' Henry Willis, and dated from 1865 and 1880, with 'improvements' by the Ginn Brothers in 1890. Little further was done apart from the addition of electrical blowing and periodic overhaul and maintenance. The specification is given in Appendix B.[120] 'By 1950, the 'whistles' were in a very sorry condition, and a rebuild was most urgently needed'.[121]

---

118 *Christchurch Times*, 21 October 1949.
119 Undated newspaper cutting, presumed from the *Christchurch Times* in late 1949 in GOT's scrapbooks.
120 Details taken from Jones, Peter, *A History of the Pipe Organ of Christchurch Priory*, Christchurch: Natula Publications, 1999, pp. 14-21. For further information on the organ prior to 1951, see Matthews, Betty, 'The Organs of Christchurch Priory'. *The Organ* 52 (208): 147-154. 1973.
121 Unattributed press cutting from GOT's scrapbooks.

The Priory Organ in the South Transept circa 1910

The Priory Organ Console, circa 1910

David Baker

The Compton Rebuild of 1951

An appeal for £7,000 had been launched in 1947,[122] and though the target sum had not been reached, 'in 1950 it was decided to make the organ worthy of the glorious building in which it stands, and the work was placed in the capable hands of the John Compton Organ Company, who commenced a rebuild on the grand scale'.[123] The builders had just completed their work on the organ of Bridlington Priory when they came to Christchurch to start work on the old organ.[124]

> The cost of these works was over £4,000 and the organ was placed in a new purpose-built gallery in the South Transept designed to support the weight of the new mechanisms at a cost of an additional £1,400 ... The rebuild involved renewing actions and providing a remote detached console placed in a 'chantry chapel' style enclosure in an arch on the north side of the Nave. Only a few new ranks were actually added and many stops were derived by borrowing or electrical extension.[125]

GOT was to have a close relationship with the Compton firm over the ensuing years.[126] A contemporary report commented:

> ... The Great organ is nearly complete; one large diapason being prepared for (there will be five). The choir organ has six at present and will be completed with fifteen stops. The Swell has nine now and will have fifteen when finished,

---

[122] Jones, Peter, *A History of the Pipe Organ of Christchurch Priory*, Christchurch: Natula Publications, 1999, p. 20.

[123] Unattributed press cutting from GOT's scrapbooks. See also Banton, Hugh, *Makin Organs History, 1972-1992*. Pamphlet available from www.organworkshop.co.uk.

[124] Undated newspaper cutting, presumed to be from the *Christchurch Times* in GOT's scrapbooks.

[125] Jones, Peter, *A History of the Pipe Organ of Christchurch Priory*, Christchurch: Natula Publications, 1999, p. 20.

[126] Information from Richard Hands.

with an additional set of 16ft, 8ft and 4ft reeds, while the pedal organ has thirteen at the moment, which will be increased to nineteen stops. Another trombone 16ft and a tuba 8ft are in the scheme … When completed, it will be very fine indeed, and it should prove an added attraction for musical folk who visit the district.[127]

Front page of the organ-builder's leaflet describing the 1951 rebuild

---

[127] Unattributed press cutting from GOT's scrapbooks.

Collections were taken at the celebrity recitals, a note at the back of the early programmes saying that 'the first part of the scheme for rebuilding the organ has been carried out at the cost of some £7,500, of which the sum of £800 is yet to be found by voluntary contribution. When this debt is entirely cleared, it is proposed to add about 20 more stops to the organ, installing each stop individually as the appropriate sum is raised'. Over time, the programmes listed the next stop or stops to be added, and the remaining funds to be raised, as for example the Tuba, for which the church was £50 short as at August 1958. By the mid-1960s, the programmes contained appeals for funds for the 'final completion of the organ', though the programme for 30 August 1967 urged audience members to be 'realistic in your donations, or our target figure may never be reached, as ever-increasing costs force it higher each year'.[128]

The Priory organ, as altered and enlarged, though incomplete, was dedicated on 2 June 1951. GOT gave a virtuoso organ recital, including Bach's Fantasia and Fugue in G minor, Liszt's Introduction and Fugue on 'Ad nos, ad salutarem undam', the Scherzo from Vierne's Second Symphony and the 'Toccata' from Widor's Fifth Symphony as well as works such as Alfred Hollins's Song of Sunshine. GOT was already in demand for 'organ openings' elsewhere, as for example St Michael's Southampton, where he gave a recital on the new instrument on 25 January 1951.

The specification of the Priory organ after 1951, including later additions made up to 1968, is given in Appendix C. The parish magazine of the time commented that the 'reconstruction of the organ … [provided] practically a new instrument worthy of the Priory, providing full opportunity for our organist, Mr. Tristram, to display his undoubted talent and to lead, with the support of the strengthened choir, the musical side of worship'.[129] It was as a teenager that Roy Massey, later Organist of Birmingham and then Hereford Cathedrals, first met GOT 'when Compton's tuner Mr. Eagle very kindly took [him] round a few Compton jobs which included the Southampton Guildhall and their new rebuild of the Father Willis at Christchurch Priory'.

---

[128] Recital programme 30 August 1967. The admission price at the time was one shilling.

[129] Christchurch Priory Parish Magazine, June? 1951.

63 speaking stops, 22 couplers and 40 pistons—with over 4,000 pipes—make substantial demands on the organist. Besides being a master musician, he must—for the proper care of the instrument be no stranger to the hidden mysteries of electrics, electronics, pneumatics, hygrology and mechanical engineering.

The 1951 Console

The Priory Choir and Sanctuary, showing the 'Chantry Chapel', 'Cage', or 'Barbershop Poles' housing the console on the left (north) side of the choir stalls

Rushworth & Dreaper, Degens & Rippin, and the 'Nave' division

John Compton, who had founded the firm in 1902, died in 1957. As well as many church instruments, Compton was well known for cinema organs, often being referred to as 'the English Wurlitzer'.[130] In 1964, the

---

[130]   Banton, Hugh, Banton, Hugh, *Makin Organs History, 1972-1992*, p.2. Pamphlet available from www.organworkshop.co.uk.

pipe organ-building side of the organisation was sold to Rushworth & Dreaper, of Liverpool. GOT was none too pleased at the way in which the new firm appears to have dealt with the changeover and wrote to other Compton customers to elicit their views.

Church Hatch,
Church St.,
Christchurch,
Hants.,

Dear

You will, no doubt, have received a letter from Rushworth & Dreaper Ltd regarding future maintenance of your organ.

It would appear from this letter that they have made arrangements with Mr. Eagle to continue his tuning contracts for pipe organs with them, but I am assured by Mr. Eagle that no such approach has been made by Rushworth & Dreaper.

In consequence, I have sent the following letter to Rushworth & Dreaper and await their reply with interest, I should be pleased to hear of your reactions and observations before making any new contract with Rushworths.

As far as I am concerned Mr. Eagle has given me every consideration and service during the past 13 years.

Yours truly,
Geoffrey Tristram

COPY OF LETTER SENT TO MESSRS. RUSHWORTH & DREAPER, LTD.

Dear Sirs,

Christchurch Priory Organ Maintenance

I have received your letter dated April 1964, contents of which I have carefully noted.

I am particularly interested in your second paragraph, in which you state – 'in effect, the existing service contracts will show little outward change, as the present tuning staff have accepted an invitation to join Rushworth & Dreaper, thereby continuing their terms of engagement'. Since the Priory Organ was rebuilt by Comptons in 1951, the maintenance has been carried out to my entire satisfaction by Compton's own representative in this area, - Mr. R.F.Eagle, 86, Merley Ways, Wimborne, Dorset. Now, I have ascertained from Mr. Eagle that he has not been offered any contract whatsoever with you. In fact, no negotiations of any kind have taken place for him to continue any terms of engagement.

I should be pleased to know exactly how you reconcile this with your statement regarding the continuation of employment of the present tuning staff.

At first sight it would appear that your letter is at least misleading and until the matter is cleared up, I have no intention whatsoever in giving your firm any contract of any kind.

Yours faithfully, etc.,

It is interesting to note that the further additions to the Priory's pipe organ after this date were carried out by Degens & Rippin (later Grant,

Degens & Rippin, then Grant, Degens & Bradbeer). GOT had given a recital (6 July 1963) on an early (opus 4) major rebuild of the organ in St Simon's Church, Southsea.[131] Maurice Forsyth-Grant, head of Grant, Degens & Rippin, wrote:

> The firm had on several occasions been asked by Geoffrey Tristram, organist of the Priory, to do minor repair work on the Compton 'rebuild' of 1948 [sic]. The whole organ was placed at the back of the south transept in a gallery with the result that the main part of the nave received no direct sound whatsoever. The organist could hear it fairly well – the detached console was placed at the front of the nave on the north side – but for a large congregation it was far from adequate, so it was decided to have a new, additional Great organ in the triforium, halfway down the nave.

> Consequently, Johnny Degens and I got down to designing and scaling the largest and loudest Great organ chorus the firm had ever done before – or since. In addition, a 32' Pedal reed and Diaphonic Contra Bass were both placed near the new Great organ to augment the chorus. Opportunity was taken at the same time to move the Compton 32' Polyphone and Tuba 8' away from the existing organ and to place them also in the triforium.

> The specification was very simple:

GREAT		PEDAL	
Open Diapason	8	Contra Posaune	32
Principal	4	Contra Bass	16
Fifteenth	2		
Mixture V	2⅔		

---

[131] Forsyth-Grant, Maurice, *Twenty-One Years of Organ-Building*. Oxford: Positif Press, pp. 77-81, especially p.79.

> All the pipes on the new Great organ were of heavy metal and were voiced 'flat out' on 5" wind.

> Geoffrey Tristram enjoyed demonstrating first the full organ 'round the corner' and then saying 'I will now add the Degens & Rippin section'. The result in the nave of the Priory was quite shattering but quite adequate for the hearty singing of a full congregation.[132]

The work was completed in 1964 as the firm's 'opus 8'. At a recital held at the Priory on 1 July of that year, the Fugue from Bach's Prelude and Fugue in D 'was played entirely on the recently completed triforium section of the organ'.[133] GOT was subsequently involved in several of the firm's rebuilds of other instruments: Holy Trinity, Bournemouth (opus 9, 1964);[134] St John's, Boscombe, near Bournemouth (opus 13, 1965) where Norman Wilson, a pupil of GOT was organist before moving to All Saints, Southbourne, GOT's previous post;[135] St Joseph's College Chapel, Birkfield, Ipswich, a de la Salle school.[136]

The Priory instrument continued to lack a case, and many stops remained 'prepared for', despite ongoing efforts at fund raising. GOT was known to complain at the lack of enthusiasm for the £5,000 job of clothing the organ saying that 'it looked like a plumber's backyard'.[137] Collections were taken at every Priory organ recital in the eager anticipation of the organ finally receiving its case by the following year. However, the money was instead used for more stops. As a result, the instrument (including the 'nave' Great) remained caseless until the 1999 rebuild and completion.

---

[132] Forsyth-Grant, Maurice, *Twenty-One Years of Organ-Building*. Oxford: Positif Press, 87.

[133] Recital programme, 1 July 1964.

[134] Forsyth-Grant, Maurice, *Twenty-One Years of Organ-Building*. Oxford: Positif Press, pp. 88-90.

[135] Forsyth-Grant, Maurice, *Twenty-One Years of Organ-Building*. Oxford: Positif Press, pp. 100-3.

[136] Forsyth-Grant, Maurice, *Twenty-One Years of Organ-Building*. Oxford: Positif Press, pp. 116-117.

[137] *Christchurch Times*, 1 January 1971.

*The 'Plumber's Backyard': Christchurch Priory Pipe
Organ as it looked from 1951 to 1999*

Compton becomes Compton Makin, then Nicholson

In the early 1970s, the Priory organ became increasingly unreliable, partly because of the various additions since the original rebuilding, together with the necessary alterations to the actions, and partly through the effects of the heating system on the instrument's mechanism. The bellows were perished. A complete rebuild was required at an estimated cost of £20,000. [138] But there were other pressing challenges. Daniel Campbell writes: 'in those days, the Priory was not exactly in the best state of repair, and it was not unusual to see a little sprinkling of dirt or plaster dust drifting down through the rays of evening sunshine when full organ was being played'. More to the point, there came a stark choice for a cash-strapped church: either a new gas-fired heating system (to replace the old 'Gurney stoves') and a much smaller two-manual pipe organ – totally unsuitable for the continuation of any recital programme - or the Compton fully restored. Dean Shearlock writes: 'it was abundantly clear that GOT loved the Priory organ and was not overly keen on the growing popularity of the relatively new electronic instruments'. 'Dad had no choice', comments Michael Tristram. Heating won the day, but GOT wanted a recital instrument and so, accepting that the reeds were never going to sound completely authentic, a four-manual state-of-the-art Compton Makin[139] electronic instrument was installed. GOT 'got a good deal for the Priory, which included upgrades to the sound systems as technical improvements were made and mothballed the pipe organ pending a dream that one day it might restored', writes Michael Tristram. The pipe organ was taken out of service on 1 December 1973. The electronic instrument was first used the same day.[140] The link with John Compton was thus re-established in a way.

Tim Norris remembers the last recital on the pipe organ:

Another such organ recital I recall, when I also page-turned for him, was when the pipe organ was to be replaced by the

---

[138] Tutte, Harold, *The Organs, Organists and Masters of the Choristers and Gentlemen of Christchurch Priory Church.* Christchurch: privately printed, [1980], p.47.

[139] For further details of the company, Banton, Hugh, *Makin Organs History, 1972-1992.* Pamphlet available from www.organworkshop.co.uk.

[140] *The Organ,* 53 (210), 1974, p.38.

all-singing and dancing electrostatic Makin organ. GOT played the first half of the recital on the outgoing, soon to be decommissioned, pipe organ, and the second half on the new Makin Organ. While playing the pipe organ in the first half there were all sorts of strange cypher, whistles and wheezing sounds heard coming from the pipes. GOT came out of "The Cage", where the console was in the North Nave Aisle, walked to the Nave and apologised to the audience before switching the old pipe organ off for the last time. Climbing aboard the new Makin organ console now in situ in the Nave for all to see he played a master of a second half of the recital, really showing-off the instrument. That was a real experience for me because, while page-turning and standing on the edge of the new console, the thing shook and moved as GOT put the new instrument through its paces.

Between the two world wars, the John Compton Organ Company had developed a pipeless organ system using a rotary electrostatic generator. The development proved popular, and the firm successfully sold several models over the years. After the sale of the pipe organ division, Compton focussed on these electrostatic instruments. Bankruptcy and reformation in 1970 led to the creation of Compton-Makin and Compton-Edwards. Compton-Makin organs began to make their mark in the church organ world thereafter.

[The installation at Christchurch Priory] proved to be a game changer, being heard live on BBC Radio a number of times. The amplification in particular was of a scale not hitherto seen on an electronic organ and included at least four 6' diameter 'Rotofon' type rotating speaker arrays, fitted with well over 70 8" loudspeakers manufactured by the Richard Allen company over in Brighouse.[141]

---

[141] Banton, Hugh, *Makin Organs History, 1972-1992*, pp. 6-7.

John Dawson from Lytham [an] accomplished church organist - became [Makin's] Sales Manager during 1975 ... He was a superb organ demonstrator and emissary for the company. He once took an extraordinary step: he possessed a tape recording of an improvisation by Geoffrey Tristram at Christchurch which brilliantly demonstrated the entire gamut of the instrument's range. John Dawson learned how to play this piece note-for-note.[142]

Dean Shearlock recalls that 'a lot of eyebrows were lifted when the Priory acquired [the Compton Makin]. There was considerable bewilderment as to why this happened'. Geoffrey Morgan, Priory Organist, writes:

G.T. was an exceptionally fine player and became very dissatisfied with the slowness of the pipe organ's mechanism. We were all surprised when he decided to abandon the pipe organ and install a large electronic instrument in its place. Compton's had since gone out of business as a pipe organ firm and were building only electronic organs, about which Geoffrey was very enthusiastic. He continued with the prestigious Priory recital series and, as he seemed to know every famous organist in existence, the recitalists' line-up was quite impressive. There was, however, one unfortunate incident! He invited a certain cathedral organist to play at the Priory, presumably trying to justify the rather-controversial electronic installation. The organist replied 'well, I shall have to come and vet the organ first'. Geoffrey was furious at the stance he had taken and snapped at him 'If that's your attitude, don't bother to come here. There are plenty of other organists, far more famous than you, who will be only too delighted to play!' By 1976, I was organ scholar at Magdalen College Oxford and Geoffrey invited me to play in the next series. I found the electronic organ very unpleasant but had no

---

[142]   Banton, Hugh, *Makin Organs History, 1972-1992*, p. 10.

scruples about giving a recital on it! Geoffrey was actually very complimentary about my programme afterwards.

So, recitals, recordings, and B.B.C. broadcasts from the Priory continued, a vindication of GOT's decision at the time. Tim Norris recalls assisting GOT with a recording of the Makin instrument:

Just before I joined the army in 1976, GOT asked me whether I would page turn for him for an LP recording session in the Priory, which I agreed to do. During the evening recording session, the newly installed central heating system began to make strange noises, as it began to cool down, and so the session had to be abandoned for a few hours. In the meantime, GOT took me and the recording engineers to the Silver Plaice Fish and Chips shop with restaurant in Tuckton over the River Stour from Christchurch. We all stayed out until about an hour and half had passed and then went back to the Priory to finish the recording. Funny how the smell of salt and vinegar still makes me recall that session.

Makin's leaflet describing the 1973 Organ with moveable console
brought to the front of the sanctuary for recitals

The specification of the Makin organ is reproduced in Appendix D. 'Although the console of the pipe organ was disconnected and removed, the Council for the Care of Churches (CCC) required that the pipework and actions be retained, allowing for restoration in the future'. [143] As Michael Tristram remembers, GOT had been 'very keen on the pipes remaining (confirmed by the CCC) because he always had a dream that the pipe organ might eventually be restored (knowing also that the electronic would have a limited shelf life)'. 'The opportunity to restore the pipe organ arose during the 900th anniversary celebrations of the Priory in 1994, when an appeal for £900,000 was launched for both building and organ restoration'.[144] Geoffrey Morgan writes: in 1999, after much fundraising and on a wave of enthusiasm after the Priory's 900th anniversary, the old pipe organ was brought back into use after a very major rebuild by Nicholson's of Malvern'. The instrument was dedicated on 17 July 1999. With various additions in 2000, 2006 and 2017, the Christchurch Priory organ now has over 4500 pipes and is a wonderfully resourceful four-manual instrument, including an 8-rank Solo division. It still boasts the 'shattering' five-rank Mixture so beloved of its designer. Geoffrey Morgan, Priory Organist, comments: 'it is now a wonderfully resourceful instrument of cathedral proportions. It is equally at home in service-playing and recital work. I consider myself most fortunate to be associated with it'. GOT would no doubt have been pleased with the result.

---

143   Jones, Peter, *A History of the Pipe Organ of Christchurch Priory,* Christchurch: Natula Publications, 1999, p. 24.

144   Jones, Peter, *A History of the Pipe Organ of Christchurch Priory,* Christchurch: Natula Publications, 1999, p. 24.

The Nave console of the 1999 Organ, together with main and nave cases (photograph courtesy of Geoffrey Morgan)

Pictures of the 1999 rebuild by Nicholson of Worcester: mechanical action console, pipework detail and case (finally!), taken by Oliver Tristram-Bishop, GOT's grandson

CHAPTER FIVE

Recitalist

First Love of a 'Magnificent Organist'

For all his many achievements in other fields, it is as performer that Geoffrey Tristram is most celebrated. Roy Massey describes GOT as being, 'above all, an absolutely magnificent organist, who was an outstanding recitalist for whom I had the greatest professional admiration'.[145] Nicolas Kynaston, then Organist at Westminster Cathedral, recalls GOT's magnificent playing there. It is reputed that George Thalben-Ball, GOT's former teacher, was in the audience at one of these Westminster recitals.[146]

GOT himself wrote: 'but of all this, my first love is still playing the organ'.[147] 'With pressure at work, I still have to do my practice, early in the morning. With a bit of luck, I can do this without waking the entire household'.[148] This was much aided in later years by the installation of a small electronic organ, with full pedal board and earphones, at 'Church Hatch', which allowed GOT to practice without having to go to 'a cold church in winter or a very noisy one in the summer. The Priory is an impossible place to practise in'.[149] There was also a Steinway in the house.

A National Reputation

Stories of GOT's prowess and his many feats during his long and illustrious career abound; 'his name is still a legend amongst older organists

---

[145] Correspondence with Roy Massey.
[146] Information supplied by Richard Hands.
[147] GOT speech.
[148] GOT speech.
[149] GOT speech.

in the area' (Geoffrey Morgan). 'He … played in many churches and Cathedrals throughout Britain, at the Royal Festival Hall, at Colston Hall, Bristol, and others. On the Continent he … played in Switzerland, Germany and France.[150] Geoffrey Morgan recollects that, on one occasion, the great Fernando Germani was booked to play at Reading Town Hall. Germani cancelled at the last minute; who should deputise for him but Geoffrey Tristram?

GOT was already well known for his recitals and broadcasts before he was appointed to the Priory, his fame as a solo performer having spread to the point where admiring audience members would queue up to get him to autograph their copy of the recital programme.[151] He was often implored to give an encore at the end of his performances, such was his hold over his listeners.[152] Daniel Campbell writes:

> We thought nothing of driving of an evening to Reading Town Hall [where GOT was a frequent performer over many years] or to St. Mary Redcliffe to hear him give a recital. One of my friends at the time was a long-distance lorry driver and he planned his journeys up and down the country to coincide with organ recitals given by Geoffrey and others, and we were often regaled with accounts of recitals at York, Durham, Liverpool and so on. The perfect employment!

---

[150] *Bournemouth Evening Echo*, 4 December 1974.

[151] As for example after recitals at St Andrew's Church, Plymouth, as noted in an undated newspaper cutting, presumed to be from the mid-1950s.

[152] *Reading Chronicle* 6 June 1968.

All the stops to success in recital

■ Mr Tristram takes a bow at the end of last night's recital.

GEOFFREY TRISTRAM'S ambitions were changed when he heard the Willis organ at Reading Town Hall.

He was just nine at the time — and last night Mr Tristram returned to the town hall to give an organ recital.

His concert was Berkshire Organists' Association's contribution to the Festival.

He was educated at Reading School, and is one-time assistant organist at St Mary's in the Butts.

Lullaby

He now gives weekly recitals at Christchurch Priory, near Bournemouth.

He also brings his choir to All Saints', Reading, for choral Evensong on occasion.

His opening number, the Prelude and Fugue in W Flat by Bach, started with an elaborate Prelude played mostly on the Great coupled to the swell organs without a great deal of change in register.

However, the Fugue weaved its way through intricate varieties with use of the choir organ to pick out the leading theme.

A Prelude, Fugue and variation by Cesar Franck was an opportunity to show the organ in its many moods, a soft choir organ prelude, a clear cut fugue, so that the melody could be easily recognised.

Two fine pieces by Vierne, a pupil of Franck followed the first almost as a lullaby, the second the pealing of bells illustrated; of all places, on the pedal organ.

Finally some brilliant work in pedal octaves in a sonata by Jongen, with all sorts of variations of the theme building up to a fast pace and tremendous power. Mr Tristram was asked for an enchore and played us one to finish.

E. A.

Press cutting, Reading Festival

141

Geoffrey Howell has a similar reminiscence to the present author's experiences of GOT's recitals at Christchurch Priory:

> There were quite a lot of organ recitals in Bournemouth during the summers of the 1960s and early 1970s, and I started going to as many as I could. The main attraction was of course Christchurch Priory, and I went there on Wednesday evenings ... The extra excitement was sometimes going by myself on the bus—either the No. 21 trolleybus via Tuckton or the direct limited-stop No. 1. Sometimes it would be Geoffrey Tristram and sometimes a visiting organist, but it was always Geoffrey Tristram's name that stuck in my mind; I remember sitting there eagerly waiting for the recital to start. In those days there were no announcements, and certainly no applause: the organ just started. I would have a programme and my challenge would be to guess which piece we were on!
>
> I remember the brightly coloured box on the north side of the chancel, and on one or two occasions I plucked up courage to stand near to it at the end. Perhaps I might have seen you outside the box on one of those Wednesday evenings! I saw people coming out of the box ... there's a possibility that I could claim to have seen Geoffrey Tristram, but I never actually spoken to him as you did!

As does Geoffrey Morgan, himself Organist of Christchurch Priory for the last 20 years:

> My connection to Christchurch Priory goes back to the early 1960s, when I used to visit the area on holiday with my parents. I had attended a few recitals at the Priory and remember being thrilled by the sound of the Compton organ at the time, especially when the recently added Tuba stop and Nave Diapason chorus came pealing down from the triforium. The great Geoffrey Tristram (Organist

and Master of the Choristers from 1949-1979) allowed me to play the Priory organ in 1964, which was a great experience for an impressionable teenager! Geoffrey T. seemed quite a formidable character to me, but later, as I gained his confidence, he let me sit with him while he played for services. Later I came to know Geoffrey T. quite well, and as I became a better organist, he allowed me to deputise for him occasionally. G.T. was an exceptionally fine player.

Broadcasts and Recordings

A later newspaper tribute commented: Mr. Tristram has lost count of the number of broadcasts he has made— most from the Priory Church. But his recording sessions have not been confined to radio'. [153] Geoffrey Morgan recalls GOT's 'magnificent broadcasts and recordings, including a recital on the Priory Compton on television - BBC2. Broadcast TV recitals were not very common then, nor are they now, but he seemed to be popular with the BBC'.

Broadcasting in those days was not the easy recording session of today. 'Everything went out live then. It was nothing to get up at one in the morning for some programme on the overseas network'.[154] GOT made several recordings with Ryemuse, the first now reproduced in digital format on CD and still available. He recorded at dead of night to avoid traffic noise and had then to be up early next day to go to school.

Daniel Campbell writes:

> I remember watching Geoffrey give two live recitals on local television which I believe was a first for anyone. He ... wore half glasses to play and only he could look up at the camera while playing and giving a little smile. Always the showman!

---

[153] *Bournemouth Evening Echo*, 4 December 1974.
[154] GOT speech.

Screenshots of one of GOT's (black and white) broadcasts from the Priory

GOT's Recordings (see Discography for details)

Technique and Performance 'Twitches'

GOT had 'a prodigious technique', according to Geoffrey Morgan, with a wonderful articulation and a clarity of rhythm, much like Cunningham, his teacher.[155] Certainly, the many and varied glowing reviews of his solo performances talk of his articulation and his rhythmic vitality, as well as a total command of the instrument, including an ability to register imaginatively and appropriately for both piece and venue, not least in quieter compositions. He was 'quite short, with stubby hands and small feet'.[156] He wore patent leather shoes at the organ so he could feel the pedals.

---

[155] G.D. CUNNINGHAM RECORDED 1926-1937 (amphion-recordings.com)
[156] Information from Richard Hands.

Dean Shearlock recollects how the correct phrasing was always important: 'it was particularly amazing that he did all this with a handspan of barely an octave!' The strain of having to get it right first time made him nervous, despite his years of experience. Daniel Campbell remembers that 'Geoffrey could be quite wound up on "performance" days, but also remarkably controlled'. GOT himself wrote: 'I have to start with something easy, or my nose starts to twitch. Or something so desperately difficult that I haven't time to think of twitches':[157] 'evidence of a great nervous energy of mind and body' as was said of G.D. Cunningham.[158]

Jeremy Blandford recalls:

> I was organist at the civic church of Southampton (St. Mary's) from 1968 to 1990. Not so long after my arrival I set up Southampton Organ Recitals with Keith Clarke in an attempt to provide regular organ concerts on the two foremost organs in the city: the majestic Willis at St. Mary's and the new-classical Grant, Degens and Rippin at the church of the Holy Family, Millbrook. Geoffrey came and played an outstanding concert for us at St. Mary's in November 1970. Three things stand out in my mind all these years on. Early in his programme he had elected to play Bach's Prelude and Fugue in D, BWV 532, with its horridly exposed initial pedal scales. The first thing Geoffrey did at St. Mary's was to leap on to the console and play this dreaded scale nonstop about thirty times without any slips. I was amazed by his energy and his mastery - and of course it was flawless in the concert too. This was in stark contrast to a renowned cathedral organist (who had better remain nameless), whom I heard play this same piece in concert in the late 60s and again about ten years later, who was felled by the scale on both occasions.

---

[157] GOT speech.
[158] G.D. CUNNINGHAM RECORDED 1926-1937 (amphion-recordings.com)

Repertoire

His musical taste changed little over the years, and he continued to draw on the same body of repertoire each year, though he played fewer transcriptions at Christchurch than during the Reading years, a trait that he held in common with most recitalists of the 1930s and 1940s, and not least his former teacher, G.D. Cunningham. On the other hand, the 'early music' movement had not fully taken hold in the 1960s and early 1970s, and GOT's playing of early English music by composers such as John Stanley was almost inevitably from arrangements for hands and feet rather than the more authentic 'manuals only' realisations.

His overall approach was described by Geoffrey Morgan as being 'of the old school' where, for example, a big Bach fugue would end with full organ, including the Tubas and 32' reeds: very much as Thalben-Ball might have done, and just as exciting! It is interesting to compare his programmes with those of the visiting recitalists in the summer series, and of other players at venues GOT regularly visited.[159] There are considerable similarities, in terms of programme planning, whether in terms of Bach or the 19th and early 20th century French, English, and, to a lesser extent, German schools of composition.

An analysis of GOT's surviving recital programmes shows that Bach's chorale prelude Ach, bleib bei uns, Herr Jesu Christ (52 times), his Prelude and Fugue in D major (51 times) and Michael Festing's Largo, Allegro, Aria and Two Variations, arranged by former teacher George Thalben-Ball (51 times) were the compositions played most frequently. It is interesting to note that these and many other of GOT's favourite pieces featured regularly in recitals by his teacher, G.D. Cunningham.[160] There were other 'lollipops' (which seldom changed) usually evident in a Tristram recital, such as Alain's Litanies, Bach's Toccata in F, Dubois's Toccata in G and Fiat Lux, Gigout's Toccata in B minor, Saint-Saëns's Fantasie in E flat, Schumann's Four Sketches for Pedal Piano, Stanford's Postlude in D

159   See, for example, a letter to GOT from David Willcocks, 5 May 1950, inviting him to give a recital at Salisbury Cathedral. The other programmes are given; many follow the same pattern as GOT's.
160   Rizzo, Jeanne, 'George Dorrington Cunningham, 1878-1948'. *The Diapason*, 67(7), June 1976, pp.4-5.

minor, among many other favourites. In later years, he might start with Francis Jackson's Fanfare. There were only eight solo recitals where Bach was not featured.

He rarely played 'dissonant' music such as works by Messaien ('though having no objection to pop', he found 'most modern organ music incomprehensible'). He occasionally played Duruflé or Langlais, as had his teacher, G.D. Cunningham.[161] This seems to have been a pattern followed by other recitalists at the Priory. Nevertheless, the closing voluntary at GOT's last Service of Nine Lessons and Carols, on 31 December 1978, was 'Transports de joie' from Messaien's L'Ascension. The order of service asks the congregation to refrain from talking during the performance! Strangely, GOT only ever seems to have played one Mendelssohn composition, the Sixth Sonata for Organ. There were few other pieces played only once during his long and illustrious career as a recitalist. Where such unica are evident, they were typically as the result of a themed concert, such as a Buxtehude recital on 30 April 1960. GOT would often 'pick up' a piece or pieces to play for a summer or two, only then to drop them and never feature the works again, as for example Armstrong Gibbs's Sketches or Franck's Pastorale. Not surprisingly, given the fact that Percy Whitlock was sometime Organist at St Stephen's and of the Pavilion Theatre, Bournemouth, he regularly played Whitlock's organ works.

He was clearly a fan of the French Romantics. Reviewers often commended his ability to play this repertoire like a French rather than an English organist, one critic likening him to Jeanne Demessieux![162] He usually ended with a flashy piece by one or other of Dubois, Dupré, Gigout, Mulet, Vierne or Widor. Vierne's Third Symphony was a special favourite, according to Geoffrey Morgan, which he broadcast from the Colston Hall, Bristol. He was renowned for his performances (he recorded the piece) of the famous Toccata from Widor's Fifth Symphony, insisting

---

[161] As for example at a recital at Birmingham Town Hall, 15 April 1942.

[162] As for example Douglas W. Churchill, in an undated review of a recital at an unnamed cathedral; details from the scrapbooks. Judging by annotations in Demessieux's recital programme at Salisbury Cathedral on 22 April 1948, GOT had attended and heard the famous French recitalist. She gave a recital in the Priory's summer series on 26 July 1951 and improvised on a theme submitted in a sealed enveloped by GOT.

on not playing it too quickly. 'Any fool can play it quickly', GOT is reputed to have said.[163] A reminiscence of Geoffrey Morgan concerns a 'spectacular performance' of Berveiller's Cadence - a study for pedals. Thalben-Ball's Variations on a Theme by Paganini for Pedals was another of his party pieces. GOT's music library also contained a complete set of Edwin Lemare's transcriptions for organ of the Wagner Overtures, which included Die Meistersinger, with its famous glissandi on the pedals.

GOT at the Makin Organ shortly after its installation

Other Performers and the Summer Recital Series

GOT often shared his recitals with other performers, including Edward Armstrong (violin), Molly Beavis (soprano), Margot Bor (piano), Lyndon Davies (piano), Robert Growcott (violin), Roy Gubby (violin), Alfred Jupp (violin), Eric Keats (bass-baritone), David Moore (baritone), Helen

---

[163] Information from Richard Hands.

Reynolds (cello), Wilson Shepherd (tenor), David Shean (violin), Pamela Stone (soprano), Bessie Tolley-Reakes (contralto), Lillian Warmington (cello), Janet Whittaker (viola) and particularly, from 1951 onwards, the violinist Raymond Mosley, with whom he recorded 'Music for the Quiet Hour' as well as performed regular radio broadcasts and Priory summer recitals. Mosley played regularly 'with all the BBC regional orchestras [and] appeared on TV … often [travelling] to the Continent to play on the Swiss radio network'.[164] GOT later regretted the fact that he only took a fee for the 'Quiet Hour' recording as it became very popular in America and more would have been earned if royalties had been paid instead!

Raymond Mosley (violin), accompanied by GOT on the Makin Organ

GOT initially gave all the recitals at the Priory himself, usually after Sunday evensong.[165] The 1951 rebuild by Compton of the organ heralded the start of the summer series of weekly recitals. The performances at the Priory were given by the elite of the day: Francis Jackson, Garth Benson, Sidney Campbell, Caleb Jarvis and many more.[166] He was especially kind

---

[164]   Undated press cutting, presumed to be from the mid-to-late 1950s.

[165]   Tutte, Harold, *The Organist's Soundboard: a comprehensive record of who have performed on Christchurch Priory Organ*. Privately printed, 1991, p.1.

[166]   Tutte, Harold, *The Organist's Soundboard: a comprehensive record of who have performed on Christchurch Priory Organ*. Privately printed, 1991. The publication is a comprehensive list, with biographies, of all the recitalists from 1951 to 1990.

to young organists starting out on their recital careers, often giving them their first 'big break'. One such was Dr Simon Lindley, now Organist Emeritus of Leeds Minster (Parish Church). Even when there was a power cut at the Priory and the organ blower would not function, the audience would not leave because GOT was the recitalist![167]

GOT was regularly the organ soloist for performances with the Bournemouth Symphony Orchestra as for example of Guilmant's Symphony for Organ and Orchestra, opus 42 at Christchurch Priory on 23 July 1959 under Charles Groves (and again at the Priory on 18 September 1964 under the baton of James Loughran) and of Saint-Saëns's Third 'Organ' Symphony at London's newly refurbished Royal Festival Hall on Sunday 16 February 1964 under Silvestri.[168] He also worked with the Bournemouth Sinfonietta, including performing with them in Christchurch Priory as well as St Peter's Bournemouth, with GOT playing Handel Organ Concertos, such as that in F, opus 4, number 4a.[169]

Royal Festival Hall 16 February 1964

[167] *Christchurch Times,* 1 January 1971.
[168] The work was also performed by GOT under Silvestri and with the BSO on 13 February 1964 at the Winter Gardens, Bournemouth, and again at the same venue on 15 April 1965.
[169] *Serenade Concerts, Bournemouth Sinfonietta, 8 July – 29 August 1970.*

GOT at the Royal Festival Hall Organ

Tributes

John Broad writes:

The reputation of Geoffrey Tristram as an organist amongst his peers was legendary, particularly for his beloved French repertoire and he was called upon to perform all over the country and abroad. While at university I managed to get to hear him play with the CBSO under Charles Groves in Birmingham and again years later at a recital he gave in York Minster. That was a particularly memorable performance and he played with tremendous virtuosity and commitment. Breath-taking stuff and only later did it emerge that in setting up the registration of stops for each manual, he had lifted the hinged music stand (behind which the various buttons were located) but had lifted it complete with his sheet music rather too high. He watched in despair as all his music disappeared into the bowels of the organ, Although the start of the recital was delayed for some time while vergers sought the missing items, he decided to press on and played most of the programme completely from memory!

YORK MINSTER

Organ Recital

by

GEOFFREY TRISTRAM

(Christchurch Priory)

Saturday, 12th August, 1978 at 6 p.m.

1. Toccata in F (BWV 540)   J. S. Bach
                                                            (1685-1750)

It is possible that this Toccata was composed some years later than the Fugue
which it so effectively overshadows. Without doubt, it is one of the finest of
the big preludial movements, with its immense and unflagging vigour, a spacious
design, and a power of development that even Bach himself rarely if ever exceeded.

2. Chorale Preludes   J. S. Bach

    (i)   'Ach bleib' bei uns.' (BWV 649)
    (ii) 'Nun danket alle Gott.' (BWV 657)

'Ach bleib bei uns' ('Abide with us'), is drawn from one of Bach's most beautiful
cantatas - that dealing with the walk to Emmaus. In its original form it is a
soprano solo, with obbligato for violoncello piccolo and continuo. Bach shortens
it in the organ arrangement, giving the vocal solo to the right hand and the
elaborate violoncello part to the left, the pedals, of course, playing the continuo.

In 'Nun danket alle Gott' ('Now thank we all our God') the music is easily followed
by the listener, as the well-known melody stands out boldly and is quite free from
any confusing ornamentation.

3. Voluntary in F (The 'Echo' Voluntary)   John Stanley
                                                            (1713-1786)

Charles John Stanley became blind at the age of two. In spite of this handicap
he made rapid progress, graduating as Mus.B. at Oxford at the age of sixteen.
Five years later he was appointed organist of the Temple Church in London.

His musical works were many and varied, including three sets, of ten each, of
organ voluntaries. His improvisations at the organ became so well known that
Handel himself would often be found amongst his appreciative listeners.

4. Pastorale   J. J. A. Roger-Ducasse
                                                            (1873-1954)

Jean Jules Aimable Roger-Ducasse was born in Bordeaux. He became a pupil of Faure
at the Paris Conservatoire, and his style derives from that of his master.

In 1935 he succeeded Paul Dukas (of the 'Sorcerer's Apprentice' fame) as a professor of composition at the Paris Conservatoire.

The Pastorale (1909) is dedicated to Nadia Boulanger. It begins disarmingly in
true pastoral style, but gradually, through many modulations and moods, builds up
to a great climax before dying away to a pianissimo conclusion. From beginning
to end, the opening theme is in constant use, either in canon, diminution, augment-
ation, metamorphosis, or even in combination with itself in several forms simultaneously.

GOT's York Minster Recital Programme, 12 August 1978

Dean Shearlock comments:

> I was a great admirer of Geoffrey and his musicianship ...
> I was in awe of his capability and enjoyed going off with
> him to act as page-turner at recitals he was invited to give
> and to see how easily he coped with whatever instrument
> that church possessed. In the days since then, I have had
> the privilege of knowing a goodly number of cathedral
> organists, but it was GOT who set the standard in my
> own mind.

CHAPTER SIX

Life at 'Church Hatch'

An 'Elegant Mansion' as House and Home

The post of Organist and Master of the Choristers at Christchurch Priory came with 'Church Hatch', an amazing Georgian house just outside the churchyard's north gate. The house was often mistaken for the Priory Vicarage, even though no vicar ever lived there. For a period in the 19th century, it was acquired by the non-Conformists for their ministers, much to the annoyance of the High Church authorities'.[170] The property was bought for the Priory's use in 1929. Living at 'Church Hatch' meant that GOT was easily able to pop over to the church at any time. Built circa 1750, the 'elegant mansion' is 'not only one of the most perfect examples of Georgian architecture to be found in Christchurch, but it has had many links with fascinating or famous personalities … The house was at one time the home of the late Mr. Walter Hutchinson, the publisher, and several former church organists … lived there'.[171] 'Church Hatch' had 'many fine features, among them beautiful ornamental railings in the front, a magnificently proportioned lounge with a curving wall and window, and a 'hanging' spiral staircase …the garden … at one time stretched down to the mill stream'.[172] Though dilapidated, Geoffrey and Rene gradually refurbished 'Church Hatch', living there from 1949 until GOT's death in 1979. Rene was also involved in the work of the Priory, running the young wives' group.

---

170 Tutte, Harold, *The Organs, Organists and Masters of the Choristers and Gentlemen of Christchurch Priory Church.* Christchurch: privately printed, [1980], p.25.

171 Undated press cutting with the heading 'Priory Organist moves in', presumed to be late 1949/early 1950, and from the *Christchurch Times*.

172 Tutte, Harold, *The Organs, Organists and Masters of the Choristers and Gentlemen of Christchurch Priory Church.* Christchurch: privately printed, [1980], p.25.

Christchurch Priory (taken by Oliver Tristram-Bishop; GOT's grandson)

*Two Pictures of 'Church Hatch', including an aerial view showing
the original garden boundary; the aerial photo is reproduced
courtesy of Denisons, 12, Castle Street, Christchurch*

The young Tristram family in the 'snug' – the smaller sitting room in Church Hatch, used for everyday living in the winter because everywhere else in Church Hatch (apart from sitting on the Aga in the kitchen) was cold! Notice the black and white TV in the background.

Family and Visitors from Far and Wide

'Church Hatch' was home for Geoffrey and Rene Tristram and their two children, Michael (born 5 August 1950), and Carolyn (born 8 May 1955) as well as a place where countless organists, singers, musicians, school parties and many others were warmly welcomed. Visiting players engaged to perform at the Priory's midweek recitalists would be treated to a typically warm 'Church Hatch' welcome. This always included a delicious dinner cooked by Rene, along with a few glasses of 'cheer'. Some stayed overnight; one guest organist (who shall remain nameless) insisted on singing hymns at breakfast! Nicolas Kynaston, then Organist of Westminster Cathedral, recalls how he was made to feel welcome whenever he visited Christchurch to play the Priory organ. 'It was not just "another booking." The place was always so happy and relaxed. Geoffrey was so charming and kind,' he said.

Dr Roy Massey, now Organist Emeritus of Hereford Cathedral, remembers the times that he was invited to Christchurch:

> Between 1965 to 1968 I was Warden of the RSCM at Addington Palace and organist of Croydon Parish Church where the junior curate was a delightful character named Michael Yorke, whose father was Vicar of Christchurch. He became a great friend and supporter of the music and said that I ought to give a recital at Christchurch and he would speak to his dad about it. Eventually, an invitation appeared, and his father looked after me and after the recital Geoffrey took me round to the Yacht Club - I think it was - for a drink, and after a glass or two let slip that mine had been one of the better offerings that year. After that I was asked several times again and accommodated over a shop quite near the Priory and, later still, my wife and I were invited to stay ... at that lovely house in the churchyard. This seemed to become an annual visit and, of course, when I moved to Hereford, we reciprocated the invitation and I vividly recall his wonderful playing of our Father Willis. Ruth remembers how absolutely charming Geoffrey always was to her and also recalls a most wonderful dinner of leg of mutton with caper sauce which Irene cooked one evening.

Carolyn Tristram writes:

> All those people, most of whom were entertained pre-recital in our dining room with Mum's delicious fare and Dad raiding the 'wine/liqueur cellar' - well the north facing pantry actually, but cellar sounds good!!! I remember being told to be on my best behaviour with a number of these organists, especially Doctor Fox but the exception was Garth Benson. He was very much a favourite of the family, I called him Uncle Garth but when he and Dad got together after his recital, it all went a bit pear-shaped!! We had a black cocker spaniel called Onyx who would be

let out of the front door and gate to do his rounds of the church yard before bedtime. My bedroom was above the front porch and steps and often I would hear Dad and Garth giggling away whilst sitting on the top step calling for the dog to return quite late at night! However, when you're a bit piddly peed, 'Onyx' is not easy to say ... I heard names like 'Oinch', 'Onshix' etc.!!! Totally hilarious!

Carolyn also recalls that:

Dad was a very social man and loved being 'mine host' to choir and school dos, indeed any excuse for a party. Church Hatch parties!! Amazing!! My godfather, Ken Smith, who was Mayor of Christchurch two or three times, was always in charge of the bar situated in the massive entrance hall. Mum's food offerings always went down a storm as they also did on bonfire night when, every year, the choirboys were treated to a Church Hatch bonfire party - toffee apples, coconut ice etc. (I have Mum's handwritten recipes). The bonfire was huge, mainly made up of old, unwanted furniture, and Michael and I built the guy and paraded him around Christchurch in a wheelbarrow collecting pennies.

The influx of foreign students from the late 50s filling the empty bedrooms made the house feel like a local United Nations where we learned about different cultures first hand and enjoyed being taught how to cook very different foods (all very new in those days.) [Carolyn and Rene once calculated the numbers: 57 in total, not only from all of the countries in western Europe and Scandinavia, but also Libya, Iran and Thailand!] Dad loved their company and the new experiences they brought as well as the contacts for the annual family driving holidays on the continent making return visits, staying in gites or, in the mid-1960s, towing a caravan along narrow mountain passes – we couldn't afford to go through the tunnel!

*GOT, assisted by Sue (from Iran) hosting one of many 'Church Hatch' parties.
Carolyn writes: 'Mum and Dad gave Sue, her husband and young daughter refuge,
having 'escaped' from the country, turning up on the front doorstep with a small
suitcase of belongings in their plight. That was what Mum and Dad did – helped
anyone in trouble or who was unhappy. The table, of course, was normally used for
the bar and it was unusual to see someone else behind it, instead of Ken Smith[173]!'*

[173] Carolyn's godfather and Mayor of Christchurch.

[Initially] Dad really wasn't keen on tasting foreign 'muck' but when Mum threatened him with school dinners instead of home-made suppers (from wherever) he decided to be polite and try ... miraculously, most offerings were enjoyed, but some needed Soda Bicarbonate in the early hours of the morning ... me too ... we would meet up and have a chat, sip, burp (or two) and giggle at the kitchen table by the warm Aga! Dad would do a stint in the kitchen every now and then, but he would leave it in a total state of chaos! Both my brother Michael and my son, Oliver, have inherited this dubious talent!

GOT, Rene, Michael, and Carolyn in the now shortened back garden of 'Church Hatch', with a group of foreign students, who were staying to gain experience of 'English life' and attending a local English language school

1971 – Rene with Michael and Carolyn in the back garden of Church Hatch with students Isabelle (Switzerland) and Godfrey (Austria) plus Michael's chaplain at Christ's College Revd Nigel McCulloch (eventually Bishop of Wakefield then of Manchester) on a visit. The group is sitting on the roof of a substantial concrete air raid shelter built in the late 1930s and under a huge mulberry tree whose leaves were much in demand by the local primary school for their silkworm collection

Michael adds:

> Dad loved his food (indeed we were always so grateful to have been introduced to cheese fondu because that was the one thing that got rid of his awful indigestion when he was recuperating at home after his first heart attack). He wasn't a cook except he loved dressing a crab, meticulously as you can imagine, from a perfectionist.
>
> Church Hatch, being a large house, was always in need of decoration and so Mum and Dad would undertake it all, and when old enough I was taught how to hang wallpaper properly as well as how to prepare wooden surfaces properly before painting. They also grew a lot of veg in the garden and at one stage had chickens and even geese (until the fox beheaded them).

Michael also remembers that:

> Although cold in winter (I was in charge of the paraffin heaters and refilling the coal-fired Aga and you had to break the ice in the toilet), [Church Hatch] was a wonderful house, enabling Dad to have a huge 00 railway layout in one of the uninhabitable rooms which he started as soon as he arrived (his sister in law Marian remembers helping lay the track on her first visits at the end of the 40s).

Picnic with relatives from Reading, late 1950s

Railways and Other Enthusiasms

GOT's heavy workload and busy schedule meant that he had limited free time. In any case, he found it hard to relax to music because, as Michael remembers, he was always automatically examining the performance or the composition. Like many organists, he was fascinated by engineering and especially (steam) railways. In addition to his 00-gauge railway on several levels in three rooms (along with one built by Michael, who was not allowed to touch his father's), he made, with the help of a friend (an engineer from de Havilland)[174] who did the lathe work, a 3 ½ inch gauge fully working Britannia steam engine. Replacing a beautiful J.M. Beeson O gauge 'Duchess', the Britannia sat proudly on the hearth in Church Hatch's formal lounge until it had to be sold to help pay for school fees!

---

[174]   Information from Richard Hands

The Beeson 'Duchess'

The Britannia, made (with help) by GOT

GOT and Gordon Hands were regular visitors around steam engine sheds in the days before Health & Safety! This iconic photo (unflattering of GOT's back view) taken in the Bournemouth sheds late 40s/early 50s. As their sons grew up, they would accompany such visits. Michael remembers in late 50s driving a steam engine for a few yards in the sidings of Eastleigh railway

Engine sheds, especially with GOT's lifelong school friend Gordon Hands, were second homes when visiting family back in Reading. When on holiday with the family on the beach in Dawlish, GOT was the only one with his deckchair facing the railway line and its back to the sea!

On the beach with Rene, Kay Hands (Gordon's wife) and their son Richard, 1949

Carolyn was a particular witness to her father's enthusiasm:

> When I was quite young, probably between 5 and 8 (1960s), on rare free Saturday mornings, Dad took me to Christchurch Station. We would go up into the signal box and while Dad chatted with the signal man and train spotted drinking a cup of tea, I cleaned the brass on the levers. The signal man gave me 6d for my labours.

Carolyn adds that 'any free time that Dad had was spent watching anything funny on television — particularly Morecambe and Wise and 'Carry on' films - but he also loved his wrestling on a Saturday afternoon, especially after a stream of back-to-back weddings!' There were so many one weekend that the choir boys went on strike because of the workload. GOT was also proud of his large Rover Coupé cars which he enjoyed driving to the many recital venues where he was the player. Jeremy Blandford recollects that GOT 'was clearly very fond of [his] three-litre Rover … asserting that he liked a car which responded to a "bit of welly".' GOT also had Minis as 'run-arounds'.

One of GOT's Rovers. There were several over the years, each one more spacious and comfortable than the last. His first car in Christchurch was a red convertible Morris Minor, which the family remembers being used for a holiday in Wales.

'WOO' – the family mini, not to be trusted on long journeys!

Michael and Carolyn Remember

Michael and Carolyn's further reminiscences follow.

Michael:

My earliest memory, other than the arrival of my sister in May 1955, was my second day at school in September which was spent in bed, with Dad in the adjoining bed, both having gone down with chicken pox!

Dad gave me the gift of music, though sadly I was not able to get to grips with a violin or indeed the piano. A big regret is that I gave up lessons, though I learned enough to be able to play to my own enjoyment, not noticing the long pause where I search for the next chord (I still hear him say that I must make the melody stand out and sing).

It seems that the generations of Tristrams have gone keyboard then voice, with Dad's Father a singer and Grandfather a pianist. I gained my choral exhibition at Christ's College, Cambridge in 1969, and singing has been such an important outlet for the whole of my life, a gift for which I shall always be so grateful to Dad, and also so grateful that he insisted I rest my voice when it started to break when I was only 13 - halfway through Stanford in G Magnificat treble solo!! - allowing it to develop and being allowed back into the choir and the back row from age 16.

Other memories include being incredibly proud when attending his performance of the Saint-Saëns Organ Symphony at the newly restored Royal Festival Hall, accompanying him on some recital tours/evenings as page-turner, map-reading for our continental driving holidays and when old enough being allowed to share the driving. Indeed 'pride' would be a key word for me in my memories. He taught me to drive, polished off with a few lessons with British School of Motoring, whose driver said I didn't need any more lessons because Dad had taught me so well, so he spent the time teaching me how to skid round corners in the ice that was lying on those winter lessons (but fortunately not on my examination.)

Domestically, I have vivid memories of my 13th birthday, when I unwrapped his present at the breakfast table of a packet of ten Richmond cigarettes, much to my Mother's surprise and indeed anger! He explained that much better for me to do it openly and learn what a horrible thing it was (Dad sadly was a heavy smoker all his life). I felt very grown up lighting my first cigarette, asking whether to suck or blow, but soon turned green and never smoked again (except a pretentious pipe for a time at Cambridge).

Indeed, Dad was so generous and selfless, committed to Carolyn and me having the best education possible, wide experiences of life and many opportunities. Money must have always been tight, with Mum trying to hold the purse strings but Dad giving his last penny to anyone he knew to be in need. I was certainly taught that if I wanted anything I had to work for it (my model railway and my sailing were all funded by weddings, Saturday and holiday jobs).

I have always wondered whether I could have had a career singing, but Dad was very insistent that I should have a proper career, because there were so many singers searching for jobs, and he wanted me to enjoy music.

Dad had a wicked sense of humour, which he delighted in sharing with any company he was in and even with some of the De La Salle Brothers from school who apparently would enjoy going for a drive with him on a Sunday afternoon to have a crafty fag and drink! One of his party pieces was playing and singing the Dvorak Humoresque 'passengers will please refrain from ...' In our toilet at Church Hatch was a stainless-steel continental railway carriage sign in Italian, French and German requiring passengers not to use the toilet whilst the train was standing at the station. Who knows how he got hold of it when on one of our continental journeys, but it was my introduction to speaking foreign languages?

Carolyn:

At the age of eight, I was given a Governor's Scholarship to Christ's Hospital Blue Coat School in Hertford. Though Mum and Dad were reluctant to send me to boarding school, it was an opportunity for an excellent education. The scholarship was as a thank you to Dad from a Mr Hubble [a Donation Governor at the school][175] for the

---

[175] Henry Dennis Hubble was one of many Donation Governors of Christ's Hospital, benefactors of the school who by donation gained the right to present pupils. Henry Hubble presented three pupils, two boys in 1947 and 1953 respectively (Horsham) and Carolyn Tristram in 1963 (Hertford). He may not have known any of the families personally. He was elected as a Governor in 1947 and died 26 December 1965. Hubble was an Old Blue, born 1 June 1902, the son of Harry Oswald Hubble and Constance. He was admitted to Christ's Hospital (under the name Harry Dennis Hubble) on 20 September 1911 (to the preparatory dept before transfer to Middleton A, a senior boarding house for about 50 boys aged 11 to 18). He left school on 21 December 1917. In 1911 the family lived at Churchover Rectory near Rugby, and in 1917 at 46 Rainbow Hill, Worcester. Information supplied by Clifford Jones, Old Blue and Museum volunteer, Christ's Hospital.

hours of pleasure he gave him listening to his recordings, BBC broadcasts and recitals.

Dad often met me off the school train at Liverpool Street Station. Our first port of call was always the local Lyons Corner House where he ordered 'chocolate sauce and a little bit of ice cream'. The waitresses there got to know us well and I am sure we had a lot more chocolate sauce than any other customer, which was part of his cunning plan. We would then catch the tube to Waterloo which went under the Thames. Dad always got me to close the windows in case any water got into the carriage, and to look out for fish!

Dad was not a good patient - when I was in my early teens, he was poorly and had to stay in bed, a very rare occurrence. I took him up a cup of tea at the usual 7am but then helped Mum in the kitchen to prepare breakfast for the foreign students. Once they had left to go to school, I remember I took Dad some toast and marmalade and a cup of coffee. It was only about 8am but I was greeted with a very grumpy 'I could have died up here and no-one would have known!'

Living with a perfectionist was not that easy. This put pressure on Michael and me to do well. If I was 'invited' into the dining room, I knew I was in trouble! Most of the time it was the day that my school report dropped through the letterbox onto the door mat or when they returned from parents' evening!!

I started to learn the violin when I was five. That didn't last long as Dad couldn't stand the screeching noises I made!! Dad often gave the impression that violins were only useful to pretend to squash flies with the bow on the back of the violin. I then took up the piano, but, lessons learned, I only practised when he was out of the house!

When I was about 16, I met a boy who promised to phone me. It was young love! However, when he phoned, Dad answered and as I was rushing down the stairs to get to the phone first, I overheard Dad say: 'I'm sorry, but there is no-one with that name here', and put the phone down. It turned out that the boy had asked to speak to 'Caro**line**'! That was the end of that!! I was pretty cross, but Dad (quite rightly) said that someone who can't even get a simple name right deserves everything he gets!

When I was about 16, Dad and I bought a sailing dinghy, a 12ft Freshman. Michael was by then a very good sailor of a larger and a better class of sailing boat. Dad bought an outboard motor and given the chance, he and I would put-put off from Christchurch Sailing Club just around the corner onto the Avon. We tied up there and Dad would have a G&T or a Cinzano Bianco and a smoke and while away the moment. It was the one place he could get some peace and quiet. I had a much weaker slurp - Michael and I were weaned on watered down wine etc. which, in retrospect, was good as it taught us how to treat alcohol with respect. These rare moments were very special as Dad was so busy with school, church, recordings, recitals and so on that we never got to see him.

In 1971, St. Peter's School opened its doors to girls from the local convent school to study A level science and maths because the nuns couldn't accommodate them. I was not a scientist nor a mathematician, but Dad was determined for me to go. It ended up with me (not from the Convent) and a private vocal student of Dad's, Margaret Belcher (née Spink), who was from the Convent, entering St. Peter's to study the arts for A level. I remember my interview with the headmaster (Brother Alan), accompanied by Dad when, upon arrival, we were offered a glass of sherry each - it went straight to my head as it still does! Margaret and I had already become firm friends as she had been coming to Church Hatch for her singing lessons for four years by that time. There were six girls in the 6th form among about 1000 boys!

When I was at St. Peter's, I attended a music appreciation lesson. We were sitting at the very top of the auditorium where the 'box of lighting and sound tricks' was. Dad put on a record and within about two minutes, he came out steaming with fury! I couldn't understand why and especially when he told me and a boy I was sitting next to, to get out! He didn't appreciate us chatting through the music, which we weren't. So, deeply hurt, we left the theatre and went up the road to the local cafe for a cup of tea! When I met up with Dad at the end of the day for a lift home, I asked him why he embarrassed me by sending me out of the lesson. His reply was: 'I knew you would be bored as you know the music, so I thought you could have the lesson off, and Simon is good boyfriend material. I hope you enjoyed having time with him!' There was no relationship as a result - that cunning plan failed!!

Dad was impatient, a trait I have inherited from him. If he decided to do something, it had to be done there and then. One Sunday morning when I was in my early 20s, Dad got back from matins. I was, as usual, helping Mum cook roast dinner. He asked me to go with him on a mission. I had no idea where we were going, and Mum was none too pleased. However, Dad took me off in his dream Rover 3.5 Coupe to Southbourne. I had no idea where we were going but ended up at a large Victorian house that had been converted into flats in Southbourne. Still none the wiser, Dad buzzed a flat number, and we were greeted by a man and a very bouncy golden retriever. It turned out that the man was a teacher at St. Peter's and he and his wife had had to move into rented accommodation, but they weren't allowed pets. Before I realised what was happening, the dog (Patsy) and I were in the car and being driven home. I always remember the look on Mum's face, already flustered at having to keep the roast warm (not an easy job), when we walked into the kitchen with a very bouncy and large dog! Patsy ended up being a well-loved dog, especially by Dad, and was the start of many more golden retrievers in Michael's family.

Rene, with golden retriever Patsy in the back garden of 'Church Hatch'

I went to the Marlborough Secretarial College in Oxford when I finished my A levels at St. Peter's and my first secretarial post was as assistant secretary to Sir Edgar Williams CB, CBE, DSO, DL, who was Warden of the Rhodes Scholarships and who was chief intelligence officer to Montgomery during the war - particularly in Egypt during the Battle of El Alamein. Dad was extremely proud of me - something that was hard to fulfil as Michael and I had so much to live up to, but he always gave us praise when it was due.

When I returned home from Oxford, after a six-month spell working in Belgium as 'governess' to a family with three girls, Mum and Dad let me have Michael's old bedroom up in the attic with a small window overlooking the Priory and churchyard. Michael by that time had bought his own house which, happily, overlooked the railway line but sadly, the day of steam had long gone! Dad often invited himself to my room to have a sneaky G&T or whatever and a cigarette away from Mum's caring eyes. I remember saying that if he wanted to join me, he would have to listen to my music, for a change. I never played my Beatles and Rolling Stones records when he was in the house! I introduced him to Genesis ... Trick of the Tail, Lamb Lies Down on Broadway etc. I will never forget what he said: 'intelligent noise'! That was a huge compliment coming from him and one I will never forget!

How music helped whilst on holiday: there were a couple of occasions that I remember well. Firstly, in Switzerland (I think), Dad was suffering from bad toothache. As we did, wherever we went, all the churches were viewed, and organs inspected. One day in a church, the organ was playing. Dad introduced himself to the organist and as if by a miracle, it turned out that he was also a dentist!! So, in return for a private recital, the dentist sorted out Dad's tooth. The other occasion was again in Switzerland (bit of a pattern here!!). Several foreign students who stayed with us were from Switzerland and many of their families had holiday chalets!! Family holidays sorted!! We were staying in a lovely chalet, halfway up a mountain - peace and quiet. One evening we went down to the local village for dinner - raclette and fondue. There was a group of men in traditional dress playing old saws and Dad just couldn't resist asking if he could have a go. Which he did and managed to get a tune! It was great entertainment value and, as a result, we ended up having a free meal!

I loved it when exams were taking place at school with Dad invigilating as this meant he had a good hour to write to me if I was not home about what was going on ... more so about my cats and what Michael was up to, as well as church niggles and the foreign students' shenanigans. The year after Dad was a judge on the 'Hymn composing competition' programme, he was invited to bring his senior choir from St. Peter's to join up with the Clarendon Road Junior school choir (now Christchurch Juniors) for the carol competition, with Fred Dinenage as presenter. It must have been either 1971 or 1972. I was one of the only three girls from the St Peter's school choir. Every Saturday for what seemed like eons, we, including Dad (how he had the time or energy!) went by coach to the television studios in Southampton to record and then to try and mime when filmed. I remember the studio lights being extremely hot and everything just had to be perfect (Dad was not alone, for once) and the little ones really struggled. We got there though ... such a shame there are no recordings in existence so my son, Oliver, cannot see me on TV, all those years ago!

Swiss N Gauge Landscape Railway – a 60ᵗʰ birthday present for GOT.

GOT playing the Makin organ, with Carolyn as page turner

Church Hatch,
Christchurch, Hants.
29th August '65.

My dear Carolyn,

At last a chance to sit
down and write to you. Actually I am
starting this letter during a long sermon
on Sunday, which I have given up
trying to follow and understand.

We have a few more choirboys back
from their holidays – Timmy Lynd is back
now, but the Cramptons have not yet
returned. Now, to cap it all, quite a few
of the choirmen are now going on holiday.
I shall be very glad to see the back of all
these comings and goings, so that we can
settle down and do some work and learn

First page of a letter to Carolyn Tristram, 29 August 1965.
An example of GOT's 'copperplate' handwriting

END NOTE

Geoffrey Tristram: a very British Organist

Death and Funeral

Geoffrey Tristram died on 5 June 1979, aged 61. He collapsed at St Peter's School at lunchtime that day. After being helped by three of the teachers, he was taken by ambulance to Boscombe Hospital,[176] where he died from a heart attack.[177] It was his third; he recovered well from the first two, but the third took him, despite every effort to save him, including by the school secretary. Though much affected by his death, colleagues at St Peter's said how GOT would have appreciated the idea of dying 'on the job'. Brother Bernard, who was with him when he died, remembers how peaceful he was.

GOT and Rene at Glyndebourne just weeks before he collapsed and died

---

[176] *Bournemouth Echo* 6 June 1979.
[177] *The Rock*, 1979.

Carolyn had a 'very deep feeling of fear and impending tragedy when during the May half-term 'Mum and Dad travelled to Sussex to go to Glyndebourne ... [with] peanut butter sandwiches for the picnic ... and drinking out of silver plate glasses that were a gift from the choir'. Carolyn continues:

> My fears were allayed as Mum and Dad returned home safely having had a plethora of Wagner! What an experience Glynebourne was ... how the rich lived with their servants and butlers setting out tressle tables with white linen tablecloths, solid silver decanters and cutlery and probs Wedgewood dinner plates etc. And there's me eating peanut butter sandwiches!!! Dad thought it was hilarious, but he made sure that not many people spotted them!!!

> At that time, I was working as a sales assistant and property auction assistant at Rumsey & Rumsey on Old Christchurch Road in Bournemouth. 5 June 1979, I headed out into town for my lunch break, but I still had a sinking feeling and was agitated. When I returned early, the receptionist looked at me and I just knew something was not good ... she said I needed to go up to Mr Phil's office (Rumsey & Rumsey were owned by Mr Phil and Mr John - how archaic was that, but we had so much respect for Victorian principles in those days). My immediate boss in the auction department was there also when I walked in and I just knew what they were going to say. Dad had collapsed and died of a major heart attack at St. Peter's School. My world just collapsed around me but, thank heavens for where I worked as a colleague of mine drove me home and then worked miracles selling the 'Tristram' grandparent bungalow extremely quickly and at a good price so that Michael and I could find somewhere for Mum and Dad's beloved golden retriever Patsy to go to.

The funeral was held at Christchurch Priory on Saturday 9 June 1979 and was attended by more than 300 people. The service was conducted by the Reverend Basil Trevor-Morgan, Vicar of Christchurch, and the Reverend Frederick Shail, Vicar of Burley, a friend of GOT and a former curate at the Priory. Before and after the service, there were muffled peals from the belfry by the Priory bellringers. The organ was played by Garth Benson, from St Mary, Redcliffe, Bristol, and GOT's long-time friend and fellow railway enthusiast. Before the service, Benson played 'Nimrod', from Elgar's Enigma Variations and Frank Bridge's Adagio in E. At the entry of the coffin, the Russian Kontakion of the Departed (a piece regularly performed at the choir's recitals) was sung. After the opening sentences, Psalm 23 was sung to Walford Davies's chant. 'Ye holy angels bright' was sung to 'Darwall's 148th and the choir performed Parry's glorious anthem 'I was glad' (GOT had been rehearsing the anthem with the choir the day before he died in preparation for the patronal festival on 10 June). The concluding voluntary was Max Reger's Chorale Prelude on 'Lobe den Herren'.

Tributes

GOT's obituary in the Parish Magazine reads as follows:

Geoffrey Tristram

The sudden and untimely passing away of Geoffrey Tristram at the age of 61 has come as a very great shock, not only to all who worship at the Priory, but also to music lovers all over the country. His death will leave a void which will be very difficult to fill.

He had been Organist and Master of the Choir for nearly 30 years and, during that time, had given of his time and talents unstintingly in the service of the Church. A brilliant soloist, he was much in demand to give recitals in cathedrals and churches throughout the country. He initiated and planned the summer series of organ recitals in the Priory which have proved so popular over the years, but which necessitated a great deal of hard work on his part, not least because he gave many recitals himself.

As Master of the Choir, it was perfectly clear that by the results which he obtained he not only was extraordinarily gifted musically but conveyed his enthusiasm and musicianship to the members of the Choir who held him in such high regard and affection that they could never give him anything but the best. In fact, for him, being a perfectionist, nothing but the best was good enough and he maintained an incredibly high standard over all his years at the Priory, a fact known and appreciated far and wide. The standards which he has set and maintained will be very hard to follow. He was so obviously devoted to the Priory and never spared himself in his efforts.

It is perhaps fitting that on his last Sunday, which was Whitsunday, we should have had what really has now become traditional, the beautiful anthem 'Come Holy Ghost our Souls Inspire'. For in his long service to the Priory, he has truly inspired the hearts of so many giving so freely of the musical gifts with which he was richly endowed.

Our love, sympathy and prayers go out to Rene, Carolyn and Michael as we look back with gratitude and pride that we have had a musician of such stature in our midst.

At a Requiem Mass at St Peter's on the Friday following GOT's death, the following address was given:

There has been no processional hymn; there is no choir; no one sits at the organ. For more than your lifetime, Geoffrey Tristram contributed greatly to our Masses and to the great musical productions. He is here no longer. We, his friends, honoured him for his prodigious gifts as a musician and for the dedication to his art that made him a great organist – one of the most distinguished in Europe. We loved him as a friend, for his humility, his kindness and his enormous good humour. When he entered a room, he created an air of expectancy. With a story, a burst of mischievous foolery, a snatch of melody, he could raise one's spirits, could leave one better for having spoken with him, yet he bore with fortitude his ill health of recent years. The recordings he has made are a permanent reminder of his art and his great talent. We should be reminded by these of the endless, dedicated practice and sheer hard work that must accompany even the greatest of gifts to produce the perfection that he brought to the performance of his music. We, here, have had the rare privilege of listening to and watching him playing the organ, and we will rejoice in the memory of a dearly loved man and friend who gave us the chance of witnessing something superlative, executed superlatively. There will be no music at the end of this Mass – no valedictory flourishes from the organ but remember with us the grand flourishes of the past as you pray for his repose.[178]

On a lighter note, an anonymous poem (perhaps written by one or more members of the Priory choir) reads as follows:

Our Choirmaster stood at the Pearly Gates
    His Face was Worn and Old
He stood before the man of Fate for admission to the Fold
    'What have you done?' St. Peter said
To gain admission here.
    'I've been a Choirmaster Sir. He said
At the PRIORY for many a Year.
    The Pearly Gates flew open wide
St. Peter touched the Bell.
    Come in, he said, and choose your HARP
You've had your share of HELL.

---

[178] *The Rock*, 1979.

David Baker

Memorials

GOT is buried in Christchurch cemetery. A memorial plaque and a choirboy music scholarship at the Priory were instigated by the Association of Friends and Parents of the Priory Choir, formed in the wake of GOT's death by David Wastie, Deputy Organist and Choirmaster, and Michael Tristram. One of the objects of the Association was 'to help enhance and maintain the standard of music at the Priory – a standard set by Geoffrey Tristram'.[179] The 'choristership' was to 'help a boy to advance in musical ability [as an] ideal way to perpetuate the memory of the late organist. [It was] worth up to £100 to go towards vocal tuition and [was] awarded annually to a chorister after a special test by [GOT's] successor at the Priory, [providing] keen competition for the choristers to attain higher personal standards of singing and so enrich the general standard of the choir'.[180] Tim Norris, both a former chorister at Christchurch Priory and a pupil of GOT's at St Peter's, then later an Assistant Organist and Choir Conductor in the 1980s became 'at a young age of only 23/24 years of age (1983 -1987) … the first chairperson of the Friends of the Priory Choir'. He continues:

> This group of friends and parents, choristers and gentlemen of the choir raised funds in numerous ways - BBQs in the garden of 'Church Hatch', concerts, and many other events to put funds to one side for especially the choir and music-making. I managed to do this on behalf of all those who remained in the Choir [and others] who had been under Geoffrey's direction before his passing. It was a very rewarding time to keep the music-making, in the beauty of holiness to the Glory of God, at the Priory in top form. Things were not always easy, and I know the finances at the Priory at the time were not always as perhaps they should have been - there were no Lottery Funds available back then.

---

[179] *Bournemouth Evening Echo*, 21 November 1979.
[180] *Bournemouth Evening Echo*, 22 April 1981.

In 1993, a prize was created in GOT's memory at Reading School to coincide with the arrival and rebuilding of the Hill organ in the chapel.

> The prize was endowed and presented by Mr. and Mrs. Gordon Hands to commemorate the achievements of Geoffrey Tristram in the world of church music and the organ in particular. To be eligible for the prize, a candidate must be at the top of the school, and be the best in the school, or have made the most progress during his last year. Geoffrey and Gordon were contemporaries at the school, interested in music, though Gordon was to make his career in banking. Geoffrey … is reputed to have said that of all the organs he had played, the one in the school chapel was by far the worst. [181]

The Hill organ itself was dedicated on 16 October 1993. The main organ voluntaries that day were the Final from Vierne's Organ Symphony I and Bach's Prelude and 'St Anne' Fugue in E flat, two favourites of GOT in his recitals.[182]

On what would have been GOT's 100th birthday, 2 August 2017, the Priory was floodlit. Rene Tristram died on 25 October 1994 aged 72. Her 100th birthday on 3 March 2022 was also commemorated with a floodlit Priory. Without her steadfast support, sheer hard work and love, much of what is being recorded and celebrated in this book would not have happened!

---

[181]   *Reading School Magazine*, September 1993, p.18.

[182]   *Service of Dedication of a new organ for the Chapel at Reading School, 16 October 1993.*

GEOFFREY TRISTRAM
MEMORIAL PRIZE

On Speech Day 1993, the first Geoffrey Tristram Memorial Prize was awarded to Richard Adams. The prize has been endowed and presented by Mr and Mrs Gordon Hands to commemorate the achievements of Geoffrey Tristram in the world of church music and the organ in particular. To be eligible for the prize a candidate must be at the top of the school, and be the best organist in the school, or have made the most progress during his last year. Geoffrey and Gordon were contemporaries at school, interested in music, though Gordon was to make his career in banking. Geoffrey's amazing talent soon showed itself, and at the age of sixteen he became an associate of the Royal College of Organists, obtaining his fellowship the following year. This remarkable achievement marked the beginning of a brilliant career as an organ recitalist combined with the post of Organist and Master of the Choristers at Christchurch Priory, which took him all over the United Kingdom and abroad as a recitalist. He is reputed to have said that of all the organs he had played, the one in the school chapel was by far the worst.

It is fitting that Mr and Mrs Hands should have endowed this prize to coincide with the arrival and rebuilding of the Hill organ in the chapel. We thank them for their continued interest in the school's music, and congratulate Richard Adams on being the first recipient of this prestigious award.

The accompanying pictures show Geoffrey Tristram at the console of Christchurch Priory organ, and a gathering of Mr and Mrs Hands, Mr and Mrs David Adams, Richard Adams, and the Director of Music outside the chapel after Choral Evensong on Speech Day, at which the existing organ had been heard officially for the last time.

G.A.I.

Details of the Geoffrey Tristram Memorial Prize
at Reading School

Legacy

Tim Norris writes:

Geoffrey Tristram's legacy is enormous with teachers, instrumentalists, singers, composers, and arrangers having all been influenced by his energy and musical skills but above all by his love of people and spheres of community music-making. Whether it be G&S in Bournemouth, at school or organ recitals and TV and radio broadcasts or recital tours. He certainly left his mark in my life and subsequently I try to emulate his enthusiasm and energies in all I do and have done for the good of music-making and music education as many of his former pupils did and still do ... People always came first for GOT and his caring and attention to detail, his ability to bring the best out in people have and will always be my motto as I know it is for so many of his former students, friends, and colleagues. Greatly missed but he was such an influence for good in so many ways.

Suffice to say that [GOT]'s fortitude, courage and kindness has stuck with me for the past 41 years, and now that I look back I can say with certainty that [he] was such a great role model for my music-making and music-education endeavours to date ... I always maintained the same standards that I always believed your father would have expected - quality, sincerity and above all everything in the beauty of holiness to, and for, the Glory of God.

Without having met, having been educated by, worked, and inspired with Geoffrey Tristram, I would not have been able to do all the things I have done musically and educationally since having first met him in 1967-1979, both at St Peter's School, Southbourne and at Christchurch Priory. He was the most influential of all

the musicians and teachers I ever met in my 62 years of
creative music-making and educating, and I have met
numerous great musicians, conductors, choral directors,
and educationalists since 1979 - 2022, but your father
was a one-off, a gem, a true gent and a marvellous laugh.

GOT had (and still has) a devoted following. Daughter Carolyn,
who lives in Christchurch, notes that 'even 43 years on from his death, I
know I often get asked if I am related to GOT [when giving my name]'.
The obituaries talk of the immense respect he enjoyed from fellow
organists throughout the country; 'his touch and interpretation were quite
outstanding'.[183] He was an 'inspirational teacher', providing that 'creative
element' for so many young people, spotting and nurturing talent and
giving them a lifelong love of music. His gifts and inspiration live on in
the family and in those he taught and encouraged. He loved music-making
and enabling others to enjoy the gift of music and find their own musical
talent. So many people would agree with Jeremy Blandford, Organist of
St Mary's Southampton, who 'found it totally refreshing to meet a person
who balanced super-human qualities with a down-to-earth understanding
of the important things in life!' GOT had singular success at Christchurch,
as choir director, teacher, accompanist and, above all, as one of the finest
recitalists of his generation, a wonderful character, and a consummate
musician.

---

[183] *Bournemouth Echo* 6 June 1979.

Memorial Plaque, 1981

GOT at the Makin Organ

Appendices

APPENDIX A

Geoffrey Tristram's application for the post of Organist and Choirmaster Christchurch Priory

In connection with my application for the position of Choirmaster & Organist of Christchurch Priory, I have ventured to compile this short Report in which I have embodied a few suggestions which I believe to be practical regarding the possibilities respecting your future musical policy.

I would stress that the following points are merely a collection of my ideas on the subject and if favoured with the appointment I would freely welcome the benefit of further ideas, alterations and additions which would foster to a higher degree the music of the Priory Church.

The major points of the issue fall naturally into three groups, namely – The Congregation, The Choir and The Organ. Let us therefore deal with each separately.

THE CONGREGATION

It must be remembered that, as a Parish Church, one must always seek to strike a happy balance between the amount of music performed by the Choir on the one hand and the Congregation on the other. I believe this to be an important detail and one that should always be borne in mind for obvious reasons.

It may be found that Congregational Practices have the effect of bring home to them their own particular responsibilities regarding the music and if this were the case, then I should be quite prepared to assist in any way possible. Needless to say, I should welcome your large Congregations and would do my best to encourage them to sing and play their part in the Services of the Church.

I would further add that it would be my wish to guard against any radical changes in the music and that any such alteration decided upon by the Authorities of the Church should be so gently and carefully introduced over a long term policy so as to cause the minimum amount of inconvenience and upset to the Congregation.

THE CHOIR

1. The Function of the Choir

    As you realise only too well the prime object of the Choir, as indeed all the music of the Church, must be –

    a) To lead all the music in which the Congregation take an active part in such a manner as to be conducive to good congregational singing.
    b) To perform Anthems as a fit and worthy offering to Almighty God and the edification of the Congregation as listeners.

    I would emphasise that it is necessary that any music performed by the Choir alone should be so carefully and sincerely interpreted so as to convey to the listeners the message of the words and the beauty of the work.

2. The Formation of the Choir

    Subject to the ever important question of the balance of parts, I would recommend that steps be taken immediately to increase the working strength of the singing boys to 16 with the possibility of a further increase to 18 with anything up to 6 probationers.

    As you will no doubt appreciate, there are various methods of recruiting boys, but it has been my experience that the following invariably produce quite satisfactory results –

    a) By making friends with headmasters of schools in the district and gaining permission to visit and talk to the boys in the schools and then, if necessary, call and see the parents of any concerned.

b) By direct appeal to the members of the congregation to encourage their sons to join the Choir.

c) To make the life of the existing Choirboys so interesting and attractive that they themselves will bring in their friends.

Naturally, it does not follow that every new member will be suitable, that is why I have suggested the need for at least 6 probationers at all times upon which to draw and to dismiss any who, after a period of anything up to 6 months' probation did not prove to be intelligently interested in the music and satisfactory from a point of view of discipline.

I would venture to suggest for your consideration, that it would appear that, for many reasons, the happiest choirboys are invariably not paid, but that a sum of money in place of this is earmarked for the provision of regular activities for the boys in sports and equipment, visits to places of interest and general enjoyment. It will be easily understood that money spent in this way will do far more to encourage the boys in their sense of fellowship and loyalty to the Church.

As it is a principle almost universally acknowledge that any choir is as good as, and no better than, its trebles, my first concern must be to spend as much time with the boys as possible in trying to produce the best results in the shortest time.

Regarding the gentlemen of the choir, it is my experience that if the standard of work is high and of an interesting nature, I am confident that there will be nothing but enthusiasm and loyalty on the part of those who so freely give of their time and without whom little or nothing could be done.

3. The Choice of Music

I would strongly emphasis the need at all times to perform music which is considered to be in good taste and which is well within the limits of the technical capabilities of the choir, giving adequate time and rehearsal to each and every work to be performed and leaving no part, however small, to chance. In the first place, I should persevere with the task of laying the foundations for good choral technique, - proper breathing, tone, production of vowel sounds, enunciation of words, clearness of diction and the many other necessary details to secure this end. Secondly, having built a basis upon which to work, the whole character of the choral music can be gradually uplifted into a thing of beauty and joy.

Regarding the actual choice of music to be performed and relying, as I should, upon the constant assistance of the gentlemen of the choir, I should at all times when the counsel and advice of its experienced members. I would add that I feel in agreement with the views expressed by the Commission appointed by the Archbishops of Canterbury and York to consider the principles of Music in Worship.

THE ORGAN

Organ playing in the Services of the Church can be a definite asset or hindrance to devotion. All accompaniments, therefore, should be sufficiently artistic in suggesting rather than imitating the character of the sung words in order to make the music live in the minds of those who attend the Services. In the same way, carefully chosen voluntaries can do much to help and assist the worshipper.

It is so often found that less care is apt to be taken by both organists and choirs in their preparation of the hymns than of any other part of the Service. The result is that hymns, instead of being inspiring and uplifting to choir and congregation alike, produce too often a sense of monotony causing physical and spiritual depression. I have found that by playing the hymns in a rhythmic manner with a certain flexibility of registration, transposed if necessary into such a key as to be within the compass of the singers in the congregation, encouragement is given and more enjoyment will result.

Now, over and above the Services of the Church, I should be happy to arrange and give a series of weekly organ recitals throughout the summer months, the entire proceeds of which could be devoted to organ or choir funds. In the course of time when the choir had become so proficient, then choral recitals and other musical Services could be introduced.

It is quite possible that the B.B.C., for whom I have the privilege of playing, would be pleased to continue my usual organ recitals from the Priory when the new organ is completed.

In closing, I would again take the opportunity of emphasising that all the various points that I have herein stated are merely intended as helpful suggestions representing a definite future policy in music, but nevertheless fully open to your discussion and criticism.

Furthermore, in order to make this or any other scheme fully practical in the shortest possible time, I should be prepared to lay aside all other musical engagement which might tend to interfere with progress, in order to devote my full energy to the task of making the music offered in Christchurch Priory worthy of the highest tradition.

Fellow of the Royal College of Organists

August, 1949

APPENDIX B

Specification of the Organ at Christchurch Priory prior to the 1951 Rebuild[184]

Great

Double Open Diapason	16
Open Diapason I	8
Open Diapason II	8
Gamba	8
Claribel Flute	8
Principal	4
Flûte Harmonique	4
Twelfth	2⅔
Fifteenth	2
Sesquialtera	III
Sharp Mixture	II
Posaune	8
Clarion	4

Swell

Double Diapason	16
Open Diapason	8
Stopped Diapason	8
Principal	4
Piccolo Harmonique	2
Sesquialtera	III
Trumpet	8
Hautbois	8
Clarion	4

---

[184] Details taken from Jones, Peter, *A History of the Pipe Organ of Christchurch Priory*, Christchurch: Natula Publications, 1999, pp. 15, 17.

Choir

Stopped Diapason	8
Viol d'Amour	8
Dulciana	8
Vox Angelica	8
Flute	4
Clarinet	8

Pedal

Open Diapason	16
Violone	16
Bourdon	16
Quint	10⅔
Principal	8
Octave	8
Mixture	II
Ophicleide	16

APPENDIX C

**Specification of the Organ at Christchurch Priory
after the 1951 Rebuild, with additions to 1968[185]**

Great

Principal	16	
Open Diapason I	8	DR (in triforium)
Open Diapason II	8	
Open Diapason III	8	
Principal	8	
Melodic Diapason	8	
Claribel Flute	8	
Flauto Dolce	8	
Flûte à Cheminée	8	
Octave	4	DR (in triforium)
Principal	4	
Gemshorn	4	
Harmonic Flute	4	
Twelfth	2⅔	
Fifteenth	2	
Sesquialtera	III	
Mixture	V	DR (in triforium)
Cymbale	III	
Double Trumpet	16	
Posaune	8	
Clarion	4	

---

[185]   Details taken from Jones, Peter, *A History of the Pipe Organ of Christchurch Priory*, Christchurch: Natula Publications, 1999, pp. 22-3.

Swell

Bourdon	16	
Open Diapason	8	
Gedackt	8	
Viola da Gamba	8	
Viole Celeste	8	DR
Principal	4	
Fifteenth	2	
Sesquialtera	III	
Contra Fagotto	16	DR
Trumpet	8	
Hautboy	8	
Clarion	4	

Choir

Stopped Diapason	8	
Dulciana	8	
Violoncello	8	
Vox Angelica	8	
Harmonic Flute	4	
Nazard	2⅔	C
Piccolo	2	C
Tierce	1&3/5	C
Larigot	1⅓	C
Sifflöte	1	C
Clarinet	8	
Tuba	8	
Tuba Clarion	4	

Pedal

Sub Bass	32	C
Contra Bass	16	DR
Open Wood	16	

Principal	16	(from Great)
Bourdon	16	
Octave Wood	8	
Principal	8	
Flute	8	
Fifteenth	4	
Fourniture	V	
Mixture	V	DR (from Great)
Harmonics IV of	32	
Harmonics IV of	16	
Fagotto	16	DR (from Swell)
Contra Trombone	32	DR (in triforium)
Ophicleide	16	
Trumpet	8	
Clarion	4	

APPENDIX D

Specification of the Compton Organ at St Peter's School, Bournemouth

Great

Double Diapason	16
Diapason	8
Hohl Flute	8
Dolce	8
Octave	4
Salicet	4
Twelfth	$2\frac{2}{3}$
Super Octave	2
Fourniture	IV
Tromba	8
Octave Tromba	4

Swell

Contre Viole	16
Geigen	8
Viola da Gamba	8
Echo Viole	8
Major Flute	8
Lieblich Gedackt	8
Octave Geigen	4
Lieblich Flute	4
Twelfth	$2\frac{2}{3}$
Fifteenth	2
Sesquialtera	II

Mixture	IV
Contra Fagotto	16
Cornopean	8
Oboe	8
Clarion	4

Choir

Lieblich Bourdon	16
Double Dulciana	16
Gemshorn	8
Rohr Flute	8
Dulciana	8
Flauto Traverso	4
Dulcet	4
Dulcet Twelfth	2⅔
Dulcet Fifteenth	2
Flautino	2
Tierce	1&3/5
Larigot	1⅓
Sifflote	1
Echo Cymbale	III
Clarinet	8
Tuba	8

Pedal

Open Wood	32
Open Wood	16
Contra Bass	16
Bourdon	16
Dulciana	16
Octave	8
Flute	8
Flute	4

Harmonics	IV
Contra Fagotto	32
Trombone	16
Fagotto	16
Trumpet	8
Schalmei	4

Specification of the Makin Organ at Christchurch Priory[186]

Pedal

Double Open Wood	32
Open Wood	16
Open Diapason	16
Violone	16
Bourdon	16
Dulciana	16
Octave	8
Bass Flute	8
Fifteenth	4
Octave Flute	4
Mixture (12.15.19.22)	IV
Contra Bombarde	32	*
Ophicleide	16	*
Clarion	8	*
Schalmei	4	*

(* = enclosed)

Great

Double Diapason	16
Bourdon	16
First Diapason	8
Second Diapason	8
Clarabella	8
Octave	4

---

186 Details taken from a company brochure, undated.

Principal	4
Waldflöte	4
Twelfth	2⅔
Fifteenth	2
Plein Jeu	VIII
Fourniture (19.22.26.29)	IV
Cymbale	III
Contra Posaune	16 *
Posaune	8 *
Clarion	4 *
(* = enclosed)	

Swell

Open Diapason	8
Lieblich Gedeckt	8
Viola da Gamba	8
Salicional	8
Vox Angelica	8
Principal	4
Lieblich Flöte	4
Fifteenth	2
Mixture	III
Mixture (15.19.22.26.29)	V
Double Trumpet	16
Trumpet	8
Horn	8
Hautboy	8
Clarion	4

Choir

Quintaten	16
Stopped Diapason	8
Höhl Flute	8

Viole	8
Principal	4
Flauto Traverso	4
Nason	4
Nazard	2⅔
Fifteenth	2
Blockflöte	2
Tierce	1&3/5
Larigot	1⅓
Sifflöte	1
Scharf (22.26.29)	III

Solo

Concert Flute	8
Viole d'Orchestre	8
Dulciana	8
Vox Angelica	8
Zauberflöte	8
Unda Maris	8
Orchestral Flute	4
Nazard	2⅔
Piccolo	2
Basset Horn	16
Orchestral Oboe	8
Orchestral Clarinet	8
Vox Humana	8
Tuba	8
Tuba Magna (unenclosed)	8

List of Recitals given by GOT, compiled from surviving programmes

RECITALS

Date	Venue	Notes	Repertoire 1	Repertoire 2	Repertoire 3	Repertoire 4
9/10/1934	Reading Minster	unknown year; pencil mark 'age 16 yrs'	Handel: Overture to Samson	Bridge: Andantino in F Minor	Bach: Prelude and Fugue in D	Rheinberger: Canzonetta
14/12/1938	Reading Town Hall	accompanied soprano Betty Palmer				
2/12/1939	Reading Minster		Bach: Prelude and Fugue in G	Brahms: Schmucke dich, o liebe Seele	Brahms: Es ist ein Ros' entsprungen	Brahms: Herzlich tut mich verlangen
6/9/1941	Reading Minster		Handel: March 'Hercules'	Festing: Largo, Allegro, Aria and Two Variations	Bach: Fantasia and Fugue in G Minor	Wesley, SS: Larghetto in F sharp Minor
8/10/1941	Trinity Congregational Church		Handel: Overture to Samson	Felton: A Little Tune	Mozart: Fantasia in F Minor	Bach: Prelude and Fugue in D
29/11/1941	St. Laurence's, Reading	Part 1	Cleramboult: Dialogue	Brahms: Schmucke dich, o liebe Seele	Brahms: Es ist ein Ros' entsprungen	Brahms: Herzlich tut mich verlangen
29/11/1941	St. Laurence's, Reading	Part 2	Yon: Humoreske	Vierne: Cathedrales	Dubois: Fiat Lux	Widor: Toccata from Symphony 5
26/5/1942	St. John the Baptist, Windsor	unknown year	Bach: Prelude and Fugue in G	Bach: Sheep may safely graze	Franck: Piece Heroique	Festing: Largo, Allegro, Aria and Two Variations
20/6/1942	Reading Minster		Bach: Prelude and Fugue in G	Bach: Sheep may safely graze	Franck: Chorale in A Minor	Bossi: Scherzo in G Minor
22/7/1942	Trinity Congregational Church		Purcell: Trumpet Tune and Air	Schumann: Canon in B minor	Bach: Toccata in F	Bach: Air on the G String
19/8/1942	Trinity Congregational Church		Bach: Toccata and Fugue in C	Bach: Jesu, Joy of Man's Desiring	Bach: All Glory, Laud and Honour	Hollins: Song of Sunshine
31/10/1942	Trinity Congregational Church		Bach: Fantasia and Fugue in G Minor	Arne: A Maggot	Wesley: Air and Gavotte	Liszt: Prelude and Fugue on B.A.C.H.
16/6/1943	Trinity Congregational Church		Bach: Prelude and Fugue in G	Wesley, SS: Larghetto in F sharp Minor	Jongen: Sonata Eroica	Vierne: Scherzo from Symphony 2

Repertoire 5	Repertoire 6	Repertoire 7	Repertoire 8	Repertoire 9	Repertoire 10	Repertoire 11
Mendelssohn: Sonata 6						
Brahms: O Welt, ich muss dich lassen	Liszt: Prelude and Fugue on B.A.C.H.	Karg Elert: Harmonies du Soir	Mendelssohn: Sonata 6	Morandi: Rondo de Campanelli	Whitlock: Scherzo	Lemmens: Finale
Elgar: Sonata in G	Franck: Piece Heroique	Hollins: Grand Choeur in D	Liszt: Prelude and Fugue on B.A.C.H.			
Guilmant: Pastorale from Sonata 1	Bonnet: Elfes-Caprice Heroique	Boellmann: Suite Gothique	Vierne: Scherzo from Symphony 2	Mulet: Toccata 'Tu es petra'		
Brahms: O Welt, ich muss dich lassen	Bach: Fantasia in G	Grace: Cradle Song	Mendelssohn: Sonata 6			
Liszt: Prelude and Fugue on B.A.C.H.	Bossi: Scherzo in G Minor	Yon: Humoreske	Vierne: Toccata from Symphony 1			
Liszt: Prelude and Fugue on B.A.C.H.	Daughtry: Jesu, Thou Joy	MacDowell: To a Wild Rose	Vierne: Carillon	Vierne: Toccata from Symphony 1		
Elgar: Sonata in G	Dvorak: Humoresque	Guilmant: Caprice in B Flat	Jongen: Chant de Mai	Karg Elert: Chorale Improvisation 'Ein' feste Burg'		
Mozart: Fantasia in F Minor	Lemare: Madrigal	Franck: Final	Dvorak: Largo from 'New World'	Vierne: Scherzo from Symphony 2	Widor: Toccata from Symphony 5	
Saint Saens: The Swan	Dubois: Fiat Lux	Hollins: Maytime	Bossi: Scherzo in G Minor	Gigout: Toccata in B Minor		
Vierne: Finale from Symphony 1						

217

30/10/1943	Reading Minster	w/ Reading Madrigal Society	Wesley, SS: Choral Song and Fugue	Wesley, SS: Larghetto in F sharp Minor		
20/4/1944	West Memorial Hall, Caversham	Guest Pianist	German: Merrie England			
25/4/1944	The Concert Hall, Reading	Hon. Conductor	German: Merrie England			
14/4/1945	St. Laurence's, Reading		Bach: Prelude and Fugue in B Minor	Wesley: Air and Gavotte	Franck: Piece Heroique	Whitlock: Folk Tune
15/7/1946	Southbourne Methodist, Bournemouth		Bach: Prelude and Fugue in G	Claremboult: Dialogue	Franck: Piece Heroique	Festing: Largo, Allegro, Aria and Two Variations
22/7/1946	Southbourne Methodist, Bournemouth		Bach: Toccata in F	Vaughan Williams: Rhosymedre	Liszt: Prelude and Fugue on B.A.C.H.	Handel: Allegro from Concerto 4 (Set 2)
29/7/1946	Southbourne Methodist, Bournemouth		Bach: Prelude and Fugue in B Minor	Bach: Sheep may safely graze	Mendelssohn: Sonata 6	Guilmant: Caprice in B Flat
12/8/1946	Southbourne Methodist, Bournemouth		Bach: Toccata and Fugue in D Minor	Karg Elert: Chorale Improvisation 'Jesu, geh 'voran'	Farrar: A Wedding Piece	Liszt: Introduction and Fugue on 'Ad nos ad salutarem undam'
19/8/1946	Southbourne Methodist, Bournemouth	w/ pianist Doris Mudge	Handel: Extracts from the 'Water Music'	Bach: Ertodt' Uns Durch Dein Güte	Bach: In Dir ist Freude	Bonnet: Elfes-Caprice Heroique
26/8/1946	Southbourne Methodist, Bournemouth		Bach: Fantasia in G	Bach: Jesu, Joy of Man's Desiring	Bach: All Glory, Laud and Honour	Wesley, SS: Larghetto in F sharp Minor
16/9/1946	Southbourne Methodist, Bournemouth		Handel: Overture to Samson	Arne: A Maggot	Bach: Prelude and Fugue in A	Rootham: Song of Victory
30/9/1946	Southbourne Methodist, Bournemouth		Bach: 'Dorian' Toccata and Fugue	Whitlock: Fidelis	Franck: Chorale in A Minor	Karg Elert: Harmonies du Soir
15/3/1947	All Saints', Bournemouth		Karg Elert: Chorale Improvisation 'Ein' feste Burg'	Whitlock: Fidelis	Jongen: Sonata Eroica	Thalben Ball: Tune in E

Boellmann: Suite Gothique	Saint Saens: The Swan	Dubois: Fiat Lux	Vierne: Berceuse	Vierne: Carillon	Hollins: Grand Choeur in D		
Jongen: Sonata Eroica	Whitlock: Scherzo	Yon: Humoreske	Lemmens: Finale				
Guilmant: Pastorale from Sonata 1	Vierne: Carillon	Vierne: Scherzo from Symphony 2	Hollins: Song of Sunshine	Vierne: Finale from Symphony 1			
Saint Saens: The Swan							
Jongen: Minuet Scherzo							
Franck: The Symphonic Variations	Boellmann: Suite Gothique	Saint Saens: The Swan	Dubois: Fiat Lux	Vierne: Berceuse	Vierne: Carillon	Hollins: Grand Choeur in D	
Handel: Concerto in B Flat	Jongen: Sonata Eroica	Whitlock: Scherzo	Yon: Humoreske	Lemmens: Finale			
Jongen: Chant de Mai	Guilmant: Pastorale from Sonata 1	Vierne: Carillon	Vierne: Scherzo from Symphony 2	Hollins: Song of Sunshine	Vierne: Finale from Symphony 1		
Jongen: Sonata Eroica	Saint Saens: The Swan	Morandi: Rondo de Campanelli	Liszt: Canzonetta del Salvator Rosa	Widor: Toccata from Symphony 5			
Morandi: Rondo de Campanelli	Jongen: Minuet Scherzo	Dubois: Fiat Lux	Lemare: Madrigal	Dvorak: Humoresque	Hollins: Concert Overture in C		

26/4/1947	All Saints', Bournemouth		Bach: Toccata and Fugue in D Minor	Arne: A Maggot	Mozart: Fantasia in F Minor	Wesley, SS: Larghetto in F sharp Minor
24/5/1947	All Saints', Bournemouth		Bach: Toccata in F	Festing: Largo, Allegro, Aria and Two Variations	Elgar: Sonata in G	Guilmant: Cantilene Pastorale
26/7/1947	All Saints', Bournemouth		Bach: Fantasia and Fugue in G Minor	Cleramboult: Dialogue	Handel: Allegro from Concerto 4 (Set 2)	Mendelssohn: Sonata 6
30/8/1947	All Saints', Bournemouth		Handel: Overture to Samson	Bach: Prelude and Fugue in B Minor	Schumann: Canon in B minor	Jongen: Sonata Eroica
27/9/1947	All Saints', Bournemouth		Bach: Prelude and Fugue in G	Bach: Sheep may safely graze	Alcock: Introduction and Passacaglia	Felton: A Little Tune
12/6/1948	All Saints', Bournemouth		Bach: Toccata and Fugue in D Minor	Festing: Largo, Allegro, Aria and Two Variations	Handel: Allegro from Concerto 4 (Set 2)	Liszt: Prelude and Fugue on B.A.C.H.
24/5/1947	All Saints', Bournemouth		Bach: Toccata in F	Festing: Largo, Allegro, Aria and Two Variations	Elgar: Sonata in G	Guilmant: Cantilene Pastorale
26/7/1947	All Saints', Bournemouth		Bach: Fantasia and Fugue in G Minor	Cleramboult: Dialogue	Handel: Allegro from Concerto 4 (Set 2)	Mendelssohn: Sonata 6
30/8/1947	All Saints', Bournemouth		Handel: Overture to Samson	Bach: Prelude and Fugue in B Minor	Schumann: Canon in B minor	Jongen: Sonata Eroica
27/9/1947	All Saints', Bournemouth		Bach: Prelude and Fugue in G	Bach: Sheep may safely graze	Alcock: Introduction and Passacaglia	Felton: A Little Tune

Liszt: Introduction and Fugue on 'Ad nos ad salutarem undam'	Franck: The Symphonic Variations					
Franck: Piece Heroique	Handel: Concerto in B Flat	MacDowell: To a Wild Rose	Bossi: Scherzo in G Minor	Hollins: Maytime	Boellmann: Suite Gothique	
Jongen: Chant de Mai	Jongen: Chant de Mai	Elgar: Allegro Maestoso from Sonata in G	Dvorak: Largo from 'New World'	Hollins: Grand Choeur in D		
Dvorak: Largo from 'New World'	Jongen: Sonata Eroica	Wesley: Air and Gavotte	Gigout: Scherzo	Mulet: Carillon Sortie		
Hollins: Concert Overture in C	Morandi: Rondo de Campanelli	Farrar: A Wedding Piece	Vierne: Cathedrales	Hollins: Maytime	Durufle: Toccata in B Minor	
Dvorak: Largo from 'New World'	Liszt: Introduction and Fugue on 'Ad nos ad salutarem undam'	Bossi: Scherzo in G Minor	Franck: Chorale in A Minor	Guilmant: Caprice in B Flat	Dubois: Toccata in G	
Franck: Piece Heroique	Handel: Concerto in B Flat	MacDowell: To a Wild Rose	Bossi: Scherzo in G Minor	Hollins: Maytime	Boellmann: Suite Gothique	
Jongen: Chant de Mai	Jongen: Chant de Mai	Elgar: Allegro Maestoso from Sonata in G	Dvorak: Largo from 'New World'	Hollins: Grand Choeur in D		
Dvorak: Largo from 'New World'	Jongen: Sonata Eroica	Wesley: Air and Gavotte	Gigout: Scherzo	Mulet: Carillon Sortie		
Hollins: Concert Overture in C	Morandi: Rondo de Campanelli	Farrar: A Wedding Piece	Vierne: Cathedrales	Hollins: Maytime	Durufle: Toccata in B Minor	

12/6/1948	All Saints', Bournemouth		Bach: Toccata and Fugue in D Minor	Festing: Largo, Allegro, Aria and Two Variations	Handel: Allegro from Concerto 4 (Set 2)	Liszt: Prelude and Fugue on B.A.C.H.
26/6/1948	All Saints', Bournemouth		Bach: Prelude and Fugue in B Minor	Arne: A Maggot	Mozart: Fantasia in F Minor	Wesley, SS: Larghetto in F sharp Minor
17/7/1948	All Saints', Bournemouth		Bach: Fantasia and Fugue in G Minor	Wesley: Air and Gavotte	Franck: Piece Heroique	Chauvet: Andantino in D Flat
31/7/1948	All Saints', Bournemouth		Bach: Toccata in F	Thalben Ball: Elegy	Mendelssohn: Sonata 6	Dubois: Fiat Lux
10/8/1948	Salisbury Cathedral		Bach: Fantasia and Fugue in G Minor	Thalben Ball: Elegy	Mendelssohn: Sonata 6	Dubois: Fiat Lux
21/8/1948	All Saints', Bournemouth		Bach: Prelude and Fugue in G	Schumann: Canon in B minor	Jongen: Sonata Eroica	Karg Elert: Harmonies du Soir
11/9/1948	All Saints', Bournemouth		Bach: Fantasia in G	Whitlock: Folk Tune	Elgar: Sonata in G	Vierne: Cathedrales
15/4/1949	Winter Gardens, Bournemouth	w/ Bournemouth Municipal Choir & Orchestra	Bach: Mass in B Minor			
11/5/1949	All Saints', Bournemouth	w/ violinist Roy Gubby	Bach: Toccata in F	Arne: A Maggot	Mozart: Fantasia in F Minor	Yon: Humoreske
21/5/1949	Salisbury Cathedral		Bach: Toccata in F	Arne: A Maggot	Mozart: Fantasia in F Minor	Wesley, SS: Larghetto in F sharp Minor
9/7/1949	Salisbury Cathedral		Bach: Prelude and Fugue in G	Darke: Meditation on 'Brother James' Air'	Alcock: Introduction and Passacaglia	Vierne: Cathedrales
24/8/1949	All Saints', Bournemouth		Bach: Toccata and Fugue in D Minor	Cleramboult: Dialogue	Liszt: Introduction and Fugue on 'Ad nos ad salutarem undam'	Darke: Meditation on 'Brother James' Air'

Dvorak: Largo from 'New World'	Liszt: Introduction and Fugue on 'Ad nos ad salutarem undam'	Bossi: Scherzo in G Minor	Franck: Chorale in A Minor	Guilmant: Caprice in B Flat	Dubois: Toccata in G		
Bossi: Scherzo in G Minor	Franck: Chorale in A Minor	Morandi: Rondo de Campanelli	Dubois: Toccata in G				
Boellmann: Suite Gothique	Hollins: Maytime	Liszt: Canzonetta del Salvator Rosa	Lemmens: Finale				
Whitlock: Scherzo	Yon: Humoreske	Mulet: Toccata 'Tu es petra'					
Bossi: Scherzo in G Minor	Mulet: Toccata 'Tu es petra'						
Bonnet: Elfes - Caprice Heroique	Farrar: A Wedding Piece	Durufle: Toccata in B Minor					
Dupre: Verset des Psaumes	Dupre: Finale 'Ave Maris Stella'	Widor: Toccata from Symphony 5					
Widor: Variations from Symphony 5							
Jongen: Sonata Eroica	Bonnet: Elfes-Caprice Heroique	Widor: Allegro Vivace from Symphony 5					
Vierne: Carillon	Yon: Humoreske	Durufle: Toccata in B Minor					
Guilmant: Scherzo Symphonique	Vierne: Finale from Symphony 1						

7/4/1950	Winter Gardens, Bournemouth	w/ Bournemouth Municipal Choir & Orchestra	Bach: St. Matthew Passion			
10/6/1950	Christchurch Priory	w/ violinist Edward Armstrong and bass baritone Eric Keats	Bach: Prelude and Fugue in D	Arne: A Maggot	Darke: Meditation on 'Brother James' Air'	Vierne: Scherzo from Symphony 2
15/7/1950	Salisbury Cathedral		Bach: Prelude and Fugue in D	Stanley: Toccata for the Flutes	Rootham: Song of Victory	Whitlock: Folk Tune
26/8/1950	Christchurch Priory	w/ tenor Wilson Shepherd	Bach: Prelude and Fugue in A	Schumann: Canon in B minor	Hollins: Song of Sunshine	Bossi: Scherzo in G Minor
2/12/1950	Avenue Methodist Church	Choir anniversary, w/ bass baritone Eric Keats		Bach: Toccata and Fugue in D Minor	Wesley: Air and Gavotte	Yon: Humoreske
25/1/1951	St. Michael's, Southampton	Opening recital	Bach: Toccata in F	Festing: Largo, Allegro, Aria and Two Variations	Franck: Chorale in A Minor	Morandi: Rondo de Campanelli
2/6/1951	Christchurch Priory	Organ dedication	Bach: Fantasia and Fugue in G Minor	Herzogenberg: Pastorale on 'Now thank we all our God'	Hollins: Song of Sunshine	Liszt: Introduction and Fugue on 'Ad nos ad salutarem undam'
12/6/1951	Christchurch Priory	w/ tenor Wilson Shepherd	Wesley, SS: Choral Song and Fugue	Stanley: Toccata for the Flutes	Darke: A Fantasy	Elgar: Sonata in G
15/6/1951	Christchurch Priory	w/ BBC West of England Singers	Bach: Toccata in F	Alcock: Introduction and Passacaglia		
11/7/1951	Christchurch Priory		Bach: Prelude and Fugue in G	Darke: Meditation on 'Brother James' Air'	Boellmann: Suite Gothique	Yon: Humoreske
1/8/1951	Christchurch Priory		Bach: Prelude and Fugue in D	Cleramboult: Dialogue	Wesley, SS: Larghetto in F sharp Minor	Dubois: Fiat Lux

224

Handel: Allegro from Concerto 4 (Set 2)	Vierne: Scherzo from Symphony 2	Dupre: Prelude and Fugue in B					
Morandi: Rondo de Campanelli							
Dubois: Fiat Lux	Handel: Allegro from Concerto 4 (Set 2)	Liszt: Canzonetta del Salvator Rosa	Karg Elert: Nun danket alle Gott				
Bossi: Scherzo in G Minor	Dubois: Fiat Lux	Hollins: Maytime	Vierne: Finale from Symphony 1				
Jongen: Minuet Scherzo	Walford Davies: Solemn Melody	Vierne: Scherzo from Symphony 2	Widor: Toccata from Symphony 5				
Vierne: Cathedrales	Vierne: Scherzetto	Dupre: Prelude and Fugue in B					
Franck: Piece Heroique	Gigout: Scherzo	Widor: Variations from Symphony 5					
Jongen: Chant de Mai	Karg Elert: Chorale Improvisation 'Ein' feste Burg'	Vierne: Berceuse	Bossi: Scherzo in G Minor	Vierne: Toccata from Symphony 1			

225

15/8/1951	Christchurch Priory		Handel: Overture to Samson	Arne: A Maggot	Mozart: Fantasia in F Minor	Guilmant: Pastorale from Sonata 1
5/9/1951	Christchurch Priory		Bach: Fantasia in G	Whitlock: Folk Tune	Jongen: Sonata Eroica	Widor: Pastorale from Symphony 2
26/9/1951	Christchurch Priory		Handel: Overture to the Occasional Oratorio		Festing: Air and Variations	Brahms: Schmucke dich, o liebe Seele
25/6/1952	St. Peter's, Bournemouth		Bach: Fantasia and Fugue in G Minor	Herzogenberg: Pastorale on 'Now thank we all our God'	Stanley: Toccata for the Flutes	Liszt: Prelude and Fugue on B.A.C.H.
1/7/1952	Guildhall, Southampton	w/ contralto Bessie Tolley-Reakes	Bach: Fantasia and Fugue in G Minor	Festing: Largo, Allegro, Aria and Two Variations	Handel: Allegro from Concerto 4 (Set 2)	Mozart: Fantasia in F Minor
16/7/1952	Christchurch Priory		Bach: Prelude and Fugue in B Minor	Cleramboult: Dialogue	Handel: Concerto in B Flat	Jongen: Chant de Mai
31/7/1952	Mortehoe Methodist Church	Organ re-opening and rededication	Bach: Fantasia and Fugue in G Minor	Festing: Largo, Allegro, Aria and Two Variations	Handel: Concerto in B Flat	Whitlock: Folk Tune
27/8/1952	Christchurch Priory		Bach: Toccata and Fugue in D Minor	Schumann: Canon in B minor	Franck: Fantasie	Hollins: Song of Sunshine
10/9/1952	Christchurch Priory	w/ violinist Raymond Mosley	Bach: Prelude and Fugue in B Minor	Herzogenberg: Pastorale on 'Now thank we all our God'	Thalben Ball: Elegy	Stanford: Postlude in D Minor
17/9/1952	Christchurch Priory		Bach: Prelude and Fugue in D	Stanley: Toccata for the Flutes	Franck: Chorale in A Minor	Darke: A Fantasy
13/12/1952	St. Mark's, Portsea		Bach: Fantasia and Fugue in G Minor	Arne: A Maggot	Handel: Allegro from Concerto 4 (Set 2)	Mozart: Fantasia in F Minor

Bonnet: Elfes-Caprice Heroique	Peeters: Abdijvrede	Morandi: Rondo de Campanelli	Mulet: Toccata 'Tu es petra'				
Handel: Allegro from Concerto 4 (Set 2)	Dvorak: Largo from 'New World'	Dubois: Toccata in G					
Brahms: Es ist ein Ros' entsprungen	Brahms: Herzlich tut mich verlangen	Dupre: Fugue in G Minor	Chauvet: Andantino in D Flat	Gigout: Scherzo	Durufle: Toccata in B Minor		
Peeters: Abdijvrede	Handel: Allegro from Concerto 4 (Set 2)	Jongen: Minuet Scherzo	Dubois: Toccata in G				
Jongen: Minuet Scherzo	Dubois: Fiat Lux	Boellmann: Suite Gothique	Yon: Humoreske	Liszt: Prelude and Fugue on B.A.C.H.			
Franck: Piece Heroique	Whitlock: Divertimento	Walford Davies: Solemn Melody	Widor: Variations from Symphony 5				
Whitlock: Scherzo	Dubois: Fiat Lux	Walford Davies: Solemn Melody	Liszt: Canzonetta del Salvator Rosa	Yon: Humoreske	Lemmens: Finale		
Liszt: Introduction and Fugue on 'Ad nos ad salutarem undam'	Vierne: Berceuse	Vierne: Scherzo from Symphony 2	Mulet: Carillon Sortie				
Dubois: Toccata in G							
Bonnet: Elfes-Caprice Heroique	Walker: Lullaby (on an old Irish Air)	Bossi: Scherzo in G Minor	Mulet: Toccata 'Tu es petra'				
Festing: Largo, Allegro, Aria and Two Variations	Franck: Chorale in A Minor	Dupre: Finale 'Ave Maris Stella'	Dubois: Fiat Lux				

Date	Venue					
22/9/1953	Guildhall, Southampton		Bach: Prelude and Fugue in B Minor	Arne: A Maggot	Elgar: Allegro Maestoso from Sonata in G	Wesley, SS: Larghetto in F sharp Minor
10/1/1954	Winchester Cathedral		Bach: Fantasia and Fugue in G Minor	Whitlock: Folk Tune	Mendelssohn: Sonata 6	Dubois: Fiat Lux
5/4/1954	East Cliff Congregational Church	w/ soprano Molly Beavis and violinist Alfred Jupp	Handel: Concerto in B Flat	Widor: Variations from Symphony 5		
7/4/1954	Christchurch Priory		Bach: Fantasia and Fugue in G Minor	Arne: A Maggot	Wesley, SS: Larghetto in F sharp Minor	Liszt: Introduction and Fugue on 'Ad nos ad salutarem undam'
17/6/1954	Christchurch Priory	w/ soprano Pamela Stone (unknown year)	Bach: Toccata and Fugue in D Minor	Festing: Air and Variations	Boellmann: Suite Gothique	Morandi: Rondo de Campanelli
7/7/1954	Christchurch Priory		Bach: Prelude and Fugue in B Minor	Cleramboult: Dialogue	Handel: Extracts from the 'Water Music'	Mozart: Fantasia in F Minor
28/7/1954	Christchurch Priory	w/ violinist Raymond Mosley	Bach: Toccata in F	Liszt: Introduction and Fugue on 'Ad nos ad salutarem undam'	Jongen: Chant de Mai	Saint Saens: Fantasie in E Flat
8/9/1954	Christchurch Priory		Handel: Overture to Samson	Stanley: Toccata for the Flutes	Bach: Prelude and Fugue in D	Wesley, SS: Larghetto in F sharp Minor
15/9/1954	Christchurch Priory	w/ cellist Lillian Warmington	Bach: Prelude and Fugue in A Minor	Festing: Largo, Allegro, Aria and Two Variations	Franck: Fantasie	Dubois: Fiat Lux
29/9/1954	Christchurch Priory	w/ tenor Jack Woodford and violinist Alfred Jupp	Handel: Concerto in B Flat	MacDowell: To a Wild Rose	Thalben Ball: Elegy	Hollins: Grand Choeur in D
16/11/1954	St. Mark's, Southampton		Bach: Fantasia and Fugue in G Minor	Bach: Ach Bleib Bei Uns, Herr Jesu Christ	Stanley: Toccata for the Flutes	Mozart: Fantasia in F Minor

Jongen: Sonata Eroica	Milford: Mr. Ben Johnson's Pleasure	Dvorak: Largo from 'New World'	Gigout: Scherzo	Widor: Variations from Symphony 5		
Bossi: Scherzo in G Minor	Vierne: Cathedrales	Mulet: Toccata 'Tu es petra'				
Whitlock: Folk Tune	Gigout: Scherzo	Widor: Variations from Symphony 5	Vierne: Berceuse	Durufle: Toccata in B Minor		
Hollins: Song of Sunshine	Dubois: Toccata in G					
Dvorak: Largo from 'New World'	Bonnet: Elfes - Caprice Heroique	Widor: Toccata from Symphony 5				
Vierne: Carillon						
Jongen: Sonata Eroica	Gigout: Scherzo	Dubois: Toccata in G				
Gigout: Scherzo	Dubois: Fiat Lux	Vierne: Berceuse	Vierne: Finale from Symphony 1			

16/2/1955	St. Michael's, Southampton		Handel: Concerto in B Flat	Stanley: Toccata for the Flutes	Mozart: Fantasia in F Minor	Wesley, SS: Larghetto in F sharp Minor
12/4/1955	St. Mary Redcliffe, Bristol		Bach: Prelude and Fugue in D	Bach: Ach Bleib Bei Uns, Herr Jesu Christ	Wesley, SS: Larghetto in F sharp Minor	Jongen: Sonata Eroica
6/7/1955	Christchurch Priory		Bach: Fantasia and Fugue in G Minor	Bach: Ach Bleib Bei Uns, Herr Jesu Christ	Stanley: Toccata for the Flutes	Mozart: Fantasia in F Minor
13/7/1955	Christchurch Priory		Bach: Toccata in F	Thalben Ball: Elegy	Mendelssohn: Sonata 6	Bonnet: Elfes - Caprice Heroique
10/8/1955	Christchurch Priory	w/ bass baritone Eric Keats	Bach: Prelude and Fugue in D	Wesley, SS: Larghetto in F sharp Minor	Handel: Concerto in B Flat	Liszt: Introduction and Fugue on 'Ad nos ad salutarem undam'
18/8/1955	Holy Trinity, Exmouth		Bach: Fantasia and Fugue in G Minor	Bach: Ach Bleib Bei Uns, Herr Jesu Christ	Stanley: Toccata for the Flutes	Mozart: Fantasia in F Minor
7/9/1955	Christchurch Priory	w/ violinist Raymond Mosley	Bach: Toccata and Fugue in D Minor	Cleramboult: Dialogue	Alcock: Introduction and Passacaglia	Franck: Chorale in A Minor
14/9/1955	Christchurch Priory	w/ cellist Lillian Warmington	Handel: Overture to Samson	Jongen: Minuet Scherzo	Darke: A Fantasy	Vierne: Finale from Symphony 1
21/9/1955	Christchurch Priory	w/ soprano Pamela Stone	Bach: Fantasia in G	Darke: Meditation on 'Brother James' Air'	Elgar: Allegro Maestoso from Sonata in G	Boellmann: Suite Gothique
5/1/1956	All Saints', Penarth		Bach: Fantasia and Fugue in G Minor	Bach: Ach Bleib Bei Uns, Herr Jesu Christ	Arne: A Maggot	Mozart: Fantasia in F Minor
3/4/1956	St. Mary Redcliffe, Bristol		Bach: Fantasia in G	Festing: Largo, Allegro, Aria and Two Variations	Handel: Allegro from Concerto 4 (Set 2)	Mendelssohn: Sonata 6

Bach: Toccata and Fugue in D Minor	Schumann: Canon in B minor	Gigout: Scherzo	Franck: Piece Heroique				
Bossi: Scherzo in G Minor	Peeters: Abdijvrede	Liszt: Introduction and Fugue on 'Ad nos ad salutarem undam'					
Gigout: Scherzo	Dubois: Fiat Lux	Widor: Variations from Symphony 5					
Walford Davies: Solemn Melody	Mulet: Toccata 'Tu es petra'						
Bossi: Scherzo in G Minor	Dubois: Fiat Lux	Widor: Variations from Symphony 5					
Gigout: Scherzo	Dubois: Fiat Lux	Vierne: Berceuse	Vierne: Finale from Symphony 1				
Bonnet: Elfes-Caprice Heroique	Vierne: Cathedrales	Mulet: Toccata 'Tu es petra'					

30/4/1956	Guildhall, Southampton	w/ Southampton Singers	Elgar: Allegro Maestoso from Sonata in G	Festing: Largo, Allegro, Aria and Two Variations	Mulet: Toccata 'Tu es petra'	
4/7/1956	Christchurch Priory	w/ the Southampton Singers	Saint Saens: Fantasie in E Flat	Bach: Ach Bleib Bei Uns, Herr Jesu Christ	Wesley, SS: Larghetto in F sharp Minor	
26/8/1956	Winchester Cathedral		Bach: Prelude and Fugue in D	Bach: Ach Bleib Bei Uns, Herr Jesu Christ	Mozart: Fantasia in F Minor	Thalben Ball: Elegy
15/9/1956	St. Peter's, Parkstone		Bach: Prelude and Fugue in D	Bach: Ach Bleib Bei Uns, Herr Jesu Christ	Wesley, SS: Larghetto in F sharp Minor	Mozart: Fantasia in F Minor
10/11/1956	Walhampton School	School Concert	Festing: Largo, Allegro, Aria and Two Variations	Handel: Allegro from Concerto 4 (Set 2)	Dubois: Fiat Lux	Arne: A Maggot
3/7/1957	Christchurch Priory	w/ violinist David Shean	Bach: Fantasia and Fugue in G Minor	Wesley, SS: Larghetto in F sharp Minor	Jongen: Sonata Eroica	Gigout: Scherzo
6/8/1957	St. Mary Redcliffe, Bristol		Handel: Overture to Samson	Wesley, SS: Larghetto in F sharp Minor	Bach: Prelude and Fugue in G	Stanley: Toccata for the Flutes
4/9/1957	Christchurch Priory	w/ cellist John Gibbs	Handel: Overture to Samson	Festing: Largo, Allegro, Aria and Two Variations	Bach: Prelude and Fugue in D	Saint Saens: Fantasie in E Flat
7/1/1958	St. Mary Redcliffe, Bristol		Jackson: Fanfare	Bach: Toccata in F	Bach: Bist du bei mir	Harwood: Allegro Appassionata from Sonata 1
22/5/1958	Sherborne Abbey		Bach: Toccata in F	Festing: Air and Variations	Jongen: Sonata Eroica	Whitlock: Chanty and Salix
18/6/1958	Christchurch Priory		Jackson: Fanfare	Handel: Overture to Samson	Festing: Air and Variations	Bach: Prelude and Fugue in D
25/6/1958	Christchurch Priory		Bach: Fantasia and Fugue in G Minor	Arne: A Maggot	Wesley, SS: Larghetto in F sharp Minor	Karg Elert: Chorale Improvisation 'Ein' feste Burg'

Liszt: Introduction and Fugue on 'Ad nos ad salutarem undam'	Vierne: Berceuse	Dubois: Toccata in G					
Handel: Allegro from Concerto 4 (Set 2)	Vierne: Berceuse	Yon: Humoreske	Dubois: Toccata in G				
Karg Elert: Nun danket alle Gott							
Mulet: Toccata 'Tu es petra'							
Franck: Piece Heroique	Gigout: Scherzo	Vierne: Berceuse	Dubois: Toccata in G				
Vierne: Scherzo from Symphony 2	Karg Elert: Nun danket alle Gott						
Bridge: Andantino in F Minor	Yon: Humoreske	Gibbs: Folk Tune	Gibbs: Jubilate Deo	Dupre: Prelude and Fugue in B			
Bach: Fugue a la Gigue	Bach: Song Tune from the Peasant Cantata	Gigout: Scherzo	Dubois: Toccata in G				
Bach: Ach Bleib Bei Uns, Herr Jesu Christ	Jongen: Sonata Eroica	Whitlock: Chanty and Salix	Dubois: Toccata in G				
Gibbs: Folk Tune	Bach: Fugue a la Gigue	Vierne: Berceuse	Liszt: Introduction and Fugue on 'Ad nos ad salutarem undam'				

2/7/1958	Christchurch Priory		Bach: Toccata and Fugue in D Minor	Bach: Song Tune from the Peasant Cantata	Mozart: Fantasia in F Minor	Handel: Allegro from Concerto 4 (Set 2)
9/7/1958	Christchurch Priory		Bach: Prelude and Fugue in B Minor	Stanley: Toccata for the Flutes	Mendelssohn: Sonata 6	Dubois: Fiat Lux
16/7/1958	Christchurch Priory	w/ violinist Raymond Mosley	Bach: Toccata in F	Bach: Bist du bei mir	Harwood: Allegro Appassionata from Sonata 1	Widor: Variations from Symphony 5
23/7/1958	Christchurch Priory	w/ the Priory choir	Handel: Concerto in B Flat	Elgar: Allegro Maestoso from Sonata in G	Vaughan Williams: Rhosymedre	Stanford: Postlude in D Minor
30/7/1958	Christchurch Priory		Alcock: Introduction and Passacaglia	Darke: Meditation on 'Brother James' Air'	Bach: Prelude and Fugue in G	Schumann: Canon in B Minor
6/8/1958	Christchurch Priory		Bach: Fantasia in G	Bach: Fugue a la Gigue	Bridge: Andantino in F minor	Liszt: Prelude and Fugue on B.A.C.H.
13/8/1958	Christchurch Priory	w/ pianist Lyndon Davies	Bach: Prelude and Fugue in G	Wesley: Air and Gavotte	Mozart: Fantasia in F Minor	Vierne: Scherzo from Symphony 2
20/8/1958	Holy Trinity, Exmouth		Jackson: Fanfare	Festing: Air and Variations	Handel: Overture to Samson	Bach: Prelude and Fugue in D
1/7/1959	Christchurch Priory		Jackson: Fanfare	Bach: Fugue a la Gigue	Handel: Overture to Samson	Wesley, SS: Larghetto in F sharp Minor
8/7/1959	Christchurch Priory	w/ cellist Lillian Warmington	Bach: Fantasia and Fugue in G Minor	Mozart: Fantasia in F Minor	Vierne: Finale from Symphony 1	
15/7/1959	Christchurch Priory		Bach: Fantasia in G	Festing: Largo, Allegro, Aria and Two Variations	Handel: Allegro from Concerto 4 (Set 2)	Harwood: Allegro Appassionata from Sonata 1
23/7/1959	Christchurch Priory	w/ BSO	Guilmant: Symphony 1			
19/8/1959	Holy Trinity, Exmouth		Bach: Fantasia in G	Thalben Ball: Elegy	Mendelssohn: Sonata 6	Handel: Allegro from Concerto 4 (Set 2)

Thalben Ball: Elegy	Gigout: Scherzo	Boellmann: Suite Gothique				
Gibbs: Jubilate Deo	Bonnet: Elfes - Caprice Heroique	Mulet: Toccata 'Tu es petra'				
Liszt: Prelude and Fugue on B.A.C.H.	Saint Saens: Fantasie in E Flat	Dvorak: Largo from 'New World'	Mulet: Carillon Sortie			
Darke: A Fantasy	Morandi: Rondo de Campanelli	Franck: Piece Heroique	Widor: Toccata from Symphony 5			
Whitlock: Fidelis	Durufle: Toccata in B Minor					
Bach: Song Tune from the Peasant Cantata	Bach: Fugue a la Gigue	Karg Elert: Chorale Improvisation 'Ein' feste Burg'	Whitlock: Chanty and Salix	Dubois: Toccata in G		
Elgar: Allegro Maestoso from Sonata in G	Whitlock: Chanty and Salix	Widor: Toccata from Symphony 5				
Gigout: Scherzo	Vierne: Berceuse	Vierne: Cathedrales	Mulet: Toccata 'Tu es petra'			
Whitlock: Folk Tune	Yon: Humoreske	Jackson: Procession	Harwood: Allegro Appassionata from Sonata 1			

2/9/1959	St. Martin's, Cardiff	on the Compton Electrone	Handel: Concerto in B Flat	Festing: Largo, Allegro, Aria and Two Variations	Gibbs: Folk Tune	Gibbs: Jubilate Deo
2/9/1959	St. Martin's, Cardiff	on the pipe organ	Elgar: Allegro Maestoso from Sonata in G	Stanley: Toccata for the Flutes	Gigout: Scherzo	Jackson: Pageant
5/1/1960	St. Mary Redcliffe, Bristol		Bach: Prelude and Fugue in B Minor	Bridge: Andantino in F Minor	Whitlock: Carol	Saint Saens: Fantasie in E Flat
30/4/1960	Farnham Parish Church	w/ the Waverley Singers	Buxtehude: Prelude and Fugue in G Minor	Buxtehude: Mit Fried und Freud ich fahr dahin	Buxtehude: Nun bitten wir den Heiligen Geist	Buxtehude: Es ist das Heil uns kommen her
1/5/1960	Sherborne Abbey	approx date	Bach: Concerto in G (Ernst)	Bach: Ach Bleib Bei Uns, Herr Jesu Christ	Bach: Bist du bei mir	Stanley: Toccata for the Flutes
31/5/1960	All Saints', Headington	Church's Golden Jubilee	Bach: Concerto in G (Ernst)	Bach: Ach Bleib Bei Uns, Herr Jesu Christ	Bach: Bist du bei mir	Bach: Fugue a la Gigue
6/7/1960	Christchurch Priory		Bach: Toccata in F	Wesley: Air and Gavotte	Handel: Allegro from Concerto 4 (Set 2)	Mendelssohn: Sonata 6
13/7/1960	Christchurch Priory		Handel: Overture to Samson	Stanley: Toccata for the Flutes	Bach: Prelude and Fugue in D	Wesley, SS: Larghetto in F sharp Minor
20/7/1960	Christchurch Priory		Bach: Prelude and Fugue in B Minor	Cleramboult: Dialogue	Handel: Extracts from the 'Water Music'	Mozart: Fantasia in F Minor
26/7/1960	All Saints', Freshwater		Bach: Toccata in F	Bach: Song Tune from the Peasant Cantata	Bach: Fugue a la Gigue	Festing: Air and Variations
27/7/1960	Christchurch Priory		Bach: Concerto in G (Ernst)	Bach: Ach Bleib Bei Uns, Herr Jesu Christ	Bach: Bist du bei mir	Bach: Fugue a la Gigue

Bach: Fugue a la Gigue	Bach: Ach Bleib Bei Uns, Herr Jesu Christ	Dubois: Fiat Lux				
Elgar: Allegro Maestoso from Sonata in G	Morandi: Rondo de Campanelli	Karg Elert: Chorale Improvisation 'Jesu, geh 'voran'	Karg Elert: Chorale Improvisation 'Ein' feste Burg'			
Buxtehude: Passacaglia in D Minor	Liszt: Prelude and Fugue on B.A.C.H.					
Elgar: Allegro Maestoso from Sonata in G	Bridge: Andantino in F Minor	Harwood: Allegro Appassionata from Sonata 1	Vierne: Berceuse	Jackson: Pageant	Liszt: Prelude and Fugue on B.A.C.H.	
Mozart: Fantasia in F Minor	Whitlock: Chanty and Salix	Gigout: Scherzo	Vierne: Berceuse	Jackson: Pageant	Dubois: Toccata in G	
Bossi: Scherzo in G Minor	Guilmant: Cantilene Pastorale	Vierne: Cathedrales	Mulet: Toccata 'Tu es petra'			
Jongen: Sonata Eroica	Thalben Ball: Elegy	Guilmant: Grand Choeur in D				
Dvorak: Largo from 'New World'	Bonnet: Elfes - Caprice Heroique	Elgar: Allegro Maestoso from Sonata in G				
Handel: Allegro from Concerto 4 (Set 2)	Mozart: Fantasia in F Minor	Whitlock: Chanty and Salix	Gigout: Scherzo	Vierne: Berceuse	Liszt: Prelude and Fugue on B.A.C.H.	
Harwood: Allegro Appassionata from Sonata 1	Whitlock: Chanty and Salix	Vierne: Scherzo from Symphony 2	Liszt: Prelude and Fugue on B.A.C.H.			

8/8/1960	St. Andrew's, Plymouth		Jackson: Pageant	Bach: Concerto in G (Ernst)	Bach: Ach Bleib Bei Uns, Herr Jesu Christ	Bach: Bist du bei mir
14/9/1960	Christchurch Priory	w/ the Priory choir	Festing: Largo, Allegro, Aria and Two Variations	Whitlock: Folk Tune	Gibbs: Jubilate Deo	Vierne: Toccata from Symphony 1
21/9/1960	Christchurch Priory		Jackson: Fanfare	Bach: Fantasia and Fugue in G Minor	Schumann: Canon in B minor	Franck: Chorale in A Minor
18/10/1960	St. Luke's, Sway		Handel: Concerto in B Flat	Festing: Largo, Allegro, Aria and Two Variations	Bach: Fugue a la Gigue	Whitlock: Folk Tune
18/12/1960	St. Matthew's, Wookey	w/ the Ebbor Singers	Jackson: Fanfare	Handel: Pastoral Symphony from Messiah	Festing: Largo, Allegro, Aria and Two Variations	Handel: Concerto in B Flat
10/5/1961	Cosham Congregational Church	w/ Drayton Choral Society	Handel: Concerto in B Flat	Festing: Largo, Allegro, Aria and Two Variations	Bach: Bist du bei mir	Bach: Fugue a la Gigue
12/7/1961	Christchurch Priory		Handel: Overture to Samson	Bridge: Andantino in F Minor	Bach: Prelude and Fugue in D	Arne: A Maggot
18/7/1961	St. Luke's, Torquay		Handel: Overture to Samson	Arne: A Maggot	Bach: Prelude and Fugue in D	Bach: Ach Bleib Bei Uns, Herr Jesu Christ
19/7/1961	Falmouth Central Methodist	w/ the church choir and the Trevaria Male Voice Quartette	Jackson: Fanfare	Bach: Fugue a la Gigue	Bach: Bist du bei mir	Handel: Concerto in B Flat
26/7/1961	Christchurch Priory		Bach: Fantasia and Fugue in G Minor	Thalben Ball: Elegy	Stanley: Toccata for the Flutes	Alcock: Introduction and Passacaglia
3/8/1961	Victoria Methodist, Weston-super-Mare	w/ the church choir	Cocker: Tuba Tune	Bridge: Andantino in F Minor	Bach: Prelude and Fugue in B Minor	Arne: A Maggot

Bach: Prelude and Fugue in D	Jongen: Sonata Eroica	Whitlock: Chanty and Salix	Vierne: Scherzo from Symphony 2	Liszt: Introduction and Fugue on 'Ad nos ad salutarem undam'		
Parry: An Old English Tune	Vaughan Williams: Rhosymedre	Morandi: Rondo de Campanelli	Whitlock: Scherzo	Karg Elert: Chorale Improvisation 'Ein' feste Burg'		
Whitlock: Scherzo	Dubois: Fiat Lux	Stanley: Toccata for the Flutes	Gibbs: Jubilate Deo	Stanford: Postlude in D Minor		
Bach: In Dulci Jubilo	Bach: Fugue a la Gigue	Whitlock: Chanty and Salix	Dubois: Fiat Lux			
Whitlock: Chanty and Salix	Vierne: Berceuse	Gibbs: Jubilate Deo	Dubois: Fiat Lux			
Harwood: Allegro Appassionata from Sonata 1	Lloyd Webber: Benedictus	Vierne: Scherzo from Symphony 2	Cocker: Tuba Tune			
Bach: Bist du bei mir	Elgar: Allegro Maestoso from Sonata in G	Lloyd Webber: Benedictus	Jackson: Pageant	Harwood: Allegro Appassionata from Sonata 1		
Guilmant: Pastorale from Sonata 1	Purcell: Trumpet Tune and Air	Walford Davies: Solemn Melody	Whitlock: Chanty and Salix	Guilmant: Grand Choeur in D		
Bossi: Scherzo in G Minor	Vierne: Cathedrales	Widor: Variations from Symphony 5				
Harwood: Allegro Appassionata from Sonata 1	Lloyd Webber: Benedictus	Widor: Toccata from Symphony 5				

30/8/1961	Holy Trinity, Exmouth		Bach: Prelude and Fugue in B Minor	Arne: A Maggot	Jongen: Sonata Eroica	Guilmant: Pastorale from Sonata 1
2/9/1961	Lansdowne Baptist, Bournemouth		Jackson: Fanfare	Bach: Fugue a la Gigue	Bach: Bist du bei mir	Handel: Concerto in B Flat
6/9/1961	Christchurch Priory		Bach: Fantasia in G	Bach: Fugue a la Gigue	Festing: Largo, Allegro, Aria and Two Variations	Saint Saens: Fantasie in E Flat
16/9/1961	Salisbury Cathedral		Handel: Overture to Samson	Bridge: Andantino in F Minor	Bach: Prelude and Fugue in D	Harwood: Allegro Appassionata from Sonata 1
20/9/1961	Christchurch Priory		Bach: Concerto in G (Ernst)	Wesley, SS: Larghetto in F sharp Minor	Mendelssohn: Sonata 6	Liszt: Canzonetta del Salvator Rosa
10/10/1961	Christchurch Priory	w/ pianist Lyndon Davies	Handel: Overture to Samson	Bridge: Andantino in F Minor	Harwood: Allegro Appassionata from Sonata 1	Dubois: Toccata in G
30/4/1962	Mint Methodist	organ reopening w/ the Mint choir	Bach: Fantasia in G	Bach: Fugue a la Gigue	Festing: Largo, Allegro, Aria and Two Variations	Harwood: Allegro Appassionata from Sonata 1
11/7/1962	Christchurch Priory		Handel: Overture to Samson	Bridge: Andantino in F Minor	Bach: Prelude and Fugue in D	Mozart: Fantasia in F Minor
18/7/1962	Christchurch Priory	Bach only	Bach: Toccata and Fugue in D Minor	Bach: Ach Bleib Bei Uns, Herr Jesu Christ	Bach: Fantasia in G	Bach: Trio Sonata 3
23/7/1962	Sherborne Abbey		Handel: Overture to Samson	Bridge: Andantino in F Minor	Bach: Prelude and Fugue in D	Mozart: Fantasia in F Minor
25/7/1962	Christchurch Priory		Handel: Concerto in B Flat	Bach: Song Tune from the Peasant Cantata	Bach: Prelude and Fugue in E Flat	Saint Saens: Fantasie in E Flat

Liszt: Canzonetta del Salvator Rosa	Vierne: Cathedrales	Lloyd Webber: Benedictus	Stanford: Postlude in D Minor			
Purcell: Trumpet Tune and Air	Guilmant: Pastorale from Sonata 1	Whitlock: Chanty and Salix	Dubois: Toccata in G			
Jongen: Sonata Eroica	Darke: Meditation on 'Brother James' Air'	Liszt: Introduction and Fugue on 'Ad nos ad salutarem undam'				
Lloyd Webber: Benedictus	Vierne: Scherzo from Symphony 2	Mulet: Toccata 'Tu es petra'				
Guilmant: Pastorale from Sonata 1	Sowerby: Holiday Trumpets	Durufle: Toccata in B Minor				
Lloyd Webber: Benedictus	Whitlock: Chanty and Salix	Liszt: Canzonetta del Salvator Rosa	Guilmant: Grand Choeur in D			
Peeters: Aria	Vierne: Scherzo from Symphony 2	Liszt: Canzonetta del Salvator Rosa	Mulet: Toccata 'Tu es petra'			
Bach: Bist du bei mir	Bach: Fugue a la Gigue	Bach: Concerto in G (Ernst)	Bach: Fantasia and Fugue in G Minor			
Peeters: Aria	Vierne: Scherzo from Symphony 2	Liszt: Canzonetta del Salvator Rosa	Parry: Toccata and Fugue (The Wanderer)			
Gigout: Scherzo	Gigout: Toccata in B Minor	Parry: Toccata and Fugue (The Wanderer)	Liszt: Introduction and Fugue on 'Ad nos ad salutarem undam'			

9/8/1962	Victoria Methodist, Weston-super-Mare	w/ the church choir	Bach: Prelude and Fugue in G	Bridge: Three Pieces	Mozart: Fantasia in F Minor	Thalben Ball: Elegy
12/9/1962	Christchurch Priory		Bach: Fantasia and Fugue in G Minor	Festing: Largo, Allegro, Aria and Two Variations	Alcock: Introduction and Passacaglia	Stanley: Toccata for the Flutes
19/9/1962	Christchurch Priory	w/ pianist Lyndon Davies	Cocker: Tuba Tune	Arne: A Maggot	Guilmant: Pastorale from Sonata 1	Harwood: Allegro Appassionata from Sonata 1
26/6/1963	Christchurch Priory		Bach: Prelude and Fugue in G	Bach: Ach Bleib Bei Uns, Herr Jesu Christ	Festing: Largo, Allegro, Aria and Two Variations	Parry: Toccata and Fugue (The Wanderer)
29/6/1963	Hereford Cathedral		Bach: Prelude and Fugue in G	Bach: Ach Bleib Bei Uns, Herr Jesu Christ	Festing: Largo, Allegro, Aria and Two Variations	Parry: Toccata and Fugue (The Wanderer)
6/7/1963	St. Simon's, Southsea		Bach: Concerto in G (Ernst)	Bach: Ach Bleib Bei Uns, Herr Jesu Christ	Bach: Fugue a la Gigue	Reger: Fantasia and Fugue on B.A.C.H.
10/7/1963	Christchurch Priory		Bach: Toccata and Fugue in D Minor	Bach: Fugue a la Gigue	Stanley: Suite in D	Harwood: Allegro Appassionata from Sonata 1
17/7/1963	Christchurch Priory		Karg Elert: Chorale Improvisation 'Ein' feste Burg'	Stanley: Toccata for the Flutes	Bach: Prelude and Fugue in D	Milford: Mr. Ben Johnson's Pleasure
23/7/1963	All Saints', Freshwater		Handel: Overture to Samson	Bridge: Andantino in F Minor	Bach: Prelude and Fugue in D	Bach: Ach Bleib Bei Uns, Herr Jesu Christ
6/8/1963	Upton Parish Church, Torquay		Handel: Overture to Samson	Festing: Largo, Allegro, Aria and Two Variations	Bach: Prelude and Fugue in D	Bach: Ach Bleib Bei Uns, Herr Jesu Christ

Parry: Toccata and Fugue (The Wanderer)	Peeters: Aria	Mulet: Toccata 'Tu es petra'				
Schumann: Four Sketches	Lloyd Webber: Benedictus	Thalben Ball: Variations on a theme by Paganini	Guilmant: Scherzo Symphonique			
Peeters: Aria	Vierne: Scherzo from Symphony 2	Cocker: Tuba Tune	Dubois: Toccata in G			
Peeters: Aria	Gigout: Scherzo	Reger: Fantasia and Fugue on B.A.C.H.				
Festing: Air and Variations	Peeters: Aria	Jackson: Pageant	Vierne: Scherzo from Symphony 2	Dubois: Toccata in G		
Whitlock: Chanty and Salix	Saint Saens: Fantasie in E Flat	Liszt: Introduction and Fugue on 'Ad nos ad salutarem undam'	Thalben Ball: Variations on a theme by Paganini			
Elgar: Allegro Maestoso from Sonata in G	Gigout: Scherzo	Reger: Fantasia and Fugue on B.A.C.H.	Mulet: Toccata 'Tu es petra'			
Harwood: Allegro Appassionata from Sonata 1	Peeters: Aria	Vierne: Scherzo from Symphony 2	Thalben Ball: Elegy	Liszt: Introduction and Fugue on 'Ad nos ad salutarem undam'		
Parry: Toccata and Fugue (The Wanderer)	Gigout: Scherzo	Peeters: Aria	Dubois: Toccata in G			

7/8/1963	Holy Trinity, Exmouth		Handel: Overture to Samson	Festing: Largo, Allegro, Aria and Two Variations	Bach: Prelude and Fugue in D	Bach: Ach Bleib Bei Uns, Herr Jesu Christ
11/8/1963	Winchester Cathedral		Bach: Fantasia in G	Festing: Largo, Allegro, Aria and Two Variations	Parry: Toccata and Fugue (The Wanderer)	Vierne: Scherzo from Symphony 2
21/8/1963	Christchurch Priory		Bach: Toccata in F	Bach: Song Tune from the Peasant Cantata	Handel: Concerto in B Flat	Franck: Chorale in A Minor
18/9/1963	Christchurch Priory	w/ the Priory choir	Festing: Largo, Allegro, Aria and Two Variations	Saint Saens: Fantasie in E Flat	Vierne: Toccata from Symphony 1	
7/12/1963	Reading Town Hall		Jackson: Fanfare	Bach: Fantasia and Fugue in G Minor	Bach: Ach Bleib Bei Uns, Herr Jesu Christ	Wesley, SS: Larghetto in F sharp Minor
13/2/1964	Winter Gardens, Bournemouth	w/ BSO	Saint Saens: Symphony 3			
16/2/1964	Royal Festival Hall	w/ BSO	Saint Saens: Symphony 3			
2/5/1964	St. Gabriel's, Aldersbrook		Handel: Overture to Samson	Festing: Largo, Allegro, Aria and Two Variations	Bach: Prelude and Fugue in D	Bach: Ach Bleib Bei Uns, Herr Jesu Christ
18/6/1964	Sherborne Abbey		Karg Elert: Chorale Improvisation 'Ein' feste Burg'	Festing: Largo, Allegro, Aria and Two Variations	Saint Saens: Fantasie in E Flat	Bach: Prelude and Fugue in B Minor
1/7/1964	Christchurch Priory		Karg Elert: Chorale Improvisation 'Ein' feste Burg'	Festing: Largo, Allegro, Aria and Two Variations	Bach: Prelude and Fugue in D	Saint Saens: Fantasie in E Flat
15/7/1964	Christchurch Priory	w/ violinist Alfred Jupp and pianist Margot Bor	Bach: Prelude and Fugue in B Minor	Harwood: Allegro Appassionata from Sonata 1		

244

Parry: Toccata and Fugue (The Wanderer)	Gigout: Scherzo	Peeters: Aria	Dubois: Toccata in G			
Reger: Fantasia and Fugue on B.A.C.H.						
Vierne: Berceuse	Bossi: Scherzo in G Minor	Sowerby: Pageant	Gigout: Toccata in B Minor			
Liszt: Introduction and Fugue on 'Ad nos ad salutarem undam'	Stanley: Toccata for the Flutes	Whitlock: Chanty and Salix	Cocker: Tuba Tune	Alain: Litanies		
Saint Saens: Fantasie in E Flat	Gigout: Scherzo	Jackson: Pageant	Liszt: Introduction and Fugue on 'Ad nos ad salutarem undam'			
Gigout: Scherzo	Gigout: Toccata in B Minor	Yon: Toccatina for Flutes	Jackson: Pageant	Alain: Litanies		
Gigout: Scherzo	Gigout: Toccata in B Minor	Yon: Humoreske	Dubois: Fiat Lux	Alain: Litanies		

245

22/7/1964	Christchurch Priory		Jackson: Fanfare	Bach: Fantasia in G	Arne: A Maggot	Parry: Toccata and Fugue (The Wanderer)
5/8/1964	Christchurch Priory		Bach: Toccata and Fugue in D Minor	Bridge: Allegretto Grazioso	Mozart: Fantasia in F Minor	Vierne: Prelude
8/8/1964	Holy Trinity, Bournemouth		Karg Elert: Chorale Improvisation 'Ein' feste Burg'	Festing: Largo, Allegro, Aria and Two Variations	Bach: Prelude and Fugue in D	Saint Saens: Fantasie in E Flat
12/8/1964	Christchurch Priory		Handel: Overture to Samson	Stanley: Toccata for the Flutes	Bach: Concerto in G (Ernst)	Reger: Fantasia and Fugue on B.A.C.H.
18/8/1964	Holy Trinity, Exmouth		Karg Elert: Chorale Improvisation 'Ein' feste Burg'	Stanley: Toccata for the Flutes	Bach: Fugue a la Gigue	Saint Saens: Fantasie in E Flat
9/9/1964	Christchurch Priory		Handel: Concerto in B Flat	Wesley, SS: Larghetto in F sharp Minor	Bach: Prelude and Fugue in B Minor	Parry: An Old English Tune
18/9/1964	Christchurch Priory	w/ BSO	Guilmant: Symphony 1			
23/9/1964	Christchurch Priory	w/ violinist Raymond Mosley	Bach: Fantasia in G	Franck: Chorale in A Minor	Vierne: Cathedrales	
30/9/1964	Christchurch Priory		Stanley: Suite in D	Bach: Fugue a la Gigue	Bach: Ach Bleib Bei Uns, Herr Jesu Christ	Karg Elert: Nun danket alle Gott
2/2/1965	St. Mary Redcliffe, Bristol		Bach: Fantasia in G	Whitlock: Folk Tune	Whitlock: Paean	Schumann: Four Sketches
23/6/1965	Christchurch Priory	w/ St. Peter's School Madrigal Society	Bach: Toccata in F	Bach: Ach Bleib Bei Uns, Herr Jesu Christ	Festing: Largo, Allegro, Aria and Two Variations	Parry: Toccata and Fugue (The Wanderer)
28/7/1965	Christchurch Priory		Bach: Prelude and Fugue in D	Wesley, SS: Larghetto in F sharp Minor	Mozart: Fantasia in F Minor	Milford: Mr. Ben Johnson's Pleasure
17/8/1965	St. Mary Redcliffe, Bristol		Bach: Toccata in F	Bach: Fugue a la Gigue	Stanley: Toccata for the Flutes	Mozart: Fantasia in F Minor

Lloyd Webber: Benedictus	Franck: Prelude, Fugue and Variation	Widor: Toccata from Symphony 5				
Howells: Psalm Prelude 1	Cocker: Tuba Tune	Sowerby: Pageant				
Harwood: Allegro Appassionata from Sonata 1	Litaize: Toccata sur le Veni Creator	Yon: Humoreske	Alain: Litanies			
Peeters: Aria	Stanford: Postlude in D Minor	Dubois: Toccata in G				
Franck: Prelude, Fugue and Variation	Dubois: Fiat Lux	Stanford: Postlude in D Minor	Alain: Litanies			
Jongen: Sonata Eroica	Vierne: Scherzo from Symphony 2	Whitlock: Paean				
Mendelssohn: Sonata 6	Dubois: Fiat Lux	Guilmant: Grand Choeur in D				
Elgar: Allegro Maestoso from Sonata in G	Lloyd Webber: Benedictus	Vierne: Prelude	Mulet: Toccata 'Tu es petra'			
Franck: Prelude, Fugue and Variation	Alain: Litanies					
Harwood: Allegro Appassionata from Sonata 1	Peeters: Aria	Thalben Ball: Variations on a theme by Paganini	Mulet: Toccata 'Tu es petra'			
Franck: Prelude, Fugue and Variation	Vierne: Sicilienne	Mulet: Carillon Sortie				

247

8/9/1965	Christchurch Priory	w/ violinist Raymond Mosley	Karg Elert: Chorale Improvisation 'Ein' feste Burg'	Bach: Ach Bleib Bei Uns, Herr Jesu Christ	Bach: Fugue a la Gigue	Saint Saens: Fantasie in E Flat
15/9/1965	Christchurch Priory	w/ the Priory choir	Parry: An Old English Tune	Mendelssohn: Sonata 6	Gigout: Toccata in B Minor	
21/9/1965	St. Mary Redcliffe, Bristol		Karg Elert: Chorale Improvisation 'Ein' feste Burg'	Bach: Prelude and Fugue in D	Bach: Song Tune from the Peasant Cantata	Harwood: Allegro Appassionata from Sonata 1
22/9/1965	Christchurch Priory		Bach: Prelude and Fugue in B Minor	Bridge: Three Pieces	Handel: Concerto in B Flat	Dubois: Toccata in G
29/9/1965	Christchurch Priory	w/ Christchurch (NZ) Harmonic Choir				
30/10/1965	St. Mary's, Weymouth		Karg Elert: Chorale Improvisation 'Ein' feste Burg'	Festing: Largo, Allegro, Aria and Two Variations	Bach: Prelude and Fugue in D	Bach: Ach Bleib Bei Uns, Herr Jesu Christ
3/11/1965	Birmingham Town Hall		Karg Elert: Chorale Improvisation 'Ein' feste Burg'	Festing: Largo, Allegro, Aria and Two Variations	Bach: Prelude and Fugue in D	Bach: Ach Bleib Bei Uns, Herr Jesu Christ
6/4/1966	Preston Parish Church		Karg Elert: Chorale Improvisation 'Ein' feste Burg'	Wesley, SS: Larghetto in F sharp Minor	Bach: Prelude and Fugue in C Minor	Bach: Ach Bleib Bei Uns, Herr Jesu Christ
20/4/1966	Clitheroe Parish Church		Karg Elert: Chorale Improvisation 'Ein' feste Burg'	Festing: Largo, Allegro, Aria and Two Variations	Bach: Prelude and Fugue in D	Bach: Ach Bleib Bei Uns, Herr Jesu Christ
3/5/1966	St. Mary Redcliffe, Bristol		Handel: Concerto in B Flat	Bach: Fantasia in G	Bach: Ach Bleib Bei Uns, Herr Jesu Christ	Parry: Toccata and Fugue (The Wanderer)
15/6/1966	Christchurch Priory		Bach: Fantasia in G	Whitlock: Paean	Parry: Toccata and Fugue (The Wanderer)	Peeters: Aria

Vierne: Sicilienne	Mulet: Carillon Sortie						
Thalben Ball: Elegy	Bossi: Scherzo in G Minor	Vierne: Cathedrales	Mulet: Toccata 'Tu es petra'				
Stanley: Suite in D	Peeters: Abdijvrede	Cocker: Tuba Tune	Mulet: Toccata 'Tu es petra'				
Mozart: Fantasia in F Minor	Stanley: Toccata for the Flutes	Franck: Prelude, Fugue and Variation	Alain: Litanies	Vierne: Prelude	Mulet: Carillon Sortie		
Franck: Prelude, Fugue and Variation	Alain: Litanies	Peeters: Aria	Litaize: Toccata sur le Veni Creator	Mulet: Carillon Sortie			
Bach: Nun Danket Alle Gott	Jongen: Sonata Eroica	Vierne: Lied	Alain: Litanies	Mulet: Carillon Sortie			
Parry: Toccata and Fugue (The Wanderer)	Peeters: Aria	Vierne: Scherzo from Symphony 2	Litaize: Toccata sur le Veni Creator	Bonnet: Elfes - Caprice Heroique			
Peeters: Aria	Vierne: Scherzo from Symphony 2	Litaize: Toccata sur le Veni Creator	Bonnet: Elfes - Caprice Heroique				
Franck: Prelude, Fugue and Variation	Alain: Litanies	Mulet: Toccata 'Tu es petra'					

22/6/1966	Christchurch Priory	w/ string quartet	Bach: Fantasia and Fugue in G Minor	Festing: Largo, Allegro, Aria and Two Variations	Mulet: Carillon Sortie	
10/8/1966	Christchurch Priory		Jackson: Fanfare	Bach: Toccata in F	Wesley, SS: Larghetto in F sharp Minor	Schumann: Four Sketches
22/8/1966	Wimborne Minster		Bach: Toccata and Fugue in D Minor	Bach: Ach Bleib Bei Uns, Herr Jesu Christ	Bach: Concerto in G (Ernst)	Litaize: Toccata sur le Veni Creator
14/9/1966	Christchurch Priory		Karg Elert: Chorale Improvisation 'Ein' feste Burg'	Festing: Largo, Allegro, Aria and Two Variations	Mendelssohn: Sonata 6	Saint Saens: Fantasie in E Flat
24/9/1966	Shepton Mallet Parish Church	Opening recital	Bach: Toccata in F	Bach: Fugue a la Gigue	Festing: Largo, Allegro, Aria and Two Variations	Mozart: Fantasia in F Minor
28/9/1966	Christchurch Priory	w/ the Priory choir	Jackson: Fanfare	Handel: Overture to the Occasional Oratorio	Sowerby: Pageant	
29/10/1966	Bath Abbey		Karg Elert: Chorale Improvisation 'Ein' feste Burg'	Festing: Largo, Allegro, Aria and Two Variations	Bach: Prelude and Fugue in C Minor	Bach: Ach Bleib Bei Uns, Herr Jesu Christ
27/5/1967	Bath Abbey		Bach: Prelude and Fugue in D	Bach: Nun Danket Alle Gott	Stanley: Toccata for the Flutes	Jongen: Sonata Eroica
28/6/1967	Christchurch Priory		Bach: Prelude and Fugue in D	Bach: Nun Danket Alle Gott	Stanley: Toccata for the Flutes	Jongen: Sonata Eroica
13/7/1967	Sidmouth Parish Church	no rep data				
31/7/1967	Wimborne Minster		Bach: Fantasia and Fugue in G Minor	Bach: Prelude and Fugue in A	Bach: Ach Bleib Bei Uns, Herr Jesu Christ	Bach: Nun Danket Alle Gott

Vierne: Prelude	Thalben Ball: Variations on a theme by Paganini	Reger: Fantasia and Fugue on B.A.C.H.				
Franck: Prelude, Fugue and Variation	Alain: Litanies	Yon: Toccatina for Flutes	Reger: Fantasia and Fugue on B.A.C.H.			
Peeters: Abdijvrede	Vierne: Cathedrales	Whitlock: Folk Tune	Whitlock: Scherzo	Whitlock: Paean	Dubois: Toccata in G	
Peeters: Abdijvrede	Litaize: Toccata sur le Veni Creator	Vierne: Prelude	Liszt: Introduction and Fugue on 'Ad nos ad salutarem undam'			
Parry: Toccata and Fugue (The Wanderer)	Peeters: Abdijvrede	Franck: Prelude, Fugue and Variation	Alain: Litanies	Vierne: Lied	Mulet: Carillon Sortie	
Franck: Pastorale	Dubois: Fiat Lux	Warlock: Andante tranquillo from 'Capriol' Suite	Mulet: Toccata 'Tu es petra'			
Franck: Pastorale	Dubois: Fiat Lux	Warlock: Andante tranquillo from 'Capriol' Suite	Mulet: Toccata 'Tu es petra'			
Stanley: Toccata for the Flutes	Parry: Toccata and Fugue (The Wanderer)	Franck: Pastorale	Mushel: Toccata			

16/8/1967	Christchurch Priory		Bach: Toccata and Fugue in D Minor	Bach: Prelude and Fugue in A	Bach: Nun Danket Alle Gott	Franck: Prelude, Fugue and Variation
23/8/1967	Christchurch Priory	w/ violinist Raymond Mosley	Bach: Fantasia and Fugue in G Minor	Franck: Chorale in A Minor	Peeters: Aria	Mulet: Carillon Sortie
30/8/1967	Christchurch Priory		Handel: Overture to Samson	Bach: Prelude and Fugue in C Minor	Bach: Fugue a la Gigue	Liszt: Evocation a la Chapelle Sixtine
6/9/1967	Victoria Methodist, Weston-super-Mare		Bach: Fantasia and Fugue in G Minor	Bach: Prelude and Fugue in A	Bach: Nun Danket Alle Gott	Festing: Largo, Allegro, Aria and Two Variations
20/9/1967	Christchurch Priory		Karg Elert: Chorale Improvisation 'Ein' feste Burg'	Wesley, SS: Larghetto in F sharp Minor	Mendelssohn: Sonata 6	Saint Saens: Fantasie in E Flat
28/10/1967	Christ Church, Bath	Christ Church Bath Festival	Bach: Fantasia and Fugue in G Minor	Bridge: Three Pieces	Harwood: Allegro Appassionata from Sonata 1	Franck: Prelude, Fugue and Variation
3/7/1968	Portsmouth Cathedral		Buxtehude: Prelude and Fugue in G Minor	Bach: Prelude and Fugue in A	Bach: Nun Danket Alle Gott	Franck: Prelude, Fugue and Variation
17/7/1968	Christchurch Priory		Buxtehude: Prelude and Fugue in G Minor	Bach: Prelude and Fugue in D	Jongen: Chant de Mai	Franck: Prelude, Fugue and Variation
7/8/1968	Christchurch Priory		Jackson: Fanfare	Arne: A Maggot	Handel: Overture to Samson	Bach: Toccata in F
21/8/1968	Christchurch Priory	w/ violinist Raymond Mosley	Bach: Toccata and Fugue in D Minor	Festing: Largo, Allegro, Aria and Two Variations	Franck: Prelude, Fugue and Variation	Vierne: Cathedrales
28/8/1968	Christchurch Priory		Bach: Concerto in G (Ernst)	Wesley, SS: Larghetto in F sharp Minor	Schumann: Four Sketches	Mendelssohn: Sonata 6
1/10/1968	St. Mary Redcliffe, Bristol		Bach: Concerto in G (Ernst)	Bach: Fugue a la Gigue	Bach: Ach Bleib Bei Uns, Herr Jesu Christ	Bach: Nun Danket Alle Gott

Dubois: Fiat Lux	Vierne: Lied	Reger: Fantasia and Fugue on B.A.C.H.	Mushel: Toccata			
Vierne: Scherzo from Symphony 2	Thalben Ball: Variations on a theme by Paganini	Liszt: Introduction and Fugue on 'Ad nos ad salutarem undam'				
Franck: Chorale in A Minor	Yon: Humoreske	Alain: Litanies	Vierne: Berceuse	Mushel: Toccata		
Peeters: Abdijvrede	Vierne: Cathedrales	Whitlock: Folk Tune	Whitlock: Scherzo	Whitlock: Paean	Dubois: Toccata in G	
Litaize: Toccata sur le Veni Creator	Peeters: Aria	Mushel: Toccata				
Dubois: Fiat Lux	Warlock: Andante tranquillo from 'Capriol' Suite	Reger: Fantasia and Fugue on B.A.C.H.	Mushel: Toccata			
Dubois: Fiat Lux	Peeters: Aria	Reger: Fantasia and Fugue on B.A.C.H.	Alain: Litanies			
Franck: Pastorale	Elgar: Finale from Sonata in G	Vierne: Berceuse	Vierne: Scherzo from Symphony 2	Widor: Toccata from Symphony 5		
Thalben Ball: Variations on a theme by Paganini	Mulet: Toccata 'Tu es petra'					
Franck: Piece Heroique	Whitlock: Folk Tune	Whitlock: Scherzo	Whitlock: Paean	Dubois: Toccata in G		
Bach: Prelude and Fugue in A	Bach: Trio Sonata 3	Bach: Prelude and Fugue in D	Reger: Fantasia and Fugue on B.A.C.H.			

2/7/1969	Christchurch Priory		Buxtehude: Prelude and Fugue in G Minor	Bach: Ach Bleib Bei Uns, Herr Jesu Christ	Bach: Nun Danket Alle Gott	Bach: Prelude and Fugue in D
30/7/1969	Westminster Cathedral		Buxtehude: Prelude and Fugue in G Minor	Bach: Ach Bleib Bei Uns, Herr Jesu Christ	Bach: Nun Danket Alle Gott	Bach: Prelude and Fugue in D
3/9/1969	Christchurch Priory	w/ baritone Stuart Harling	Handel: Overture to Samson	Franck: Chorale in A Minor	Mulet: Toccata 'Tu es petra'	
1/10/1969	Christchurch Priory	w/ the Priory choir	Mozart: Fantasia in F minor			
17/3/1970	St. Peter's, Bournemouth	Bach only	Bach: Toccata and Fugue in D Minor	Bach: Prelude and Fugue in A	Bach: Fantasia in G	Bach: Ach Bleib Bei Uns, Herr Jesu Christ
23/5/1970	Salisbury Cathedral		Alain: Litanies	Buxtehude: Prelude and Fugue in G Minor	Bach: Ach Bleib Bei Uns, Herr Jesu Christ	Bach: Nun Danket Alle Gott
24/6/1970	Christchurch Priory		Handel: Overture to Samson	Bach: Prelude and Fugue in D	Festing: Largo, Allegro, Aria and Two Variations	Mozart: Fantasia in F Minor
8/7/1970	Christchurch Priory		Jackson: Fanfare	Bach: Prelude and Fugue in E Flat	Bach: Fugue a la Gigue	Schumann: Four Sketches
12/8/1970	Christchurch Priory	w/ violinist Raymond Mosley	Bach: Fantasia in G	Stanley: Toccata for the Flutes	Warlock: Andante tranquillo from 'Capriol' Suite	Franck: Piece Heroique
26/8/1970	Christchurch Priory		Karg Elert: Chorale Improvisation 'Ein' feste Burg'	Bach: Prelude and Fugue in G	Bach: O Mensch, bewein' dein' Sunde gross	Saint Saens: Fantasie in E Flat
30/9/1970	Christchurch Priory	w/ the Priory choir	Franck: Prelude, Fugue and Variation			
7/10/1970	Christchurch Priory		Bach: Toccata and Fugue in D Minor	Wesley, SS: Larghetto in F sharp Minor	Mendelssohn: Sonata 6	Franck: Piece Heroique
9/12/1970	Christchurch Priory		Bach: Concerto in G (Ernst)	Bach: Wachet auf	Wesley, SS: Larghetto in F sharp Minor	Elgar: Allegro Maestoso from Sonata in G

Franck: Prelude, Fugue and Variation	Vierne: Arabesque	Vierne: Cathedrales	Vierne: Scherzo from Symphony 2	Alain: Litanies	Mulet: Carillon Sortie	
Franck: Prelude, Fugue and Variation	Vierne: Arabesque	Vierne: Cathedrales	Vierne: Scherzo from Symphony 2	Alain: Litanies	Mulet: Carillon Sortie	
Bach: Nun Danket Alle Gott	Bach: Prelude and Fugue in D	Bach: Concerto in G (Ernst)	Bach: Sheep may safely graze	Bach: Fugue a la Gigue	Bach: Prelude and Fugue in E Flat	
Bach: Prelude and Fugue in D	Mozart: Fantasia in F Minor	Franck: Prelude, Fugue and Variation	Vierne: Arabesque	Mulet: Carillon Sortie		
Franck: Chorale in A Minor	Vierne: Arabesque	Mushel: Toccata	Liszt: Prelude and Fugue on B.A.C.H.			
Jongen: Chant de Mai	Alain: Litanies	Vierne: Carillon de Westminster				
Widor: Toccata from Symphony 5						
Arne: A Maggot	Elgar: Allegro Maestoso from Sonata in G	Vierne: Lied	Vierne: Scherzo from Symphony 2	Vierne: Carillon	Mulet: Toccata 'Tu es petra'	
Whitlock: Folk Tune	Whitlock: Scherzo	Whitlock: Paean	Thalben Ball: Variations on a theme by Paganini	Durufle: Toccata in B Minor		
Saint Saens: Fantasie in E Flat	Vierne: Scherzo from Symphony 2	Boellmann: Suite Gothique	Liszt: Introduction and Fugue on 'Ad nos ad salutarem undam'			

Date	Venue	With/Notes	Piece 1	Piece 2	Piece 3	Piece 4
6/1/1971	Christchurch Priory	Christmas music w/ the Priory choir	Handel: Overture to the Occasional Oratorio	Handel: Pastoral Symphony from Messiah	Bach: In Dulci Jubilo	
3/3/1971	Christchurch Priory		Bach: Prelude and Fugue in E Flat	Peeters: Aria	Stanley: Toccata for the Flutes	Franck: Piece Heroique
7/4/1971	Christchurch Priory		Buxtehude: Prelude and Fugue in G Minor	Brahms: Schmucke dich, o liebe Seele	Brahms: Herzlich tut mich verlangen	Bach: 'Dorian' Toccata and Fugue
16/6/1971	Christchurch Priory		Jackson: Fanfare	Bach: 'Dorian' Toccata and Fugue	Franck: Piece Heroique	Roger-Ducasse: Pastorale
30/6/1971	Reading Town Hall		Bach: Prelude and Fugue in E Flat	Bach: Ach Bleib Bei Uns, Herr Jesu Christ	Bach: Nun Danket Alle Gott	Stanley: Toccata for the Flutes
11/8/1971	Christchurch Priory	w/ violinist Raymond Mosley	Bach: Prelude and Fugue in E Flat	Stanley: Toccata for the Flutes	Elgar: Allegro Maestoso from Sonata in G	Mulet: Toccata 'Tu es petra'
18/8/1971	Christchurch Priory		Handel: Overture to Samson	Bach: Prelude and Fugue in D	Bach: Liebster Jesu, wir sind hier	Bach: Nun Danket Alle Gott
22/9/1971	Christchurch Priory	w/ the Priory choir	Franck: Chorale in A Minor	Widor: Toccata from Symphony 5		
29/9/1971	Christchurch Priory	on the Compton Makin Westmorland Organ	Bach: Prelude and Fugue in D	Brahms: Schmucke dich, o liebe Seele	Festing: Largo, Allegro, Aria and Two Variations	Mozart: Fantasia in F Minor
30/10/1971	King's College, Cambridge		Bach: Prelude and Fugue in D	Bach: Ach Bleib Bei Uns, Herr Jesu Christ	Bach: Nun Danket Alle Gott	Roger-Ducasse: Pastorale
3/11/1971	Christchurch Priory		Bach: Toccata in F	Bach: Nun Komm' der Heiden Heiland	Stanley: Toccata for the Flutes	Stanley: Trumpet Voluntary
13/11/1971	Christ's College, Cambridge		Bach: Toccata in F	Bach: Nun Komm' der Heiden Heiland	Stanley: Toccata for the Flutes	Stanley: Trumpet Voluntary
5/1/1972	Christchurch Priory	Christmas music w/ the Priory choir	Mulet: Noel	Handel: Overture to the Occasional Oratorio	Bach: In Dulci Jubilo	

Bossi: Scherzo in G Minor	Roger-Ducasse: Pastorale	Vierne: Arabesque	Vierne: Carillon			
Franck: Prelude, Fugue and Variation	Elgar: Allegro Maestoso from Sonata in G	Parry: An Old English Tune	Alain: Litanies	Mulet: Toccata 'Tu es petra'		
Whitlock: Chanty and Salix	Stanford: Postlude in D Minor	Vierne: Carillon de Westminster				
Mozart: Fantasia in F Minor	Franck: Prelude, Fugue and Variation	Vierne: Berceuse	Vierne: Carillon	Bossi: Scherzo in G Minor	Jongen: Sonata Eroica	
Bach: Fugue a la Gigue	Franck: Piece Heroique	Festing: Largo, Allegro, Aria and Two Variations	Mushel: Toccata	Alain: Litanies		
Vierne: Berceuse	Bossi: Scherzo in G Minor	Jongen: Sonata Eroica				
Bossi: Scherzo in G Minor	Vierne: Arabesque	Vierne: Carillon				
Parry: Toccata and Fugue (The Wanderer)	Vierne: Lied	Saint Saens: Fantasie in E Flat	Mulet: Carillon Sortie			
Franck: Chorale in A Minor	Vierne: Scherzo from Symphony 2	Langlais: Incantation				

2/2/1972	Christchurch Priory		Bach: Toccata and Fugue in D Minor	Vaughan Williams: Rhosymedre	Elgar: Allegro Maestoso from Sonata in G	Franck: Chorale in A Minor
5/4/1972	Christchurch Priory		Handel: Overture to the Occasional Oratorio	Bach: Prelude and Fugue in A	Stanley: Trumpet Voluntary	Franck: Prelude, Fugue and Variation
18/5/1972	Worcester Cathedral		Bach: Prelude and Fugue in D	Bach: Ach Bleib Bei Uns, Herr Jesu Christ	Bach: Nun Danket Alle Gott	Festing: Largo, Allegro, Aria and Two Variations
3/6/1972	Chester Cathedral		Bach: Prelude and Fugue in D	Bach: Ach Bleib Bei Uns, Herr Jesu Christ	Bach: Nun Komm' der Heiden Heiland	Bach: Nun Danket Alle Gott
21/6/1972	Christchurch Priory		Bach: Prelude and Fugue in D	Bach: Ach Bleib Bei Uns, Herr Jesu Christ	Bach: Nun Komm' der Heiden Heiland	Bach: Nun Danket Alle Gott
5/7/1972	Christchurch Priory		Bach: Toccata in F	Arne: A Maggot	Franck: Prelude, Fugue and Variation	Dubois: Fiat Lux
11/10/1972	Christ Church, Reading	Festival of Music	Bach: Toccata in F	Bach: Ach Bleib Bei Uns, Herr Jesu Christ	Bach: Nun Komm' der Heiden Heiland	Arne: A Maggot
30/10/1972	Birmingham Cathedral		Bach: Prelude and Fugue in D	Bach: Ach Bleib Bei Uns, Herr Jesu Christ	Bach: Nun Komm' der Heiden Heiland	Bach: Nun Danket Alle Gott
20/6/1973	Christchurch Priory		Karg Elert: Chorale Improvisation 'Ein' feste Burg'	Festing: Largo, Allegro, Aria and Two Variations	Bach: Toccata in F	Bach: Nun Komm' der Heiden Heiland
2/7/1973	Christchurch Priory		Alain: Litanies	Bach: Fugue a la Gigue	Mozart: Fantasia in F Minor	Peeters: Aria
4/7/1973	Christchurch Priory	w/ the Priory choir	Franck: Chorale in A Minor			
5/7/1973	Christchurch Priory	w/ violinist Raymond Mosley	Handel: Concerto in B Flat	Saint Saens: Fantasie in E Flat	Vierne: Carillon de Westminster	

Widor: Pastorale from Symphony 2	Widor: Scherzo from Symphony 4	Widor: Toccata from Symphony 5	Langlais: Incantation				
Vierne: Carillon de Westminster	Whitlock: Chanty and Salix	Reger: Fantasia and Fugue on B.A.C.H.					
Mushel: Toccata	Vierne: Cathedrales	Vierne: Clair De Lune	Bossi: Scherzo in G Minor	Reger: Fantasia and Fugue on B.A.C.H.			
Franck: Piece Heroique	Mushel: Toccata	Vierne: Cathedrales	Vierne: Clair de Lune	Vierne: Carillon	Bossi: Scherzo in G Minor	Reger: Fantasia and Fugue on B.A.C.H.	
Franck: Piece Heroique	Vierne: Arabesque	Vierne: Cathedrales	Vierne: Clair de Lune	Vierne: Toccata from Symphony 1	Vierne: Carillon		
Elgar: Allegro Maestoso from Sonata in G	Vierne: Berceuse	Mushel: Toccata	Mulet: Toccata 'Tu es petra'				
Mozart: Fantasia in F Minor	Roger-Ducasse: Pastorale	Bossi: Scherzo in G Minor	Langlais: Incantation	Vierne: Clair De Lune	Reger: Fantasia and Fugue on B.A.C.H.		
Roger-Ducasse: Pastorale	Bossi: Scherzo in G Minor	Mushel: Toccata	Reger: Fantasia and Fugue on B.A.C.H.				
Bach: Ach Bleib Bei Uns, Herr Jesu Christ	Gigout: Scherzo	Gigout: Toccata in B Minor	Vierne: Cathedrales	Vierne: Clair De Lune	Vierne: Carillon		
Roger-Ducasse: Pastorale	Vierne: Symphony 3						

6/7/1973	Christchurch Priory	w/ the BBC West of England Singers	Bach: Prelude and Fugue in D	Gigout: Scherzo	Gigout: Toccata in B Minor	
1/8/1973	Christchurch Priory		Buxtehude: Prelude and Fugue in G Minor	Stanley: Toccata for the Flutes	Franck: Prelude, Fugue and Variation	Elgar: Allegro Maestoso from Sonata in G
8/8/1973	Christchurch Priory		Handel: Overture to the Occasional Oratorio	Bach: Prelude and Fugue in E Flat	Franck: Chorale in A Minor	Vierne: Clair de Lune
29/8/1973	Christchurch Priory		Bach: Fantasia in G	Festing: Largo, Allegro, Aria and Two Variations	Mendelssohn: Sonata 6	Schumann: Canon in B Minor
26/9/1973	Christchurch Priory		Bach: Fantasia and Fugue in G Minor	Stanley: Trumpet Voluntary	Schumann: Four Sketches	Vierne: Cathedrales
1/12/1973	Christchurch Priory	Opening recital	Jackson: Fanfare	Parry: Toccata and Fugue (The Wanderer)	Stanley: Voluntary in F	Bach: Toccata and Fugue in D Minor
26/6/1974	Christchurch Priory		Bach: Prelude and Fugue in D	Bach: Ach Bleib Bei Uns, Herr Jesu Christ	Bach: Nun Danket Alle Gott	Mozart: Fantasia in F Minor
3/7/1974	Christchurch Priory		Karg Elert: Chorale Improvisation 'Ein' feste Burg'	Stanley: Trumpet Voluntary	Bach: Toccata in F	Franck: Chorale in A Minor
6/8/1974	St. Peter's, Bournemouth		Buxtehude: Prelude and Fugue in G Minor	Stanley: Toccata for the Flutes	Wesley, SS: Larghetto in F sharp Minor	Franck: Chorale in A Minor
7/8/1974	Christchurch Priory		Handel: Overture to Samson	Stanley: Toccata for the Flutes	Bach: Prelude and Fugue in G	Bach: Nun Komm' der Heiden Heiland
21/8/1974	Christchurch Priory		Buxtehude: Prelude and Fugue in G Minor	Arne: A Maggot	Wesley, SS: Larghetto in F sharp Minor	Jongen: Sonata Eroica

260

Whitlock: Folk Tune	Whitlock: Scherzo	Whitlock: Paean	Vierne: Arabesque	Vierne: Carillon	Mulet: Carillon Sortie	
Jongen: Sonata Eroica	Cocker: Tuba Tune					
Franck: Piece Heroique	Bossi: Scherzo in G Minor	Widor: Toccata from Symphony 5				
Vierne: Arabesque	Vierne: Allegro maestoso from Symphony 3	Karg Elert: Chorale Improvisation 'Ein' feste Burg'				
Roger-Ducasse: Pastorale	Vierne: Intermezzo from Symphony 3	Karg Elert: Chorale Improvisation 'Jesu, geh 'voran'	Liszt: Introduction and Fugue on 'Ad nos ad salutarem undam'			
Bossi: Scherzo in G Minor	Franck: Prelude, Fugue and Variation	Vierne: Clair De Lune	Liszt: Introduction and Fugue on 'Ad nos ad salutarem undam'			
Roger-Ducasse: Pastorale	Vierne: Cortege	Vierne: Berceuse	Widor: Allegro from Symphony 6			
Peeters: Abdijvrede	Vierne: Carillon	Vierne: Arabesque	Vierne: Cortege	Vierne: Scherzo from Symphony 2	Vierne: Allegro from Symphony 2	
Franck: Piece Heroique	Morandi: Rondo de Campanelli	Vierne: Symphony 3				
Peeters: Abdijvrede	Vierne: Carillon	Vierne: Berceuse	Mushel: Toccata	Cocker: Tuba Tune		

261

11/9/1974	Christchurch Priory	w/ violinist Raymond Mosley	Bach: Fantasia and Fugue in G Minor	Saint Saens: Fantasie in E Flat	Elgar: Allegro Maestoso from Sonata in G	
2/10/1974	Christchurch Priory		Bach: Fantasia and Fugue in G Minor	Stanley: Voluntary in F	Mendelssohn: Sonata 6	Vierne: Allegro from Symphony 2
5/12/1974	St. Peter's, Southbourne		Bach: Fantasia and Fugue in G Minor	Wesley, SS: Larghetto in F sharp Minor	Stanley: Toccata for the Flutes	Mozart: Fantasia in F Minor
28/6/1975	Christchurch Priory	w/ the Priory choir	Handel: Concerto in B Flat			
9/7/1975	Christchurch Priory		Bach: Prelude and Fugue in D	Festing: Largo, Allegro, Aria and Two Variations	Franck: Prelude, Fugue and Variation	Mushel: Toccata
6/8/1975	Christchurch Priory		Bach: Fantasia and Fugue in G Minor	Stanley: Toccata for the Flutes	Roger-Ducasse: Pastorale	Weitz: Stella Maris
20/8/1975	Christchurch Priory		Bach: Fantasia in G	Wesley, SS: Larghetto in F sharp Minor	Franck: Chorale in A Minor	Morandi: Rondo de Campanelli
1/10/1975	Christchurch Priory	w/ the Priory choir	Elgar: Allegro Maestoso from Sonata in G			
9/6/1976	Christchurch Priory		Bach: Prelude and Fugue in D	Bach: Ach Bleib Bei Uns, Herr Jesu Christ	Bach: Nun Danket Alle Gott	Stanley: Toccata for the Flutes
30/6/1976	Christchurch Priory		Bach: Toccata in F	Bach: Fugue a la Gigue	Stanley: Voluntary in F	Cocker: Tuba Tune
10/8/1976	St. Mary Redcliffe, Bristol		Handel: Arrival of the Queen of Sheba	Arne: A Maggot	Bach: Toccata in F	Roger-Ducasse: Pastorale
1/9/1976	Christchurch Priory		Handel: Overture to Samson	Festing: Largo, Allegro, Aria and Two Variations	Bach: Prelude and Fugue in C Minor	Elgar: Allegro Maestoso from Sonata in G
22/9/1976	Christchurch Priory		Bach: Prelude and Fugue in G	Bach: Nun Komm' der Heiden Heiland	Mozart: Fantasia in F Minor	Stanley: Voluntary in F

262

Bonnet: Elfes - Caprice Heroique	Weitz: Stella Maris						
Bonnet: Elfes - Caprice Heroique	Franck: Prelude, Fugue and Variation	Bossi: Scherzo in G Minor	Weitz: Stella Maris				
Guilmant: Verset	Bossi: Scherzo in G Minor	Liszt: Canzonetta del Salvator Rosa	Vierne: Intermezzo from Symphony 3	Vierne: Final from Symphony 3			
Cocker: Tuba Tune	Vierne: Clair de Lune	Mulet: Carillon Sortie					
Bonnet: Elfes - Caprice Heroique	Alain: Litanies	Vierne: Berceuse	Vierne: Carillon	Mulet: Toccata 'Tu es petra'			
Karg Elert: Chorale Improvisation 'Ein' feste Burg'	Mushel: Toccata	Guilmant: Verset	Weitz: Stella Maris	Liszt: Canzonetta del Salvator Rosa	Vierne: Final from Symphony 3		
Roger-Ducasse: Pastorale	Bossi: Scherzo in G Minor	Vierne: Berceuse	Messiaen: Transports de Joie				
Liszt: Canzonetta del Salvator Rosa	Vierne: Clair de Lune	Vierne: Final from Symphony 2					
Franck: Prelude, Fugue and Variation	Whitlock: Chanty and Salix	Vierne: Final from Symphony 2					
Franck: Chorale in A Minor	Vierne: Arabesque	Vierne: Carillon	Alain: Litanies				

10/8/1977	Christchurch Priory		Stanford: Postlude in D Minor	Bridge: Three Pieces	Bach: Prelude and Fugue in G	Jongen: Sonata Eroica
17/8/1977	Christchurch Priory		Bach: Toccata in F	Bach: Fugue a la Gigue	Festing: Largo, Allegro, Aria and Two Variations	Roger-Ducasse: Pastorale
7/6/1978	Christchurch Priory	w/ Bournemouth Sinfonietta Choir	Widor: Allegro Vivace from Symphony 5			
14/6/1978	Christchurch Priory		Karg Elert: Chorale Improvisation 'Ein' feste Burg'	Bach: Fantasia in G	Jongen: Chant de Mai	Vierne: Arabesque
5/7/1978	Christchurch Priory	w/ baritone Ian Caddy	Elgar: Allegro Maestoso from Sonata in G	Vierne: Cathedrales		
12/8/1978	York Minster		Bach: Toccata in F	Bach: Ach Bleib Bei Uns, Herr Jesu Christ	Bach: Nun Danket Alle Gott	Stanley: Voluntary in F
16/8/1978	Christchurch Priory		Bach: Toccata in F	Bach: Ach Bleib Bei Uns, Herr Jesu Christ	Bach: Nun Danket Alle Gott	Stanley: Voluntary in F
4/10/1978	St. Mary Redcliffe, Bristol	Redcliffe Organ Festival	Buxtehude: Prelude and Fugue in G Minor	Couperin: Soeur Monique	Bach: Ach Bleib Bei Uns, Herr Jesu Christ	Bach: Nun Danket Alle Gott
	Reading Minster		Bach: Toccata in F	Schumann: Canon in B minor	Elgar: Allegro Maestoso from Sonata in G	Guilmant: Cantilene Pastorale
	Reading Minster		Bach: Prelude and Fugue in G	Bach: Sheep may safely graze	Franck: Chorale in A Minor	Bossi: Scherzo in G Minor

Warlock: Andante tranquillo from 'Capriol' Suite	Vierne: Arabesque	Vierne: Berceuse	Vierne: Carillon	Guilmant: Verset	Mulet: Toccata 'Tu es petra'		
Mushel: Toccata	Vierne: Clair de Lune	Vierne: Intermezzo from Symphony 3	Vierne: Final from Symphony 3				
Vierne: Carillon	Weitz: Stella Maris	Berveiller: Intermezzo	Langlais: Dialogue sur les Mixtures	Widor: Allegro from Symphony 6			
Roger-Ducasse: Pastorale	Weitz: Stella Maris	Berveiller: Intermezzo	Langlais: Dialogue sur les Mixtures	Vierne: Symphony 3			
Roger-Ducasse: Pastorale	Weitz: Stella Maris	Berveiller: Intermezzo	Langlais: Dialogue sur les Mixtures	Vierne: Intermezzo from Symphony 3	Vierne: Final from Symphony 3		
Bach: Fugue a la Gigue	Bach: Toccata in F	Roger-Ducasse: Pastorale	Berveiller: Cadence	Vierne: Final from Symphony 2			
Liszt: Introduction and Fugue on 'Ad nos ad salutarem undam'	Saint Saens: The Swan	Hollins: Song of Sunshine	Hollins: Concert Overture in C				
Liszt: Prelude and Fugue on B.A.C.H.	Daughtry: Jesu, Thou Joy	MacDowell: To a Wild Rose	Vierne: Cathedrales	Vierne: Toccata from Symphony 1			

REPERTOIRE

Piece	Instances
Alain: Litanies	23
Alcock: Introduction and Passacaglia	7
Arne: A Maggot	26
Bach: Ach Bleib Bei Uns, Herr Jesu Christ	53
Bach: Air on the G String	1
Bach: All Glory, Laud and Honour	2
Bach: Bist du bei mir	11
Bach: Concerto in G (Ernst)	13
Bach: 'Dorian' Toccata and Fugue	3
Bach: Ertodt' Uns Durch Dein Güte	1
Bach: Fantasia and Fugue in G Minor	34
Bach: Fantasia in G	23
Bach: Fugue a la Gigue	33
Bach: In Dir ist Freude	1
Bach: In Dulci Jubilo	3
Bach: Jesu, Joy of Man's Desiring	2
Bach: Liebster Jesu, wir sind hier	1
Bach: Mass in B Minor	1
Bach: Nun Danket Alle Gott	24
Bach: Nun Komm' der Heiden Heiland	9
Bach: O Mensch, bewein' dein' Sunde gross	1
Bach: Prelude and Fugue in A	9
Bach: Prelude and Fugue in A Minor	1
Bach: Prelude and Fugue in B Minor	17
Bach: Prelude and Fugue in C Minor	4
Bach: Prelude and Fugue in D	53
Bach: Prelude and Fugue in E Flat	7
Bach: Prelude and Fugue in G	20
Bach: Sheep may safely graze	6
Bach: Song Tune from the Peasant Cantata	7

Bach: St. Matthew Passion	1
Bach: Toccata and Fugue in C	1
Bach: Toccata and Fugue in D Minor	20
Bach: Toccata in F	34
Bach: Trio Sonata 3	2
Bach: Wachet auf	1
Berveiller: Cadence	1
Berveiller: Intermezzo	3
Boellmann: Suite Gothique	10
Bonnet: Elfes - Caprice Heroique	17
Bossi: Scherzo in G Minor	32
Brahms: Es ist ein Ros' entsprungen	3
Brahms: Herzlich tut mich verlangen	4
Brahms: O Welt, ich muss dich lassen	2
Brahms: Schmucke dich, o liebe Seele	5
Bridge: Allegretto Grazioso	1
Bridge: Andantino in F Minor	12
Bridge: Three Pieces	4
Buxtehude: Es ist das Heil uns kommen her	1
Buxtehude: Mit Fried und Freud ich fahr dahin	1
Buxtehude: Nun bitten wir den Heiligen Geist	1
Buxtehude: Passacaglia in D Minor	1
Buxtehude: Prelude and Fugue in G Minor	11
Chauvet: Andantino in D Flat	2
Cleramboult: Dialogue	9
Cocker: Tuba Tune	11
Couperin: Soeur Monique	1
Darke: A Fantasy	4
Darke: Meditation on 'Brother James' Air'	7
Daughtry: Jesu, Thou Joy	2
Dubois: Fiat Lux	34
Dubois: Toccata in G	25
Dupre: Finale 'Ave Maris Stella'	2

Dupre: Fugue in G Minor	1
Dupre: Prelude and Fugue in B	3
Dupre: Verset des Psaumes	1
Durufle: Toccata in B Minor	8
Dvorak: Humoresque	2
Dvorak: Largo from 'New World'	9
Elgar: Allegro Maestoso from Sonata in G	25
Elgar: Finale from Sonata in G	1
Elgar: Sonata in G	5
Farrar: A Wedding Piece	3
Felton: A Little Tune	2
Festing: Air and Variations	7
Festing: Largo, Allegro, Aria and Two Variations	52
Franck: Chorale in A Minor	25
Franck: Fantasie	2
Franck: Final	1
Franck: Pastorale	4
Franck: Piece Heroique	21
Franck: Prelude, Fugue and Variation	27
Franck: The Symphonic Variations	1
German: Merrie England	2
Gibbs: Folk Tune	3
Gibbs: Jubilate Deo	6
Gigout: Scherzo	29
Gigout: Toccata in B Minor	8
Grace: Cradle Song	1
Guilmant: Cantilene Pastorale	3
Guilmant: Caprice in B Flat	3
Guilmant: Grand Choeur in D	4
Guilmant: Pastorale from Sonata 1	8
Guilmant: Scherzo Symphonique	3
Guilmant: Symphony 1	2
Guilmant: Verset	3

Handel: Allegro from Concerto 4 (Set 2)	17
Handel: Arrival of the Queen of Sheba	1
Handel: Concerto in B Flat	21
Handel: Extracts from the 'Water Music'	3
Handel: March 'Hercules'	1
Handel: Overture to Samson	31
Handel: Overture to the Occasional Oratorio	6
Handel: Pastoral Symphony from Messiah	2
Harwood: Allegro Appassionata from Sonata 1	20
Herzogenberg: Pastorale on 'Now thank we all our God'	3
Hollins: Concert Overture in C	3
Hollins: Grand Choeur in D	4
Hollins: Maytime	5
Hollins: Song of Sunshine	8
Howells: Psalm Prelude 1	1
Jackson: Fanfare	16
Jackson: Pageant	8
Jackson: Procession	1
Jongen: Chant de Mai	9
Jongen: Minuet Scherzo	5
Jongen: Sonata Eroica	27
Karg Elert: Chorale Improvisation 'Ein' feste Burg'	27
Karg Elert: Chorale Improvisation 'Jesu, geh 'voran'	3
Karg Elert: Harmonies du Soir	3
Karg Elert: Nun danket alle Gott	4
Langlais: Dialogue sur les Mixtures	3
Langlais: Incantation	3
Lemare: Madrigal	2
Lemmens: Finale	5
Liszt: Canzonetta del Salvator Rosa	13
Liszt: Evocation a la Chapelle Sixtine	1
Liszt: Introduction and Fugue on 'Ad nos ad salutarem undam'	24

Liszt: Prelude and Fugue on B.A.C.H.	17
Litaize: Toccata sur le Veni Creator	7
Lloyd Webber: Benedictus	9
MacDowell: To a Wild Rose	4
Mendelssohn: Sonata 6	22
Messiaen: Transports de Joie	1
Milford: Mr. Ben Johnson's Pleasure	3
Morandi: Rondo de Campanelli	14
Mozart: Fantasia in F Minor	41
Mulet: Carillon Sortie	17
Mulet: Noel	1
Mulet: Toccata 'Tu es petra'	33
Mushel: Toccata	15
Parry: An Old English Tune	4
Parry: Toccata and Fugue (The Wanderer)	17
Peeters: Abdijvrede	10
Peeters: Aria	20
Purcell: Trumpet Tune and Air	3
Reger: Fantasia and Fugue on B.A.C.H.	16
Rheinberger: Canzonetta	1
Roger-Ducasse: Pastorale	15
Rootham: Song of Victory	2
Saint Saens: Fantasie in E Flat	22
Saint Saens: Symphony 3	2
Saint Saens: The Swan	4
Schumann: Canon in B minor	10
Schumann: Four Sketches	6
Sowerby: Holiday Trumpets	1
Sowerby: Pageant	3
Stanford: Postlude in D Minor	8
Stanley: Suite in D	3
Stanley: Toccata for the Flutes	38
Stanley: Trumpet Voluntary	5

Stanley: Voluntary in F	6
Thalben Ball: Elegy	13
Thalben Ball: Tune in E	1
Thalben Ball: Variations on a theme by Paganini	7
Vaughan Williams: Rhosymedre	4
Vierne: Allegro from Symphony 2	2
Vierne: Allegro maestoso from Symphony 3	1
Vierne: Arabesque	13
Vierne: Berceuse	26
Vierne: Carillon	19
Vierne: Carillon de Westminster	4
Vierne: Cathedrales	25
Vierne: Clair De Lune	10
Vierne: Cortege	2
Vierne: Final from Symphony 2	3
Vierne: Final from Symphony 3	4
Vierne: Finale from Symphony 1	9
Vierne: Intermezzo from Symphony 3	4
Vierne: Lied	5
Vierne: Prelude	5
Vierne: Scherzetto	1
Vierne: Scherzo from Symphony 2	33
Vierne: Sicilienne	2
Vierne: Symphony 3	3
Vierne: Toccata from Symphony 1	7
Wagner: The Ride of the Valkyries	1
Walford Davies: Solemn Melody	5
Walker: Lullaby (on an old Irish Air)	1
Warlock: Andante tranquillo from 'Capriol' Suite	5
Weitz: Stella Maris	7
Wesley, SS: Larghetto in F sharp Minor	35
Wesley, SS: Choral Song and Fugue	2
Wesley: Air and Gavotte	7

Whitlock: Carol	1
Whitlock: Chanty and Salix	18
Whitlock: Divertimento	1
Whitlock: Fidelis	3
Whitlock: Folk Tune	16
Whitlock: Paean	8
Whitlock: Scherzo	12
Widor: Allegro from Symphony 6	2
Widor: Allegro Vivace from Symphony 5	4
Widor: Pastorale from Symphony 2	2
Widor: Scherzo from Symphony 4	1
Widor: Toccata from Symphony 5	16
Widor: Variations from Symphony 5	10
Yon: Humoreske	16
Yon: Toccatina for Flutes	2

VENUES

Venue	Instances
Christchurch Priory	148
All Saints', Bournemouth	14
St. Mary Redcliffe, Bristol	12
Southbourne Methodist, Bournemouth	8
Holy Trinity, Exmouth	6
Salisbury Cathedral	6
Reading Minster	7
Sherborne Abbey	4
Guildhall, Southampton	3
Reading Town Hall	3
St. Laurence's, Reading	3
St. Peter's, Bournemouth	3
Victoria Methodist, Weston-super-Mare	3
Winchester Cathedral	3
Winter Gardens, Bournemouth	3
All Saints', Freshwater	2
Bath Abbey	2
St. Martin's, Cardiff	2
St. Michael's, Southampton	2
Wimborne Minster	2
All Saints', Headington	1
All Saints', Penarth	1
Avenue Methodist Church	1
Birmingham Cathedral	1
Birmingham Town Hall	1
Chester Cathedral	1
Christ Church, Bath	1

Christ Church, Reading	1
Christ's College, Cambridge	1
Clitheroe Parish Church	1
Cosham Congregational Church	1
East Cliff Congregational Church	1
Falmouth Central Methodist	1
Farnham Parish Church	1
Hereford Cathedral	1
Holy Trinity, Bournemouth	1
King's College, Cambridge	1
Lansdowne Baptist, Bournemouth	1
Mint Methodist	1
Mortehoe Methodist Church	1
Portsmouth Cathedral	1
Preston Parish Church	1
Royal Festival Hall	1
Shepton Mallet Parish Church	1
Sidmouth Parish Church	1
St. Andrew's, Plymouth	1
St. Gabriel's, Aldersbrook	1
St. John the Baptist, Windsor	1
St. Luke's, Sway	1
St. Luke's, Torquay	1
St. Mark's, Portsea	1
St. Mark's, Southampton	1
St. Mary's, Weymouth	1
St. Matthew's, Wookey	1
St. Peter's, Parkstone	1
St. Peter's, Southbourne	1

St. Simon's, Southsea	1
The Concert Hall, Reading	1
Trinity Congregational Church	5
Upton Parish Church, Torquay	1
Walhampton School	1
West Memorial Hall, Caversham	1
Westminster Cathedral	1
Worcester Cathedral	1
York Minster	1

APPENDIX G

Sample List of Visiting Recitalists' Programmes (1963-1979)

RECITALS

Date	Name	Location	Notes	Repertoire			
6/19/1963	Garth Benson	St. Mary Redcliffe, Bristol					
7/3/1963	John Langdon	King's College, Cambridge					
7/24/1963	Alwyn Surplice	Winchester Cathedral					
7/31/1963	Richard Popplewell	St. Paul's Cathedral					
8/7/1963	John Turner	Cheltenham College					
8/14/1963	Christopher Dearnley	Salisbury Cathedral					
8/28/1963	Richard Lloyd	Salisbury Cathedral					
9/4/1963	Norman Wilson	St. John's, Boscombe					
9/11/1963	Simon Preston	Westminster Abbey					
9/25/1963	Melville Cook	Hereford Cathedral					
10/2/1963	Frederick Fea	Sherborne Abbey					
6/17/1964	Douglas Fox	Great St. Mary, Cambridge		Handel: Overture to Athaliah	Bach: Jesus Christ, our Saviour, turn from us the wrath of God	Bach: To God alone be Glory	Bach: Bide with us, Lord Jesus
6/24/1964	Sidney Campbell	St. George's Chapel, Windsor		Gibbons: A Fancy for Double Organ	Clemamboult: Basse et dessus de trompette	Bach: Toccata, Adagio and Fugue	Vierne: Lied
7/11/1964	Norman Wilson	St. John's, Boscombe		Bach: Toccata and Fugue in D minor	Handel: Concerto 3	Schumann: Canon in B minor	Hurford: Two Chorale Preludes
7/29/1964	Garth Benson	St. Mary Redcliffe, Bristol		Stanley: Prelude and Bell Allegro	Martini: Sarabande and Balletto	Bach: Fantasia and Fugue in G minor	Lang: Three Choral-Preludes
8/19/1964	Garth Benson	St. Mary Redcliffe, Bristol		Stanley: Prelude and Bell Allegro	Martii: Sarabande and Balletto	Bach: Fantasia and Fugue in G minor	Lang: Three Choral-Preludes

Reger: Introduction and Passacaglia	Bridge: Adagio in E	Arthur Wills: Elegy	Peeters: Holy God, we praise Thy Name	Whitlock: Scherzo in G flat	McKie: Romance in G minor	Harwood: Sonata 1 (Third mvmt.)	
Roger-Ducasse: Pastorale	Gordon Phillips: Minuet (Suite in F minor)	Monnikendam: Toccata	Franck: Choral 2				
Guilmant: March on a theme by Handel	Karg Elert: Now thank we all our God	Vierne: Berceuse	Vierne: Carillon				
Guridi: Offertoire	Healey Willan: Elegy	Parry: Toccata and Fugue 'The Wanderer'	Guilmant: March on a theme of Handel				
Guridi: Offertoire	Healey Willan: Elegy	Parry: Toccata and Fugue (The Wanderer)	Guilmant: March on a theme of Handel				

8/26/1964	Caleb Jarvis	St. George's Hall, Liverpool		Maleingreau: Toccata	Jarvis: Sarabande	Jarvis: Meditation on a Hereford shire tune	Bach: Variations 'O Gott du frommer Gott'
9/2/1964	John Birch	Chichester Cathedral		Murrill: Carillon	Bach: Fantasia and Fugue in C minor	SS Wesley: Andante in E flat	Stanley: Voluntary in C
9/16/1964	Richard Lloyd	Salisbury Cathedral		Bach: Prelude and Fugue in A	Franck: Pastorale: Boyce: Voluntary in D	Byrd: Pavane	Alcock: Introduction and Passacaglia
7/14/1965	John Sanders	Chester Cathedral		Bach: Prelude in E flat	Whitlock: Five short pieces	Hurford: Two Dialogues	Franck: Choral in A minor
7/21/1965	Garth Benson	St. Mary Redcliffe, Bristol		Raison: Offertoire on 'Vive le Roi'	Couperin: Musette	Stanley: Suite in D	Bach: Prelude and Fugue in A minor
8/4/1965	Christopher Robinson	Worcester Cathedral		Parry: Fantasia and Fugue in G	Sweelinck: Variations on 'Mein junges leben hat ein end'	Bach: Toccata, Adagio and Fugue in C	Mozart: Andante in F
8/11/1965	Arthur Wills	Ely Cathedral		Dandrieu: Offertoire 'O Filii et Filiae'	Bach: Fantasia and Fugue in G minor	Franck: Choral in B minor	Liszt: Fantasia and Fugue on B.A.C.H.
8/18/1965	Robert Joyce	Llandaff Cathedral		Bach: Prelude and Fugue in G	Whitlock: Five short pieces	Franck: Choral 3	Vaughan Williams: Three Preludes on Welsh Hymn Tunes
8/25/1965	Charles Myers	Clitheroe Parish Church		Cook: Fanfare	Rossi: Miniature	Sumsion: Introduction and Theme (Ostinato)	Frantisek Tuma: Suite for Organ
9/1/1965	Stanley Sackett	St. Helier Parish Church		Stanley: Trumpet Tune	Vaughan Williams: Prelude on 'Rhosymedre'	Bach: Wachet auf, ruft uns die Stimme	Bach: Wo soll ich fliehen hin
6/29/1966	Robert Munns	Holy Trinity, Brompton		Tournemire: Te Deum	Durufle: Scherzo	Leighton: Prelude, Scherzo and Passacaglia	Franck: Pastorale

Peeters: Lied to the Flowers	Peeters: Lied to the Mountains	Franck: Choral 3					
Brahms: Es ist ein Ros' entsprungen	Britten: Prelude and Fugue on a theme of Vittoria	Vierne: Berceuse	Harvey Grace: Resurgam	Harris: Reverie	Brockless; Prelude, Toccata and Chaconne		
Parry: Chorale Prelude on Melcombe	Couperin: Rondo: 'Soeur Monique'	Handel: Concerto 5					
Walond: Voluntary in E major	Parry: Chorale Prelude on the Old 104th	Peeters: Variations on 'King Jesus hath a garden'	Vaughan Williams: Hymn Tune Prelude on 'Rhosymedre'	Bach: Fugue in E flat			
S Wesley: Air and Gavotte	Guilmant: March on a theme of Handel	Guridi: Ofertoria	Alcock: Introduction and Passacaglia				
Dupre: Prelude and Fugue in G minor	Mathias: Processional	Preston: Alleluyas					
Vierne: Scherzo and Final from Symphony 2	Wills: Prelude and Fugue						
Liszt: Fugue on 'Ad nos ad Salutarem undam'							
Howells: Rhapsody op. 17 no. 3	Beethoven: Allegro and Scherzo	Whitlock: Exultemus from Seven Psalm Sketches	JC Oley: Two Chorale Preludes	Handel: Concerto in F	Richard Jones: Toccata in D minor	du Mage: Basse de Trompette	Andriessen: Toccata
Bach: Fantasia and Fugue in G minor	Sydney Campbell: Canterbury Interlude	Franck: Choral 1	Bossi: Divertimento in the form of a jig	Widor: Toccata from Symphony 5			
Mushel: Aria	Vierne: Impromptu	Vierne: Carillon de Westminster					

7/6/1966	Sidney Campbell	St. George's Chapel, Windsor		Mendelssohn: Sonata in A	Reger: Benedictus	Bach: Passacaglia	Franck: Pastorale
7/13/1966	John Birch	Chichester Cathedral		Bach: Fantasia in G	S Wesley: Air and Gavotte	Peeters: Aria	Howells: Paean
7/20/1966	Garth Benson	St. Mary Redcliffe, Bristol		Stanley: Prelude and Bell Allegro	Stanley: Toccata for the Flutes	Bach: Prelude and Fugue in A minor	Mendelssohn: Sonata 3
7/27/1966	George Guest	St. John's College, Cambridge		Anon: Voluntary in D minor	Daquin: Noel in G	Buxtehude: Prelude and Fugue in D minor	Haydn: Three Clock Pieces
8/3/1966	Garth Benson	St. Mary Redcliffe, Bristol	Played for GOT at short notice	Handel: Overture to the Occasional Oratorio	Pachelbel: Chaconne in D minor	Stanley: A Fancy	Bach: Fantasia and Fugue in G minor
8/17/1966	Charles Myers	Clitheroe Parish Church		Blow: Toccata	Sumsion: Canzona	Nares: Prelude and Fugue in E flat	Elgar: Allegro maestoso from Sonata 1
8/31/1966	Stanley Curtis	Westminster Chapel		Stanley: Suite in D	Bach: Come, Redeemer of our Race BWV 659	Bach: Come, Holy Ghost BWV 651	MacDowell: AD 1620
9/7/1966	John Mingay	Crewkerne Parish Church		Reger: Introduction and Passacaglia in D minor	Haydn: 4 Pieces for a Mechanical Clock	Robert Cundick: Sonatina	Bach: Dorian Toccata and Fugue
6/14/1967	Peter Stevenson	Portsmouth Cathedral		Bach: 'Great' Prelude and Fugue in C	Stanley: Voluntary 7	Andriessen: Third Chorale	Walton: Three Pieces for Organ
7/5/1967	Lillian Wu		Piano	Schubert: Sonata in A	Prokofiev: Sonata 3	Chopin: Andante Spianato	Grande Polonaise Brillante
7/12/1967	Roy Massey	Croydon Parish Church		Widor: Symphony 5 1st mvmt.	Bach: Prelude and Fugue in A minor	Whitlock: Divertimento	Byrd: Pavana - The Earle of Salisbury

Franck: Piece Heroique	Bach: Dorian Toccata and Fugue							
Langlais: Trois meditations sur la Sainte Trinity	Greene: Voluntary 13	Reger: Chorale Fantasia: 'Hallelujah! Gott zu Loben'						
Leonard Butler: Capriccietto	Howells: Psalm Prelude Set 1 No. 1	Reger: Introduction and Passacaglia	Franck: Finale in B flat					
Bach: Fantasia and Fugue in C minor	von Herzogenberg: Pastorale on 'Nun danket alle Gott'	Langlais: Triptyque						
Howells: Psalm Prelude Set 1 No. 3	Gurindi: Ofertoria	Alcock: Introduction and Passacaglia						
Arne: A Maggot	Howells: Siciliano for a High Ceremony	SS Wesley: Holsworthy Church Bells	Wolstenholme: Voluntary	Mathias: Allegro non troppo	Avison: Concerto in D	Whitlock: Fanfare	
Kitson: Chorale Prelude on 'Irish'	Webber: Postlude on 'Miles Lane'	Haydn: Air and variations from Symphony in D	Widor: Andante cantabile from Symphony 4	Rheinberger: Toccata from Sonata 14	Bairstow: Evening Song	Vierne: Finale from Symphony 1	
Jongen: Chant de Mai	Bossi: Scherzo in G minor	Peeters: Concert Piece						
Mathias: Partita op. 19	Bonnet: Romance sans paroles	Peeters: Toccata, Fugue and Hymn 'Ave Maris Stella'						
Anon: From the Mulliner Book	Mendelssohn: Sonata 6	Durufle: Toccata						

Date	Performer	Venue		Piece 1	Piece 2	Piece 3	Piece 4
7/19/1967	Garth Benson	St. Mary Redcliffe, Bristol		Raison: Offertoire on 'Vive le Roi'	Festing: Largo, Allegro, Aria and Variations	Bach: Prelude and Fugue in G minor	Darke: Prelude on a theme of Tallis
7/26/1967	Cyril Diplock	Alton Parish Church		Mendelssohn: Sonata 2	Messiaen: Apparition de l'eglise Eternelle	Lang: Tuba tune in D	Bach: Prelude and Fugue in B minor
8/2/1967	Robert Joyce	Llandaff Cathedral		Bach: Prelude and Fugue in C minor	Robinson: Voluntary in A minor	Derek Healey: Three Preludes on French Hymn Tunes	Reger: Introduction and Passacaglia in D minor
8/9/1967	Robert Gillings	Bridgwater Parish Church		Bach: Toccata, Adagio and Fugue	Schumann: Sketch in D flat	Andriessen: Theme and Variations	Jackson: Arabesque
9/6/1967	John Marsh	Clifton College		Dandrieu: Offertoire 'O Filii et Filiae'	Buxtehude: Prelude and Fugue in F sharp minor	Whitlock: Canzona	Cook: Fanfare
9/13/1967	Stanley Curtis	Westminster Chapel		Stanley: Trumpet Voluntary	Dienel: Chorale Prelude 'If thou but suffer God to guide thee'	Bach: Sinfonia to Cantata 106	Bach: Sinfonia to Cantata 29
9/27/1967	Garth Benson	St. Mary Redcliffe, Bristol		Stanley: Prelude and Bell Allegro	Paradies: Aria and Andante	Bach: Fugue on the Magnificat	Bach: Chorale Prelude on the Nunc Dimittis
6/12/1968	Garth Benson	St. Mary Redcliffe, Bristol		Handel: Overture to Ptolemy	Handel: Passepied from the Aylesford pieces	Festing: Largo, Aria, Allegro and Variations	Bach: Fantasia and Fugue in G minor
6/19/1968	George Guest	St. John's College, Cambridge		Sweelinck: Variations on 'Mein junges Leben Hat ein End'	Bach: Prelude and Fugue in B minor	Reger: Benedictus	Elgar: Sonata 2
7/3/1968	James Dalton	The Queen's College, Oxford		Bach: Fantasia in G	Blitheman: Etherne rerum Conditor	Bull: Prelude and Carol 'Laet ons met herten reijne'	Purcell: Voluntary on the 100th Psalm Tune

284

Hollins: A Trumpet Minuet	Howells: Psalm Prelude Set 1 No. 1	Reger: Introduction and Passacaglia	Franck: Finale in B flat				
Franck: Andantino in G minor	Schumann: Sketch 1	Mulet: Carillon Sortie					
Camidge: Concerto 2	Mathias: Processional	Guilmant: Sonata 1					
Alain: Un jardin suspendu	Franck: Choral 3						
Bonnet: Romance sans Paroles	Vierne: Cathedrales	Jongen: Chant de Mai	Peeters: Toccata and Hymn 'Ave Maris Stella'				
Searle Wright: Prelude on 'Brother James's Air'	Rheinberger: Sonata 12	Vierne: Allegro vivace from Symphony 1	Grieg: At the cradle	Brahms: Lullaby	Mushel: Toccata		
Bach: Prelude and Fugue in A minor	Mendelssohn: Sonata 2	Howells: Psalm Prelude Set 1 No. 3	Lang: Three hymn-tune preludes	Alcock: Introduction and Passacaglia			
Guiridi: Offertoria	Rheinberger: Cantilene	Franck: Choral 3	Liszt: Fantasia and Fugue on B.A.C.H.				
Whitlock: Five short pieces	Cooke: Prelude, Intermezzo and Finale						
Bach: Fugue in G minor	Bach: Chorale 'Wachet auf, ruft uns die Stimme'	Bach: Fugue in B minor on a theme of Corelli	Vaughan Williams: Three preludes on Welsh Tunes	Bach: Toccata in D minor			

285

7/10/1968	Yapp Ket Siong	RAM		Bach: Prelude and Fugue in C	Bach: Trio Sonata in E flat	Bach: Chorale Prelude on 'Dies sind die heil'gen zehn gebot'	Franck: Choral 2
7/24/1968	Richard Lloyd	Hereford Cathedral		Buxtehude: Prelude and Fugue in F	Felton: Concerto in B flat	Langlais: Suite Medievale	Harris: A Fancy
7/31/1968	Melville Cook	Toronto		Handel: Concerto 5	Bach: Passion Chorale	Brahms: Passion Chorale	Bach: Dorian Toccata and Fugue
8/14/1968	Nicolas Kynaston	Westminster Cathedral		Bach: Aus tiefer Noth Schrei' ich zu dir	Bach: Christe, under Herr zum Jordan kam	Bach: Prelude and Fugue in D	Franck: Choral 3
9/11/1968	Garth Benson	St. Mary Redcliffe, Bristol		Handel: Overture to the Occasional Oratorio	Stanley: A Fancy	Stanley: Introduction, Adagio and Trumpet Tune	Bach: Prelude and Fugue in A minor
9/18/1968	Francis Jackson	York Minster		Nares: Introduction and Fugue in F	Bach: Chorale Prelude 'Schmucke dich, O liebe Seele'	Jackson: Toccata, Chorale and Fugue	Gigout: Scherzo
9/25/1968	Gordon Thorne	Manchester					
10/2/1968	Richard Seal	Salisbury Cathedral		Bach: Fantasia in G	Bach: Kommst du nun, Jesu	Bach: Allein Gott in der Hoh sei Ehr	Kelly: Introduction and Allegro
6/25/1969	Peter Stevenson	Ex Portsmouth Cathedral		Andriessen: Theme and Variations	Bach: Meine Seele erhebt den Herren	Bach: Kommst du nun, Jesu	Ian Parrott: Toccata
7/9/1969	Dudley Holroyd	Bath Abbey		Andriessen: Thema met Variations	Buxtehude: Ciacona in E minor	Sweelinck: Fantasia in echo	Bach: Toccata, Adagio and Fugue in C
7/16/1969	Nicolas Kynaston	Westminster Cathedral		Bach: Prelude and Fugue in B minor	Alain: Fantaisie 2	Alain: Litanies	Vierne: Scherzo from Symphony 6

286

Messiaen: Dieu parmi nous	Reubke: Sonata							
Harris: A Prelude	Brockless: Introduction, Passacaglia and Coda	Mathias: Processional						
Sweelinck: Variations: 'Mein Junges Leben Hat ein End'	Micheelson: Orgelkonzert	Boellmann: Suite Gothique						
Franck: Pastorale	Tournemire: Improvisation on Victimae Paschali	Vierne: Carillon de Westminster						
Parry: When I survey the wondrous Cross	Howells: Master Tallis' Testament	Stanford: Postlude in D	Reger: Introduction and Passacaglia					
Liszt: Ad nos, ad salutarem undam								
SS Wesley: Larghetto in F sharp minor	Arne: A Maggot	Franck: Prelude, Fugue and Variation	Liszt: Fantasia and Fugue on the name B.A.C.H.					
Langlais: Trois Paraphrases Gregoriennes	Widor: Symphony 6							
Langlais: Plainte and Dialogue sur les Mixtures from Suite Breve	Peeters: Aria op. 51	Reger: Fantasia on the chorale 'Hallelujah! Gott zu loben'						
Liszt: Fantasia and Fugue on Ad nos, ad salutarem undam								

7/23/1969	Garth Benson	St. Mary Redcliffe, Bristol		Arne: Overture to Comus	Zipoli: Sarabande and Giga	Bach: The Wedge Prelude and Fugue in E	Rheinberger: Cantilena
7/30/1969	Peter Goodman	Hull		Smart: Overture in D	Sweelinck: Variations 'Ballatto del granduca'	Bach: Toccata and Fugue in F	Bach: Fantasia in G
8/6/1969	Eric Hemery	Cartmel Priory		Alcock: Introduction and Passacaglia	Howells: Rhapsody 1	Vaughan Williams: Three Preludes on Welsh Hymn Tunes	Bach: Fantasia and Fugue in G minor
8/13/1969	Robert Joyce	Llandaff Cathedral		Leighton: Paean	Bach: Prelude and Fugue in C	Howells: Rhapsody op. 17 no. 2	Karg-Elert: O my soul, rejoice with gladness
8/18/1969	John Birch	Chichester Cathedral		Bach: Prelude and Fugue in C	Camidge: Concerto 2	Howells: Rhapsody 4	Hindemith: Sonata 3
8/20/1969	Jennifer Bate	London		Purcell: Trumpet Tune and Air	Krebs: Trio in B flat	Bach: Toccata in F	Schroeder: 2 Kleine Praeludien
8/27/1969	John Marsh	Clifton College, Bristol		Walton: Suite	Bach: Great Prelude and Fugue in C minor	Doles: Three Chorale Preludes	Nieland: Toccata
9/10/1969	Garth Benson	St. Mary Redcliffe, Bristol		Raison: Offertoire on 'Vive le Roy'	Pachelbel: Chaconne in D minor	Festing: Largo, Aria, Allegro and Two Variations	Bach: Prelude and Fugue in A minor
9/19/1969	George Thalben-Ball	The Temple Church, London		Stanley: Suite in D	Couperin: Rondeau - Les Sylvides	Bach: Prelude and Fugue in G minor	Walford Davies: Interlude
9/24/1969	Richard Seal	Salisbury Cathedral		Reger: Toccata and Fugue in D minor and D major	Bach: Fugue a la gigue	Bach: Sheep may safely graze	Buxtehude: Prelude and Fugue in G minor

Healey Willan: Elegy and Chaconne	Parry: When I survey the Wondrous Cross	Howells: Rhapsody 3	Mushel: Toccata				
Karg-Elert: Legende	Whitlock: Folk Tune and Scherzo	Hindemith: Sonata 2	Durufle: Toccata				
Bach: It certainly is time	Bach: He who lets only beloved God rule	Sibelius: Intrada and Sorgmusik	Whitlock: Fanfare				
Karg-Elert: I thank thee, dearest Lord	Derek Healey: Three Preludes on French Hymn-Tunes	Stanley: Concerto in A	Whitlock: Plymouth Suite				
Krebs: O God hear my sighing	Brahms: O wie selig	Brian Brockless: Introduction, Passacaglia and Coda	Schumann: Canon in B minor	Reger: Dankpsalm			
Mendelssohn: Sonata 3	Ropartz: Meditation	Pierne: Prelude, Cantilene and Scherzando	Peeters: Largo	Peeters: Concert Piece			
Seth Bingham: Rhythmic Trumpet	Rheinberger: Idyll and Toccata (Sonata 14 in C major)	Bonnet: Intermezzo	Langlais on the Te Deum				
Howells: Psalm Prelude Set 1 No. 1	Leonard Butler: Capricietto	Reger: Introduction and Passacaglia	Franck: Finale in B flat				
Liszt: Variations on Weinen, Klagen, Sorgen, Sagen	Widor: Andante cantabile from Symphony 4	Thaarup Sark: Toccata Primi Toni op. 11	Bedell: In Paradisum	Paul Creston: Finale (Suite)			
Leighton: Paean	Yon: Humoresque	Handel: Concerto 2	Peeters: Toccata, Fugue and Hymn 'Ave Maris Stella'				

6/17/1970	Derek Cantrell	Manchester Cathedral		Murrill: Carillon	CPE Bach: Sonata 5	Leighton: Prelude, Scherzo and Passacaglia	Franck: Prelude, Fugue and Variation
7/1/1970	Dudley Holroyd	Bath Abbey		Couperin: Messe pour les Paroisses	Dandrieu: Noel	Bach: Prelude and Fugue in B minor	Widor: Allegro vivace from Symphony 5
7/15/1970	Raymond Isaacson	High Wycombe		Greene: Voluntary 13	Hollins: Concert Overture in C minor	Bach: Toccata and Fugue in E	Kellner: Chorale Prelude on Was Gott tut
7/22/1970	Gary Desmond	City Parish Church, Bristol		Raison: Offerte upon 'Vive le Roy'	Stanley: Introduction and Trumpet Tune	Brahms: Schmucke Dich	Bach: Prelude and Fugue in F minor
7/29/1970	Martin White	Armagh Cathedral		Myron Roberts: Homage to Perotin	Boyce: Introduction and Trumpet Tune	Bohm: Prelude and Fugue in C	Bach: Trio in C minor
8/5/1970	Garth Benson	St. Mary Redcliffe, Bristol		Handel: Overture to the Occasional Oratorio	Stanley: A Fancy	Boyce: Introduction and Trumpet Tune	Bach: Dorian Toccata and Fugue
8/19/1970	Peter Bullett	Christ's College, Cambridge		Stanley: Trumpet Tune	Bach: Jesus Christus, unser Heiland, der von uns	Bach: Nun komm, der Heiden Heiland	Bach: Fantasia and Fugue in G minor
9/2/1970	Simon Lindley	St. Olave's, London		Bach: Fantasia in G	Bach: Sei gegrusset, Jesu gutig	Mathias: Toccata Giocosa	Greene: Voluntary in C minor
9/9/1970	Frederick Hewitt	Christchurch Priory		Bach: Toccata and Fugue in F	Langlais: Three Meditations on the Holy Spirit	Buxtehude: Ach herr, mich armen Sunder	Liszt: Fantasia and Fugue on B.A.C.H.
9/16/1970	Garth Benson	St. Mary Redcliffe, Bristol		Handel: Overture to Ptolemy	William Felton: Minuet	Stanley: Introduction, Largo and Trumpet Tune	Bach: Prelude and Fugue in A minor
9/23/1970	Francis Jackson	York Minster		Camidge: Concerto in G minor	Bach: Prelude and Fugue in A minor	Peeters: Modale Suite	Sweelick: Variations on 'Est-ce Mars?'
11/4/1970	Nicolas Kynaston	Westminster Cathedral		Bach: Prelude and Fugue in A minor	Saint-Saens: Fantaisie in D flat	Franck: Choral 2	Jongen: Toccata in D flat

Vaughan Williams: Rhosymedre	Howells: Psalm Prelude Set 1 No. 3	Bach: Prelude and Fugue in G					
Messiaen: Le Banquet Celeste	Vierne: Final from Symphony 1						
Messiaen: Apparition de l'Eglise Eternelle	Franck: Fantaisie in A	Walton: Three Pieces from Richard III	Reubke: Introduction and Fugue (94th Psalm)				
Rheinberger: Introduction and Passcaglia from Sonata 8	Peeters: Aria	Widor: Symphony 6 Mvmt. 1					
Franck: Choral 2	Whitlock: Canzona	Alain: Litanies	Improvisation on a theme				
Mendelssohn: Sonata 3	Lang: Three Hymn-tune Preludes	Franck: Choral 3					
Arne: Ayre and Gavot	Walton: Three Pieces for Organ	Peeters: Variations on 'Herr Jesu hat ein Gartchen'	Ireland: Villanella	Messiaen: Joie et clarte des corps glorieux	Bonnet: Elfes	Cocker: Tuba Tune	
Brahms: Herzlich tut mich erfreuen	Brahms: Es ist ein ros' entsprungen	Jongen: Sonata Eroica					
Buxtehude: Nun bitten wir den heiligen Geist	Bach: Toccata and Fugue in D minor						
Wesley: Air and Gavotte	Stanford: Postludes 3 & 6	Guilmant: March on a theme of Handel					
Jackson: Sonata in G minor							
Reubke: Sonata in C minor							

Date	Performer	Venue		Piece 1	Piece 2	Piece 3	Piece 4
2/3/1971	Garth Benson	St. Mary Redcliffe, Bristol		Stanley: Suite in D	Dandrieu: Rondeau (La Musette)	Bach: Mit Fried' und Freud' ich fahr' Dahin	Bach: Mein Seele erhebt den Herren
6/23/1971	John Wycliffe-Jones	St. Mary's, Weymouth		Handel: Occasional Overture	Bach: Canzona in D minor	Stanley: Trumpet Voluntary	William Hine: Flute Piece
6/30/1971	Garth Benson	St. Mary Redcliffe, Bristol		Purcell: Voluntary on the Old Hundredth	Purcell: Trumpet Tune and Air	Battishill: Corant and Minuet	Bach: The Wedge Prelude and Fugue in E
7/7/1971	Dudley Holroyd	Bath Abbey		Mendelssohn: Prelude and Fugue in C minor	Stanley: Voluntary in C	Bach: Art of Fugue	Peeters: Aria op. 51
7/14/1971	Roger Fisher	Chester Cathedral		Alcock: Introduction and Passacaglia	Bach: Chorale Prelude 'Allein Gott'	Philip Cranmer: Galliard	Mozart: Andante in F major
7/21/1971	Peter Boorman	St. David's Cathedral		Benjamin Cooke: Introduction and Fugue in C minor	Karg-Elert: Harmonies du soir	Mozart: Fantasia in F minor and major	Rossi: Miniature for portable organ
7/28/1971	Roy Massey	Birmingham Cathedal		Widor: Symphony 5 Mvmt. 1	Bach: Fantasia and Fugue in G minor	SS Wesley: Holsworth Church Bells	Mendelssohn: Sonata 6
8/4/1971	Garth Benson	St. Mary Redcliffe, Bristol		Buxtehude: Prelude and Fugue in G minor	Dandrieu: Rondeau (La Musette)	Stanley: Suite for Organ	Bach: Fantasia in G
8/19/1971	Peter Bullett	Christ's College, Cambridge					
8/25/1971	Anthony Crossland	Wells Cathedral		Bach: Toccata and Fugue in D minor	SS Wesley: Larghetto in F sharp minor	Bach: Nun komm, der Heiden Heiland	Brahms: Herzlich tut mich verlangen
9/1/1971	Nicolas Kynaston			de Grigny: Dialogue in A minor	de Grigny: Dialogue de Flute pour l'Elevation	Bach: Toccata and Fugue in F	Reger: Trauerode
9/8/1971	Frederick Hewitt						

Bach: Fugue on the Magnificat	Whitlock: Lantana	Whitlock: Salix	Rheinberger: Sonata 4	Vierne: Carillon de Westminster				
John Bennett: Voluntary in F	William Walond: Cornet Voluntary	Cocker: Tuba Tune	Salome: Grand Choeur	Peeters: Aria	Guilmant: Pastorale and Final from Sonata 1			
Saint-Saens: Breton Rhapsody 3	Elgar: Nimrod	Peeters: Preludium, Canzona e Ciacona	Cook: Fanfare					
Messiaen: La Nativite								
Saint-Saens: Allegretto	Jongen: Sonata Eroica	Arthur Wills: Introduction and Allegro						
Bach: Toccata in F	Felton: Concerto in E flat	Reger: Canzona in E flat	Buxtehude: Prelude and Fugue in G minor					
Whitlock: Divertimento	Pierne: Cantilene	Dupre: Variations on a Noel						
Parry: Elegy	Franck: Chorale in A minor	Vierne: Carillon de Westminster						
Karg-Elert: Nun danket alle Gott	Schumann: Sketch in D flat	Bridge: Adagio in E	Blow: Toccata for a double organ	Mendelssohn: Sonata 2				
Durufle: Prelude and Fugue on the name ALAIN	Healey Willan: Introduction, Passacaglia and Fugue in E flat minor	Vierne: Final from Symphony 1						

293

9/15/1971	Ian Hare	King's College, Cambridge		Buxtehude: Prelude and Fugue in G minor	Bach: Two Chorale Preludes upon 'Allein Gott, in der Hoh' sei Ehr'	Bach: Trio Sonata in C minor	Reger: Chorale Fantasia upon 'Wachet auf, ruft uns die Stimme'
10/6/1971	Noel Rawsthorne	Liverpool Cathedral		Bach: Sinfonia from Cantata 29	Bach: Three Schubler Preludes	Bach: Toccata and Fugue in D minor	Howells: Psalm Prelude Set 1 No. 1
12/1/1971	Christopher Jenkins	Southwark Cathedral		Bach: The Giant Fugue in D minor	Bach: Fantasia in G	Bach: Great Prelude and Fugue in A minor	Stanford: Three Pieces
3/1/1972	Robin Jackson	Christ Church, Lancaster Gate, London		Buxtehude: Prelude and Fugue in F	Gigout: Toccata	Haydn: Three Pieces for musical clocks	Jongen: Sonata Eroica
5/3/1972	Dudley Holroyd	Bath Abbey		Vivaldi-Bach: Concerto in G	Sweelinck: Variations on 'Mein junges Leben hat ein End'	Bach: Sleepers wake!	Bach: My soul doth magnify the Lord
6/7/1972	Garth Benson	St. Mary Redcliffe, Bristol		William Walond: Introduction and Toccata	Pachelbel: Chaconne in D minor	Festing: Largo, Allegro, Aria and Variations	Bach: Prelude and Fugue in B minor
6/28/1972	Peter Boorman	St. David's Cathedral		Bach: Prelude in E flat	Best: Air and Variations	Schroeder: Toccata on 'Veni Creator Spiritus'	Philip Marshall: Morning Canticle
7/12/1972	Gary Desmond	City Parish Church, Bristol		Cocker: Tuba Tune	Bach: Prelude and Fugue in C	Festing: Largo, Allegro, Aria and Two Variations	Franck: Choral 1
7/19/1972	Arthur Wills	Ely Cathedral		Bach: Prelude and Fugue in E flat	Buxtehude: Chaconne in E minor	Franck: Choral in B minor	Widor: Intermezzo, Adagio and March Pontificale from Symphony 1
7/26/1972	Garth Benson	St. Mary Redcliffe, Bristol		Stanley: Suite in D	Paradies: Aria and Andante	Bach: Prelude and Fugue in A minor	Rheinberger: Cantilena
8/2/1972	Nicolas Kynaston			Karg-Elert: Toccata on the Choral 'Jerusalem, Du Hochgebaute Stadt'	Mozart: Phantasie in F minor	Vierne: Symphony 6	

Durufle: Scherzo	Jongen: Toccata						
Franck: Choral in A minor	Yon: Toccatina for Flutes	Liszt: Prelude and Fugue on B.A.C.H.					
Vierne: Berceuse	Pierne: Prelude	Alain: Litanies					
Bach: Fantasia in G	Cocker: Tuba Tune	Vierne: Finale from Symphony 1					
Bach: Ah remain with us, Lord Jesus Christ	Bach: Passacaglia and Fugue in C minor	Franck: Choral 3	Peeters: Suite Modale				
Bridge: Adagio	Leonard Butler: Vapriccietto	Peeters: Preludium, Canzona e Ciacona	Cook: Fanfare				
Rheinberger: Fantasie- Sonata 2	Croft: Voluntary in D	Jean Absil: Pastorale on an old Flemish carol	Alcock: Legend: Bach: Fugue in E flat				
Haydn: Two Pieces for Musical Clock	Widor: Two Movements from Symphony 5						
Durufle: Scherzo	Wills: Introduction and Allegro						
Andriessen: Theme and Variations	Guilmant: March on a theme of Handel	Franck: Finale in B flat					

8/9/1972	Christopher Gower	Portsmouth Cathedral		Walther: Concerto in B minor	Sweelinck: Echo Fantasia	Blow: Echo Voluntary in G	Bach: Toccata, Adagio and Fugue
8/16/1972	Rosalyn Charles	St. David's Cathedral		Schroeder: Prelude	Bach: Dorian Toccata and Fugue in D minor	Whitlock: Carol	Philip Marshall: Processional - Fanfare
8/23/1972	Michael Nicholas	Norwich Cathedral		Leighton: Paean	Howells: Saraband	Buxtehude: Prelude and Fugue in D	Reubke: Introduction and Fugue from Sonata on the 94th Psalm
8/30/1972	John Bishop	Worksop College		Rheinberger: Sonata 7	Daquin: Noel Suisse	Messiaen: Dieu parmi nous	Stanley: Voluntary in F
9/6/1972	Garth Benson	St. Mary Redcliffe, Bristol		du Mage: Grand Jeu	Dandrieu: Rondeau (La Musette)	Bach: Dorian Toccata and Fugue in D minor	Guridi: Offertoire
9/13/1972	Christopher Robinson	Worcester Cathedral		Parry: Fantasia and Fugue in G	Bach: Prelude and Fugue in B minor	Widor: Variations from Symphony 5	Bach: Schmucke dich, O liebe Seele
10/4/1972	Martin White	Armagh Cathedral		Murill: Carillon	Stanley: Voluntary in G minor	Raison: Two Pieces from 'Messe du Premier Ton'	Bach: Prelude and Fugue in C minor
6/12/1973	George Guest						
7/10/1973	Nicolas Kynaston						
7/17/1973	George Thalben-Ball	The Temple Church, London					
7/18/1973	Roger Fisher	Chester Cathedral		Bach: Toccata, Adagio and Fugue in C	Telemann: Concerto per la Chiesa	Roger-Ducasse: Pastorale	Reubke: Sonata on the 94th Psalm
7/25/1973	Garth Benson	St. Mary Redcliffe, Bristol		Raison: Offertoire on 'Vive le Roy'	Battishill: Corante and Minuet	Stanley: Introduction, Largo and Trumpet Tune	Bach: Wenn wir in hochsten noten sein
8/1/1973	Roy Massey	Birmingham Cathedal					

Brockless: Prelude, Toccata and Chaconne	Haydn: Six pieces for musical clocks	Howells: Master Tallis's Testament	Elgar: Sonata 2				
Peeters: Largo	Bonnet: Etude de Concert	Reger: Fantasia on the Chorale 'Straf' mich nicht in deinen Zorn'					
Bach: Trio Sonata 5 in C	Peeters: Aria	Messiaen: Three Pieces from 'La Nativite du Seigneur'					
Liszt: Fantasia and Fugue 'Ad nos, ad salutarem undam'							
Parry: When I survey the Wondrous Cross	Reger: Introduction and Passacaglia	Vierne: Carillon de Westminster					
Bach: Jesu Christus unser Heiland	Mathias: Invocation						
Franck: Choral 1	Vaughan Williams: Rhosymedre	Vierne: Final from Symphony 1	Improvisation on a submitted theme				
Bach: Prelude and Fugue in C minor	Howells: Rhapsody 2 in D flat	Stanford: Postlude in D	Liszt: Prelude and Fugue on B.A.C.H.				

8/15/1973	Peter Boorman	St. David's Cathedral		Cleramboult: Caprice	Reger: Canzona in B flat	Mozart: Fantasia in F minor	Herman Schroeder: Fantasie-Ricercare
8/22/1973	John Marsh	Clifton College, Bristol		Cleramboult: Suite on the First Tone	Lidon: Sonata for Trompeta Real	Lubeck: Prelude and Fugue in G major	Karg-Elert: Harmonies du Soir
9/5/1973	Garth Benson	St. Mary Redcliffe, Bristol		Handel: Overture to the Occasional Oratorio	Stanley: A Fancy	Bach: Chorale Prelude and Fugue on the Magnificat	Howells: Psalm Prelude Set 1 No. 3
9/19/1973	Dudley Holroyd	Bath Abbey		Bach: Pieces from Part 3 of the Clavierubung	Joaoa de Sousa Carvalho: Allegro	Franck: Choral 3	Messiaen: Le Banquet Celeste
7/10/1974	Nicolas Kynaston						
7/17/1974	George Thalben-Ball	The Temple Church, London					
7/24/1974	Garth Benson	St. Mary Redcliffe, Bristol		Stanley: Suite in D	Dandrieu: Rondeau (La Musette)	Pachelbel: Chaconne	Krebs: Chorale Prelude 'O God, Hear my Crying'
7/31/1974	Roy Massey	Hereford Cathedral		Mozart: Adagio and Fugue in C minor	Bach: Prelude and Fugue in D	Mendelssohn: Sonata 4	Guilmant: Canzona in A minor
8/14/1974	Dudley Holroyd	Bath Abbey					
8/28/1974	Margaret Cobb	St. Lawrence Jewry, London		Mathias: Processional	Sweelinck: Variations on 'My Young Life hath an end'	Bach: Fantasia in G	Langlais: Trois Meditations sur la Saint Trinite
9/4/1974	Garth Benson	St. Mary Redcliffe, Bristol		Stanley: Introduction and Bell Allegro	Festing: Largo, allegro, aria and variations	Zipoli: Sarabande and Giga	Bach: Prelude and Fugue in A minor
9/18/1974	Christopher Robinson	Worcester Cathedral		Mendelssohn: Sonata 4	Elgar: Four Vesper Voluntaries	Bach: Prelude and Fugue in A minor	John McCabe: Sinfonia op. 6
9/25/1974	Nicolas Kynaston			Sebastian Anguilera de Herdia: Obra de Tono VIII Alto	Bach: Concerto 4 in C	Bach: Prelude and Fugue in A minor	Liszt: Trauerode

Bach: Prelude and Fugue in A	Bach: O Lamm Gottes unschuldig	Bach: Concerto in C	Howells: Psalm Prelude Set 1 No. 1	Wesley: Prelude and Fugue in A				
Whitlock: Scherzetto	Elgar: Sonata 2	Widor: Finale from Symphony 6						
Wesley: Air and Gavotte	Franck: Chorale in A minor	Alcock: Introduction and Passacaglia						
Parry: Fantasia and Fugue in G								
Bach: Dorian Toccata and Fugue in D minor	Charles Macpherson: Andante	Howells: Rhapsody 3	Vierne: Carillon de Westminster					
Salome: Menuet Symphonique	Vierne: Impromptu	Reger: Chorale Fantasia 'Wie schon leuchtet uns der Morgenstern'						
Franck: Choral 2	Wiedermann: Berceuse	Liszt: Prelude and Fugue on BACH						
Bridge: Adagio in E	Healey Willan: Elegy and Chaconne	Alcock: Introduction and Passacaglia						
Bridge: Three Pieces	Jongen: Chant de May	Widor: Marche Pontificale						
Tournemire: Pastorale Fantaisie - Improvisation sur l'Ave maris stella	Alain: Intermezzo	Germani: Toccata op. 12	Berveiller: Cadence-Etude de Concert	Widor: Finale from Symphony 8				

10/2/1974	Fernando Germani						
6/11/1975	Simon Lindley	Leeds Parish Church					
6/18/1975	Peter Boorman	St. David's Cathedral		Bach: Sinfonia to Cantata 29	Howells: Rhapsody in D flat op. 17 no. 1	Harris: Flourish for an Occasion	Perotin-le-Grand: Deux Points d'Orgue en triple
7/16/1975	Stanley Curtis	Westminster Chapel		Bach: Prelude in C minor	Bach: Chorale 'Mortify us by Thy goodness'	Handel: Two Bourrees 'The faithful Shepherd'	Karg-Elert: O God, Thou faithful God
7/23/1975	Malcolm Pearce	Gli Amici della Musica, Bournemouth		Vaughan Williams: Prelude and Fugue in C minor	Howells: Master Tallis's Testament	Whitlock: Scherzo	Cocker: Tuba Tune
7/30/1975	Dudley Holroyd	Bath Abbey		Mendelssohn: Prelude and Fugue in C	Stanley: Voluntary in E minor	Bach: Passacaglia and Fugue in C minor	Bach: Chorale Prelude 'Nun komm, der Heiden Heiland'
8/13/1975	Roy Massey	Hereford Cathedral		Reger: Introduction and Passacaglia in D minor	Bach: Prelude and Fugue in A	Mozart: Fantasia in F minor	Franck: Prelude, Fugue and Variation
8/27/1975	David Patrick	Exeter		Bach: Toccata and Fugue in D minor	Bach: Pastorale in F	Vivaldi-Bach: Concerto in A minor	Alain: Choral Dorien
9/3/1975	Garth Benson	St. Mary Redcliffe, Bristol					
9/10/1975	Richard Lloyd	Durham Cathedral		Walther: Chorale with Variations 'Meinen Jesus lass ich nicht'	Handel: Concerto 5 in F	Bach: Passacaglia and Fugue	Parry: Melcombe
9/17/1975	John Turner	Glasgow Cathedral		Handel: Concerto in D	Reger: Fantasia on 'Wachet auf'	Bach: Allein Gott (2 claviers and pedal)	Bach: Allein Gott (Trio)
9/24/1975	John Birch	Chichester Cathedral		Bach: Allabreve in D major	Sweelinck: Variations on 'Mein junges leben hat ein end'	Hollins: Trumpet minuet	Kittel: Three Preludes

Bach: Toccata, Adagio and Fugue in C	Peeters: Largo in E flat	Jose Lidon: Sonata de 1e tono para organo con trompeta real	Derek Bourgeois: Serenade	Parry: Fantasia and Fugue in G				
Parry: Chorale Prelude on the Old 104th	Haydn: Air and Variations	Rheinberger: Two Movements from Sonata 14	Whitlock: Fidelis and Scherzo	Widor: Andante Cantabile from Symphony 4	Felton: A little tune	Guilmant: Scherzo from Sonata 5		
Vivaldi-Bach: Concerto in A minor	Alain: Deux Fantasies	Saint-Saens: Fantasie in E flat	Vierne: Carillon de Westminster					
Jongen: Sonata Eroica	Yon: Humoresque	Dupre: Prelude and Fugue in G minor						
Whitlock: Two Short Pieces	Dupre: Variations sur un Noel							
Jongen: Sonata Eroica								
Vaughan Williams: Rhosymedre	Franck: Chorale 3 in A minor							
Bach: Dorian Toccata and Fugue in D minor	Messiaen: Dieu parmi nous							
Pierne: Prelude, Cantilene and Scherzando	Howells: Sarabande for the 12th day of any October	Schumann: Fugue 2 on B.A.C.H.	SS Wesley: Andante in G	Mulet: Toccata 'Tu es petra'				

Date	Performer	Venue					
6/16/1976	Garth Benson	St. Mary Redcliffe, Bristol		Handel: Overture to the Occasional Oratorio	Zipoli: Sarabande and Giga	Bach: Fantasia and Fugue in G minor	Wesley: Air and Gavotte
6/23/1976	John Belcher	St. Peter's, Bournemouth		SS Wesley: Choral Song and Fugue	Telemann: Concerto per la Chiesa	Bach: Prelude and Fugue in G minor	Mozart: Andante in F
7/7/1976	Michael Peterson	Tewkesbury Abbey					
7/14/1976	Harold Britton	Walsall Town Hall		Handel: Concerto 4	Wesley: Holsworthy Church Bells	Mendelssohn: Sonata 1	Bossi: Scherzo
7/21/1976	Dudley Holroyd	Bath Abbey		Andriessen: Thema met Variaties	Buxtehude: Prelude and Fugue in G minor	Sweelinck: Variations on 'Mein junges Leben hat ein End'	Bach: Toccata, Adagio and Fugue in C
7/28/1976	Martin White	Armagh Cathedral		Bossi: Etude Symphonique	Couperin: Dialogue sur les Trompettes	Bach: Passacaglia in C minor	Franck: Pastorale
8/4/1976	David Seward	Loughborough Parish Church		Leighton: Fanfare	Scarlatti: Sonata in D	Pachelbel: Chorale Partita 'Was Gott thut, das ist wohlgetan'	Bach: Vom Himmel hoch da komm ich her
8/11/1976	Anthony Crossland	Wells Cathedral		Vierne: Carillon	Bach: Partita on the Choral 'O Gott, du frommer Gott'	Pachelbel: Two Chorale Preludes on 'Vom Himmel hoch'	Bridge: Adagio in E
8/18/1976	Simon Lindley	Leeds Parish Church	Guilmant: Sonata 1	SS Wesley: Andante in G	Whitlock: Four Extemporisations	Haydn: Four Pieces for Musical Clock	Healey Willan: Introduction, Passacaglia and Fugue
8/25/1976	Norman Pope		David Johnson: Trumpet Tune in C	Bach: Toccata, Adagio and Fugue in C	Stanley: A Fancy	Guilmant: Sonata 1	Jongen: Chant de Mai

Smart: Postlude in C	Dupre: Lamento	Liszt: Prelude and Fugue on B.A.C.H.					
Franck: Chorale in B minor	Harris: A Fancy	Reger: Fantasia on the Chorale 'Hallelujah! Gott zu loben'					
Wolstenholme: Allegretto in E flat	Whitlock: After an Old French Air	Whitlock: Fidelis	Wagner: The Ride of the Valkyries				
Dupre: Cortege et Litanie	Franck: Prelude, Fugue and Variation	Liszt: Fantasia and Fugue on B.A.C.H.					
Brian Brockless: Prelude, Toccata and Chaconne	Whitlock: Folk Tune and Scherzo	Peeters: Toccata on 'Pascal Alleluia'					
Bach: Liebster jesu, wir sind hier	Bach: In Dulci Jubilo	Greene: Voluntary in E flat	Dubois: Grand Choeur	Vierne: Berceuse	Vierne: Arabesque	Boellmann: Suite Gothique	
Vivaldi: Concerto in A minor	Howells: Psalm Prelude Set 1 No. 3	Franck: Piece Heroique					
Dupre: Prelude and Fugue in B							
Ives: Variations on America							

8/28/1976	Dudley Savage	BBC	A Concert of his Favourite Pieces' including selections from his Radio Two programme 'As Prescribed'	Guilmant: Paraphrase (sur un choeur de Judas Machabee de Handel)	Stanley: Voluntary	Binge: Holiday for Bells	S Wesley: Gavotte	
9/8/1976	Geoffrey Morgan	Magdalen College, Oxford		Bach: Prelude and Fugue in A minor	Schumann: Canon	Post: Partite Diverse Sopre 'De Lofzang Van Maria'	Franck: Choral No. 2	
9/15/1976	Roy Massey	Hereford Cathedral						
6/15/1977	Garth Benson	St. Mary Redcliffe, Bristol		Handel: Overture to the Occasional Oratorio	Dandrieu: Rondeau la Musette	Pachelbel: Chaconne in D minor	Bach: Fugue on the Magnificat	
6/22/1977	Christopher Robinson	St. George's Chapel, Windsor						
7/6/1977	Harry Bramma	Southwark Cathedral		Handel: Organ Concerto 7	Bach: Fantasia and Fugue in C minor	Whitlock: Plymouth Suite	Bridge: Allegretto grazioso	
7/13/1977	Geoffrey Morgan	Magdalen College, Oxford						
8/24/1977	Anthony Crossland	Wells Cathedral		Mendelssohn: Sonata 2	Howells: Sarabande	Bach: Nun komm, der Heidan Heiland	Bach: Herzlich tut mich verlangen	
9/7/1977	Marcus Sealy	Bath Abbey		Karg Elert: Choral Improvisation on 'Sleepers Wake'	Daquin: Noel in G	Bach: Toccata and Fugue in F	Karg Elert: Choral Improvisation on 'Jesu, help us conquer death'	
9/14/1977	John Birch	Chichester Cathedral						

Handel: Finale from Music for the Royal Fireworks	Saint-Saens: Le Cygne	Favourite Themes from Famous Overtures arr. Savage	Bach: Schafe konnen sicher weiden	Bach: Wir glauben all' an einen Gott	Haydn: Pieces for Musical and Mechanical Clocks	Beethoven: Ode to Joy	Strauss: Radetzky March
					Lemare: Andantino in D flat	Handel: Arrival of the Queen of Sheba	Widor: Toccata from Symphony 5
Peeters: Concert Piece	Hollins: A Song of Sunshine	Dupre: Prelude and Fugue in B					
Dupre: Lamento	Howells: Rhapsody in C sharp minor	Parry: Chorale Fantasia on 'When I survey the wondrous Cross'	Vierne: Carillon de Westminster				
Wolsten holme: Final in D flat	Hollins: Spring Song	Franck: Choral 3	Vierne: Berceuse	Reger: Dankpsalm			
Schumann: Sketch in D flat	Bach: Prelude and Fugue in C	Mozart: Andante in F	Liszt: Fantasia and Fugue on B.A.C.H.				
Durufle: Prelude and Fugue on the name 'Alain'	Peeters: Aria	Reger: Fantasia on 'Hallelujah, praise the Lord'					

Date	Performer	Venue		Piece 1	Piece 2	Piece 3	Piece 4
9/21/1977	John Belcher	St. Peter's Church, Bournemouth		Guilmant: March on a Theme of Handel	Robinson: Voluntary in A minor	Bach: Prelude and Fugue in F minor	Bach: Chorale Prelude on 'O Lamm Gottes, unschuldig'
9/28/1977	Francis Jackson	York Minster					
7/12/1978	John Wycliffe-Jones	St. Mary's Church, Weymouth					
7/19/1978	Dudley Holroyd	Bath Abbey		Cook: Fanfare	Sweelinck: Variations on 'Mein junges Leben hat ein end'	Bach: Prelude and Fugue in E minor	Howells: Psalm Prelude Set 1 No. 1
7/20/1978	Dudley Holroyd	Bath Abbey					
7/26/1978	Garth Benson	St. Mary Redcliffe, Bristol	GOT has a sprained wrist	Greene: Voluntary in C minor	Paradies: Aria and Andante	Bach: Fantasia in G	Walther: Lobe den Herren
8/2/1978	Roy Massey	Hereford Cathedral		Handel: Overture to Athalia	Bach: Toccata, Adagio and Fugue in C	Franck: Prelude, Fugue and Variation	Bossi: Scherzo in G minor
8/9/1978	Lucian Nethsingha	Exeter Cathedral		Bach: Prelude and Fugue in C	Vivaldi: Concerto in A minor	Stanley: Voluntary in E minor	Bach: Toccata and Fugue in D minor
8/23/1978	Michael Smith	Llandaff Cathedral		Alcock: Introduction and Passacaglia	Gerber: Three Inventions	Whitlock: Two Short Pieces	Mendelssohn: Sonata 3
8/30/1978	Cyril Diplock	Alton Parish Church		Rheinberger: Sonata 1	Healey Willan: Chorale Preludes	Bach: Prelude and Fugue in A minor	Bach: O Mensch, bewein'
9/27/1978	Garth Benson	St. Mary Redcliffe, Bristol		du Mage: Grand Jeu	Stanley: Echo Voluntary	Stanley: Introduction, Largo and Trumpet Tune	Bach: Fugue on the Magnificat
6/27/1979	David Victor-Smith	St. Thomas-on-the-Bourne, Farnham		Buxtehude: Toccata and Fugue in F	Albinoni: Adagio in G minor	Bach: Toccata and Fugue in D minor BWV 565	Haydn: Four Pieces for Musical Clock

Best: Introduction, Variations and Finale on 'God Save the Queen'	Karg Elert: Benediction	Reger: Fantasia on 'Wachet auf, ruft uns die Stimme'						
Reger: Introduction and Passacaglia in D minor	Messiaen: Le Banquet Celeste	Vierne: Symphony 3						
Merkel: Lobe den Herren	Reger: Lobe den Herren	Michaelson: Lobe den Herren	Reger: Variations and Fugue on the National Anthem	Howells: Psalm Prelude Set 1 No. 3	Alcock: Introduction and Passacaglia			
Liszt: Prelude and Fugue on B.A.C.H.	Bonnet: Elfes	Janacek: Finale from Glagolitic Mass	Rossi: Miniature	Dupre: Prelude and Fugue in B				
Franck: Pastorale	Peeters: Sleepers Awake	Peeters: How brightly shines the morning star	Boellmann: Toccata from Suite Gothique					
Yon: Humoresque	Cocker: Tuba Tune	Vierne: Allegro vivace from Symphony 1	Vierne: Finale from Symphony 1					
Peeters: Variations on 'Herr Jesu hat ein Gartden'	Lindberg: Gammal faboldpsalm	Franck: Piece Heroique						
Bach: Chorale Prelude on the Nunc Dimittis	Mendelssohn: Sonata 3	Bridge: Adagio in E	Franck: Choral 3					
Franck: Choral 3	Vierne: Impromptu	Liszt: Prelude and Fugue on B.A.C.H.						

7/4/1979	Colin Andrews			Bach: Fantasia in C minor BWV 562	Bach: Little Fugue in G minor BWV 578	Bach: O Mensch, bewein' BWV 622	Bach: Herr Jesu Christ BWV 655
7/11/1979	John Marsh	Clifton College					
7/18/1979	Dudley Holroyd	Bath Abbey		Guilmant: Grand Choeur in D	Bach: Nun komm, der Heiden Heiland	Bach: Prelude and Fugue in C minor	Dupre: Cortege et Litanie
7/25/1979	Garth Benson	St. Mary Redcliffe, Bristol		Handel: Overture to the Occasional Oratorio	Pachelbel: Chaconne in D minor	Festing: Largo, Allegro, Aria and Variations	Bach: Prelude and Fugue in A minor
8/1/1979	Martin White	Armagh Cathedral		Bach: Toccata, Adagio and Fugue in C BWV 564	Scronx: Echo Fantasia	Guilmant: Priere et Berceuse	Lang: Tuba Tune
8/8/1979	Ian Shaw	St. John's College, Cambridge		Bach: Prelude and Fugue in A minor	Bach: Chorale Prelude on 'O Lamm Gottes, unschulding'	Vivaldi-Bach: Concerto in A minor	Vierne: Final from Symphony 1
8/15/1979	Marcus Sealy	Bath Abbey		Bohm: Prelude and Fugue in C	Pergolesi: Sonata in F	Bach: Dorian Toccata	Bach: Nun komm, der Heiden Heiland
8/22/1979	John Birch	Chichester Cathedral		Bach: Contrapuncti 1, 9, 12 and 11 from the Art of Fugue	Kittel: Three Preludes	Hollins: Trumpet Minuet	Pierne: Prelude, Cantilene and Scherzando
8/29/1979	Michael James	Wimborne Minster		Bach: Toccata and Fugue in D minor BWV 565	Gabrieli: Fuga del 9o tono	Tomkins: A Verse of 3 Parts	Elgar: Sonata in G op. 28 1st mvmt.
9/5/1979	Francis Jackson	York Minster		Boyce: Voluntary in D	Mathias: Partita op. 19	Jackson: Sonata 3 op. 50	Bach: Ach bleib bei uns, Herr Jesu Christ BWV 649

Bach: Nun komm, der Heiden Heiland BWV 659	Bach: Gigue Fugue BWV 577	Hindemith: Sonata 3	Liszt: Variations on a theme of Bach				
Vierne: Symphony 1							
Healey Willan: Elegy and Chaconne	Parry: Chorale Fantasia on 'When I survey the wondrous Cross'	Vierne: Carillon de Westminster					
Bonnet: Variations de Concert	Whitlock: Canzona	Verschraegen: Partita on 'Veni Creator Spiritus'	Peeters: Elegie	Franck: Piece Heroique			
Jongen: Chant de Mai	Franck: Choral 3						
Bach: Prelude and Fugue in A minor	Cocker: Interlude	Guilmant: Sonata 1	Harris: Reverie	Guy Weitz: Stella Maris			
Harvey Grace: Resurgam	S Wesley: Andante in G	Reger: Dankpsalm					
Ireland: Meditation on Keble's Rogationtide Hymn	Langlais: Dialogue sur les Mixtures	Messiaen: Le Banquet Celeste	Vierne: Toccata in B minor	Galuppi: Sonata per Flauto	Liszt: Fantasia and Fugue on B.A.C.H.		
Bach: In dir ist Freude BWV 615	Debussy: Andante from the Quartet	Franck: Final					

9/12/1979	Paul Morgan	Exeter Cathedral		Bach: Prelude and Fugue in D BWV 532	John James: Echo Voluntary	SS Wesley: Larghetto in F sharp minor	Reger: Chorale Fantasia on 'Hallelujah, Gott zu loben'
9/19/1979	Roy Massey	Hereford Cathedral					
9/26/1979	Garth Benson	St. Mary Redcliffe, Bristol		Raison: Offertoire on 'Vive le Roi'	Dandrieu: Rondeau (La Musette)	Stanley: Prelude and Allegro	Bach: Chorale Prelude and Fugue on the Magnificat

Howells: Siciliano for a High Ceremony	Cocker: Tuba Tune	Durufle: Scherzo Op. 2	Vierne: Final from Symphony 1				
Michaelson: Lobe den Herren	Walther: Lobe den Herren	Reger: Lobe den Herren	Bridge: Adagio in E	Franck: Chorale in A minor			

RECITALISTS

Name	Frequency
Garth Benson	31
Dudley Holroyd	11
Nicolas Kynaston	8
Roy Massey	8
John Birch	6
Christopher Robinson	4
Francis Jackson	4
John Marsh	4
Martin White	4
Peter Boorman	4
Richard Lloyd	4
Anthony Crossland	3
George Guest	3
George Thalben-Ball	3
Robert Joyce	3
Simon Lindley	3
Stanley Curtis	3
Arthur Wills	2
Charles Myers	2
Cyril Diplock	2
Frederick Hewitt	2
Gary Desmond	2
Geoffrey Morgan	2
John Belcher	2
John Turner	2
John Wycliffe-Jones	2
Marcus Sealy	2
Melville Cook	2
Norman Wilson	2
Peter Bullett	2

Peter Stevenson	2
Richard Seal	2
Roger Fisher	2
Sidney Campbell	2
Alwyn Surplice	1
Caleb Jarvis	1
Christopher Dearnley	1
Christopher Gower	1
Christopher Jenkins	1
Colin Andrews	1
David Patrick	1
David Seward	1
David Victor-Smith	1
Derek Cantrell	1
Douglas Fox	1
Dudley Savage	1
Eric Hemery	1
Fernando Germani	1
Frederick Fea	1
Gordon Thorne	1
Harold Britton	1
Harry Bramma	1
Ian Hare	1
Ian Shaw	1
James Dalton	1
Jennifer Bate	1
John Bishop	1
John Langdon	1
John Mingay	1
John Sanders	1
Lillian Wu	1
Lucian Nethsingha	1
Malcolm Pearce	1

Margaret Cobb	1
Michael James	1
Michael Nicholas	1
Michael Peterson	1
Michael Smith	1
Noel Rawsthorne	1
Norman Pope	1
Paul Morgan	1
Peter Goodman	1
Raymond Isaacson	1
Richard Popplewell	1
Robert Gillings	1
Robert Munns	1
Robin Jackson	1
Rosalyn Charles	1
Simon Preston	1
Stanley Sackett	1
Yapp Ket Siong	1

APPENDIX H

Analysis of GOT'S Collection of Recital
Programmes by G.D. Cunningham

RECITALS

Date	Venue	Notes	Repertoire 1	Repertoire 2	Repertoire 3	Repertoire 4
		No date or venue	Bach: Fantasia and Fugue in G minor	Haydn: Andante Cantabile from Symphony in C minor	Mozart: Fantasia in F minor	S Wesley: Two Short Piece
11/11/1937	West London Synagogue	Opening recital of series	Bach: Prelude and Fugue in E minor	Brahms: Schmucke dich, o liebe Seele	Brahms: O wie selig seid ihr doch, ihr Frommen	Brahms: Es ist ein Ros' entsprungen
9/3/1941	Birmingham Town Hall		Handel: Concerto in F	Bonnet: Elves	Mulet: Carillon-Sortie	Mendelssohn: Overture from 'Ruy Blas'
9/10/1941	Birmingham Town Hall		Dubois: Fiat Lux	Haydn: Andante Cantabile from Symphony in C minor	Bach: Toccata and Fugue in C	Walker: Prelude on a hymn-tune
4/15/1942	Birmingham Town Hall		Smart: Postlude in D	Schumann: Andante con moto vivace	Bach: Prelude and Fugue in A minor	Mendelssohn: Overture from 'Hebrides'
4/22/1942	Birmingham Town Hall		Bach: Fantasia in G	Haydn: Andante Cantabile from Symphony in C minor	Mozart: Fantasia in F minor	Franck: Prelude, Fugue and Variation
9/26/1942	Trinity Congregational Church, Reading		Bach: Fantasia and Fugue in G minor	Haydn: Andante Cantabile from Symphony in C minor	Mozart: Fantasia in F minor	SS Wesley: Larghetto in F sharp minor
11/11/1942	Birmingham Town Hall		Purcell: Toccata in A	SS Wesley: Larghetto in F sharp minor	Bach: Prelude and Fugue in D	Guilmant: Lamentation
4/21/1943	Birmingham Town Hall		Beethoven: Overture from 'Egmont'	Boely: Andante con moto	Bach: Prelude and Fugue in A minor	Reubke: Sonata in C minor
5/12/1943	Birmingham Town Hall		Frescobaldi: Prelude and Fugue in G minor	Bach: Wachet auf	Guilmant: Sonata 1	Weber: Overture from 'Der Freischutz'
6/16/1943	Birmingham Town Hall		Pachelbel: Chaconne	Bach: Herzlich tut mich verlangen	Bach: In dulci jubilo	Bach: Prelude and Fugue in D
6/6/1945	Birmingham Town Hall		Buxtehude: Prelude and Fugue in F sharp minor	Cleramboult: Prelude	Bach: Passacaglia in C minor	Reubke: Sonata in C minor

316

Repertoire 5	Repertoire 6	Repertoire 7	Repertoire 8	Repertoire 9	Repertoire 10
Franck: Chorale in A Minor	Chauvet: Andantino in D flat	Schumann: Canon	Widor: Allegro vivace from Symphony 5	Gigout: Scherzo	Guilmant: Scherzo Symphonique
Brahms: Herzlich tut mich verlangen	Brahms: O Welt, ich muss dich lassen	Sowerby: Symphony in G			
Bach: Passacaglia in C minor	Franck: Prelude, Fugue and Variation	Beethoven: Finale from Symphony 5			
Weber: Overture from 'Euryanthe'	Elgar: Chanson de Matin	Rheinberger: Sonata 5			
Mulet: Carillon-Sortie	Guilmant: Meditation in F sharp minor	Durufle: Toccata			
Guilmant: Scherzo Symphonique	Howells: Psalm Prelude Set 1 No. 2	Merkel: Sonata in E minor			
Liszt: Introduction and Fugue on 'Ad nos ad salutarem undam'	Gigout: Scherzo	Franck: Chorale in A Minor	Schumann: Canon	Mulet: Toccata	
Jongen: Sonata Eroica	Wolstenholme: Canzona	Smart: Grand Solemn March			
Guilmant: Caprice in B flat	Widor: Marcia from Symphony 3				
SS Wesley: Air 'Holsworthy Church Bells'	Rootham: Epinikion				
Wolstenholme: Allegretto in E flat	Handel: Concerto in F	Bossi: Scherzo in G minor	Mendelssohn: Sonata 5		
Bridge: Adagio in E	Guilmant: Finale in E flat				

6/27/1945	Birmingham Town Hall		Bach: Fantasia in G	Gluck: Gavotte from 'Iphegenie'	Mendelssohn: Sonata 3	Jongen: Minuet-Scherzo
9/11/1945	Birmingham Town Hall		Bach: Little Fugue in G minor	Beethoven: Romance in G	Mendelssohn: Sonata 4	Franck: Prelude, Fugue and Variation
10/3/1945	Birmingham Town Hall		Pachelbel: Chaconne	Haydn: Andante Cantabile from Symphony in C minor	Bach: 'St Anne' Prelude and Fugue	Elgar: Sursum Corda
10/17/1945	Birmingham Town Hall		Handel: Concerto in F	Bach: Prelude and Fugue in A minor	Widor: Symphony 6	Bairstow: Scherzo in A flat
10/24/1945	Birmingham Town Hall		Handel: Overture from 'Otho'	Boely: Andante con moto	Bach: Toccata and Fugue in F	Franck: Chorale in A Minor
11/6/1945	Birmingham Town Hall		Bach: Prelude and Fugue in C	MacDowell: Maestoso 'AD 1620'	Handel: Concerto in G minor	Dvorak: Largo from 'New World'
11/14/1945	Birmingham Town Hall		Handel: Concerto in B flat	Haydn: Andante from 'Surprise' Symphony	Vierne: Symphony 3	Wolstenholme: The Question
11/21/1945	Birmingham Town Hall		Beethoven: Overture from 'Coriolan'	Bach: Prelude and Fugue in B minor	Franck: Pastorale	Guilmant: Sonata 1
11/28/1945	Birmingham Town Hall		Bach: Fugue in B minor	Handel: Bourree from 'Pastor Fido'	Dupre: Prelude and Fugue in G minor	Guilmant: Caprice in B flat
1/9/1946	Birmingham Town Hall		Parry: Fantasia and Fugue in G	Bach: Helft mir Gottes Gute preisen	Bach: Das alte Jahr vergangen ist	Bach: In dir ist Freude
2/27/1946	Birmingham Town Hall		Buxtehude: Chaconne in E minor	Haydn: Air and Variations from Symphony in D	Bach: Toccata and Fugue in C	Guilmant: Lamentation
3/6/1946	Birmingham Town Hall		Guilmant: March on 'Lift up your Heads'	SS Wesley: Larghetto in F sharp minor	Bach: Dorian Toccata	Elgar: Prelude from 'Dream of Gerontius'
3/12/1946	Birmingham Town Hall		Handel: Overture from 'Samson'	Bach: Nun komm, der Heiden Heiland	Parry: Toccata and Fugue 'The Wanderer'	Beethoven: Air and Variations from 'Septet'
5/15/1946	Birmingham Town Hall		Krebs: Fugue in G	Bennett: Barcarolle	Bach: Prelude and Fugue in F minor	MacDowell: Maestoso 'AD 1620'

Reger: Fantasia and Fugue on B.A.C.H.	Brahms: Schmucke dich, o liebe Seele	Brahms: Herzlich tut mich verlangen	Franck: Piece Heroique		
Boellmann: Suite Gothique	Guilmant: Prayer and Cradle Song	Harwood: Dithyramb			
Mozart: Fantasia in F minor	Reger: Intermezzo	Guilmant: Scherzo Symphonique			
Smart: Air and Variations with finale fugato					
Mendelssohn: Overture from 'Ruy Blas'	Guilmant: Canzona in A minor	Widor: Marcia from Symphony 3			
Jongen: Sonata Eroica	Ireland: Villanella	Howells: Psalm Prelude Set 2 No. 3			
Wolstenhole: The Answer	Saint-Saens: Prelude and Fugue in E flat				
Whitlock: Allegretto	Whitlock: Scherzo	Morandi: Allegretto Vivace in A minor			
Rheinberger: Sonata 7	Smyth: Du, O Schones Weltgebaude	Karg-Elert: Jesu, meine Freude			
Bach: Toccata and Fugue in D minor	Dubois: March of the Magi	Mendelssohn: Sonata 6	Gigout: Scherzo	Beethoven: Finale from Symphony 5	
Franck: Chorale in E	Walker: Prelude on a hymn-tune	Rootham: Epinikion			
Mendelssohn: Sonata 5	Hollins: Pastorale 'In Springtime'	Stanford: Toccata in D minor			
Mulet: Carillon-Sortie	Lemare: Gavotte Moderne	Harwood: Paean			
Guilmant: Sonata 5	Whitlock: Allegretto	Whitlock: Scherzo	Vierne: Finale from Symphony 1		

4/16/1947	Birmingham Town Hall		Handel: Concerto in A	Boely: Andante con moto	Bach: Fantasia and Fugue in G minor	Brahms: Schmucke dich, o liebe Seele
4/23/1947	Birmingham Town Hall		Handel: Concerto in G minor	Cleramboult: Prelude	Bach: Prelude and Fugue in B minor	Smart: Air and Variations with finale fugato
6/25/1947	Birmingham Town Hall		Saint-Saens: Prelude and Fugue in C	Haydn: Largo cantabile from Symphony in D	Bach: Passacaglia in C minor	Karg-Elert: Legend
6/28/1947	All Saints', Bournemouth	Reference to GOT; included a congregational hymn	Bach: Prelude and Fugue in D	Haydn: Andante Cantabile from Symphony in C minor	Stanford: Toccata in D minor	Karg-Elert: Legend
7/9/1947	Birmingham Town Hall		Handel: Overture from 'Occasional Oratorio'	Bach: Prelude and Fugue in A	Mendelssohn: Sonata 4	Franck: Chorale in B Minor
7/15/1947	Birmingham Town Hall		Widor: Marcia from Symphony 3	Bach: Trio Sonata 2	Guilmant: Scherzo Symphonique	Brahms: Herzlich tut mich erfreuen

Brahms: Herzlich tut mich verlangen	Mendelssohn: Sonata 1	Turner: Scherzo in F minor	Stanford: Toccata in D minor		
Mendelssohn: Sonata 5	Saint-Saens: Le Cygne	Hollins: Concert Overture in C minor			
Franck: Chorale in A Minor	Howells: Psalm Prelude Set 1 No. 1	Gigout: Allegro con brio			
Liszt: Prelude and Fugue on B.A.C.H.	Widor: Pastorale from Symphony 2	Widor: Finale from Symphony 2	Whitlock: Scherzetto	Franck: Final in B flat	
Hollins: Concert Overture in C minor	Whitlock: Scherzetto	Dubois: Fiat Lux			
Brahms: Es ist ein Ros' entsprungen	Reger: Fantasia and Fugue on B.A.C.H.	Franck: Andantino in G minor	Hollins: Grand Choeur in G minor		

REPERTOIRE

Piece	Instances
Haydn: Andante Cantabile from Symphony in C minor	6
Franck: Chorale in A Minor	4
Guilmant: Scherzo Symphonique	4
Mozart: Fantasia in F minor	4
Bach: Fantasia and Fugue in G minor	3
Bach: Passacaglia in C minor	3
Bach: Prelude and Fugue in A minor	3
Bach: Prelude and Fugue in D	3
Boely: Andante con moto	3
Brahms: Herzlich tut mich verlangen	3
Brahms: Schmucke dich, o liebe Seele	3
Franck: Prelude, Fugue and Variation	3
Gigout: Scherzo	3
Handel: Concerto in F	3
Mendelssohn: Sonata 5	3
Mulet: Carillon-Sortie	3
SS Wesley: Larghetto in F sharp minor	3
Stanford: Toccata in D minor	3
Widor: Marcia from Symphony 3	3
Bach: Fantasia in G	2
Bach: Prelude and Fugue in B minor	2
Bach: Toccata and Fugue in C	2
Beethoven: Finale from Symphony 5	2
Brahms: Es ist ein Ros' entsprungen	2
Cleramboult: Prelude	2
Dubois: Fiat Lux	2
Guilmant: Caprice in B flat	2
Guilmant: Lamentation	2
Guilmant: Sonata 1	2
Handel: Concerto in G minor	2
Hollins: Concert Overture in C minor	2

Jongen: Sonata Eroica	2
Karg-Elert: Legend	2
MacDowell: Maestoso 'AD 1620'	2
Mendelssohn: Overture from 'Ruy Blas'	2
Mendelssohn: Sonata 4	2
Pachelbel: Chaconne	2
Reger: Fantasia and Fugue on B.A.C.H.	2
Reubke: Sonata in C minor	2
Rootham: Epinikion	2
Schumann: Canon	2
Smart: Air and Variations with finale fugato	2
Walker: Prelude on a hymn-tune	2
Whitlock: Allegretto	2
Whitlock: Scherzetto	2
Whitlock: Scherzo	2
Bach: 'St Anne' Prelude and Fugue	1
Bach: Das alte Jahr vergangen ist	1
Bach: Dorian Toccata	1
Bach: Fugue in B minor	1
Bach: Helft mir Gottes Gute preisen	1
Bach: Herzlich tut mich verlangen	1
Bach: In dir ist Freude	1
Bach: In dulci jubilo	1
Bach: Little Fugue in G minor	1
Bach: Nun komm, der Heiden Heiland	1
Bach: Prelude and Fugue in A	1
Bach: Prelude and Fugue in C	1
Bach: Prelude and Fugue in E minor	1
Bach: Prelude and Fugue in F minor	1
Bach: Toccata and Fugue in D minor	1
Bach: Toccata and Fugue in F	1
Bach: Trio Sonata 2	1
Bach: Wachet auf	1
Bairstow: Scherzo in A flat	1
Beethoven: Air and Variations from 'Septet'	1

Beethoven: Overture from 'Coriolan'	1
Beethoven: Overture from 'Egmont'	1
Beethoven: Romance in G	1
Bennett: Barcarolle	1
Boellmann: Suite Gothique	1
Bonnet: Elves	1
Bossi: Scherzo in G minor	1
Brahms: Herzlich tut mich erfreuen	1
Brahms: O Welt, ich muss dich lassen	1
Brahms: O wie selig seid ihr doch, ihr Frommen	1
Bridge: Adagio in E	1
Buxtehude: Chaconne in E minor	1
Buxtehude: Prelude and Fugue in F sharp minor	1
Chauvet: Andantino in D flat	1
Dubois: March of the Magi	1
Dupre: Prelude and Fugue in G minor	1
Durufle: Toccata	1
Dvorak: Largo from 'New World'	1
Elgar: Chanson de Matin	1
Elgar: Prelude from 'Dream of Gerontius'	1
Elgar: Sursum Corda	1
Franck: Andantino in G minor	1
Franck: Chorale in B Minor	1
Franck: Chorale in E	1
Franck: Final in B flat	1
Franck: Pastorale	1
Franck: Piece Heroique	1
Frescobaldi: Prelude and Fugue in G minor	1
Gigout: Allegro con brio	1
Gluck: Gavotte from 'Iphegenie'	1
Guilmant: Canzona in A minor	1
Guilmant: Finale in E flat	1
Guilmant: March on 'Lift up your Heads'	1
Guilmant: Meditation in F sharp minor	1
Guilmant: Prayer and Cradle Song	1

Guilmant: Sonata 5	1
Handel: Bourree from 'Pastor Fido'	1
Handel: Concerto in A	1
Handel: Concerto in B flat	1
Handel: Overture from 'Occasional Oratorio'	1
Handel: Overture from 'Otho'	1
Handel: Overture from 'Samson'	1
Harwood: Dithyramb	1
Harwood: Paean	1
Haydn: Air and Variations from Symphony in D	1
Haydn: Andante from 'Surprise' Symphony	1
Haydn: Largo cantabile from Symphony in D	1
Hollins: Grand Choeur in G minor	1
Hollins: Pastorale 'In Springtime'	1
Howells: Psalm Prelude Set 1 No. 1	1
Howells: Psalm Prelude Set 1 No. 2	1
Howells: Psalm Prelude Set 2 No. 3	1
Ireland: Villanella	1
Jongen: Minuet-Scherzo	1
Karg-Elert: Jesu, meine Freude	1
Krebs: Fugue in G	1
Lemare: Gavotte Moderne	1
Liszt: Introduction and Fugue on 'Ad nos ad salutarem undam'	1
Liszt: Prelude and Fugue on B.A.C.H.	1
Mendelssohn: Overture from 'Hebrides'	1
Mendelssohn: Sonata 1	1
Mendelssohn: Sonata 3	1
Mendelssohn: Sonata 6	1
Merkel: Sonata in E minor	1
Morandi: Allegretto Vivace in A minor	1
Mulet: Toccata	1
Parry: Fantasia and Fugue in G	1
Parry: Toccata and Fugue 'The Wanderer'	1
Purcell: Toccata in A	1

Reger: Intermezzo	1
Rheinberger: Sonata 5	1
Rheinberger: Sonata 7	1
S Wesley: Two Short Piece	1
Saint-Saens: Le Cygne	1
Saint-Saens: Prelude and Fugue in C	1
Saint-Saens: Prelude and Fugue in E flat	1
Schumann: Andante con moto vivace	1
Smart: Grand Solemn March	1
Smart: Postlude in D	1
Smyth: Du, O Schones Weltgebaude	1
Sowerby: Symphony in G	1
SS Wesley: Air 'Holsworthy Church Bells'	1
Turner: Scherzo in F minor	1
Vierne: Finale from Symphony 1	1
Vierne: Symphony 3	1
Weber: Overture from 'Der Freischutz'	1
Weber: Overture from 'Euryanthe'	1
Widor: Allegro vivace from Symphony 5	1
Widor: Finale from Symphony 2	1
Widor: Pastorale from Symphony 2	1
Widor: Symphony 6	1
Wolstenhole: The Answer	1
Wolstenholme: Allegretto in E flat	1
Wolstenholme: Canzona	1
Wolstenholme: The Question	1

Composer	Instances
Bach	36
Guilmant	16
Franck	13
Brahms	11
Handel	11
Mendelssohn	11
Haydn	9
Widor	7
Beethoven	6
Whitlock	6
Gigout	4
Hollins	4
Mozart	4
Mulet	4
SS Wesley	4
Smart	4
Boely	3
Dubois	3
Elgar	3
Howells	3
Jongen	3
Karg-Elert	3
Reger	3
Saint-Saens	3
Schumann	3
Stanford	3
Wolstenholme	3
Buxtehude	2
Cleramboult	2
Harwood	2
Liszt	2
MacDowell	2

Pachelbel	2
Parry	2
Reubke	2
Rheinberger	2
Rootham	2
Vierne	2
Walker	2
Weber	2
Bairstow	1
Bennett	1
Boellmann	1
Bonnet	1
Bossi	1
Bridge	1
Chauvet	1
Dupre	1
Durufle	1
Dvorak	1
Frescobaldi	1
Gluck	1
Ireland	1
Krebs	1
Lemare	1
Merkel	1
Morandi	1
Purcell	1
S Wesley	1
Smyth	1
Sowerby	1
Turner	1

APPENDIX I

List of Broadcasts by Geoffrey Tristram on the
BBC according to BBC Genome Website
Compiled by Michael Tristram
all from Christchurch Priory unless otherwise stated
ORGANISED CHRONOLOGICALLY BY NETWORK

BBC Home Service

08.10.47	18.30	Organ (no other details of this 15 min programme on Home Service West)
24.02.48	22.15	Organ (no other details of this 15 min programme on Home Service West)
24.09.48	22.15	Organ (no other details of this 30 min programme on Home Service West)
21.12.49	22.40	Organ (no other details of this 20 min programme on Home Service West)
19.11.50	09.30	Morning service (Choral Mattins)
15.06.51	19.30	Festival of Arts with BBC West of England Singers
04.04.52	22.00	Organ & Cello Recital with Lillian Warmington
20.04.52	16.00	Choral Evensong
22.03.53	16.00	Choral Evensong
07.06.53	22.00	Organ & Baritone Recital with Frederick Harvey
21.10.53	22.00	Organ & Baritone Recital with Henry Cummings
23.05.54	19.45	Evening Service ('Act of Praise & Intercession')
06.06.54	22.15	Organ & Baritone Recital with Henry Cummings
13.02.55	22.15	Organ & Violin with Raymond Mosley
10.08.55	16.00	Choral Evensong
17.08.55	16.00	Choral Evensong
01.01.56	22.35	Organ Recital (25 mins for end of New Year's Day – no details of programme)
04.01.56	16.00	Choral Evensong
24.02.56	19.45	'Faith in the West' with GOT Interlude

28.03.57	19.00	with Southampton Singers
16.06.57	10.00	with Poole Grammar School Choir 'Anthology of Readings and Music for Trinity Sunday'
04.09.57	16.00	Choral Evensong
18.10.57	19.00	with Southampton Singers
29.01.59	22.15	Organ
12.08.59	16.00	Choral Evensong
05.08.59	16.00	Choral Evensong
03.08.60	16.00	Choral Evensong
28.12.60	16.00	Choral Evensong
23.08.61	16.00	Choral Evensong
27.12.61	09.10	Sung Eucharist
16.08.64	09.45	Choral Mattins
12.01.65	21.00	With Bournemouth Brass Ensemble
15.06.65	21.00	With Bournemouth Brass Ensemble
10.11.65	16.00	Choral Evensong
04.01.67	16.00	Choral Evensong

BBC Light Service

22.03.53	20.30	Community hymn singing mass choirs conducted by GOT

Network Three

31.08.59	19.00	Organ Recital Mendelssohn Prelude & fugue in G; Rheinberger : Monologue in D Flat; Karg-Elert :Chorale Improvisation Jesu geh voran; Francis Jackson: Fanfare, Procession, Pageant,
05.05.60	18.10	Organ Recital from Portsmouth Guildhall (no details of programme)
13.09.62	18.30	Organ Recital Scherzo Symphonique. Guilmant
04.11.62	18.30	Organ Recital from The Colston Hall, Bristol (no details of programme)
26.05.63	14.40	Organ Recital from The Colston Hall, Bristol (no details of programme)
15.09.63	14.40	Organ Recital (no details of programme)
16.01.64	14.00	Organ Recital (no details of programme)
27.09.65	11.20	Organ Recital (no details of programme)

06.01.66	18.00	Organ Recital (no details of programme)
10.10.66	15.00	Organ Recital (no details of programme)
30.03.67	10.15	Organ Recital (no details of programme)
01.05.67	17.55	Organ Recital (no details of programme)
29.11.67	10.45	Organ Recital from The Colston Hall, Bristol (no details of programme)

Radio Three

01.05.68	10.20	Organ Recital (no details of programme)
16.10.68	10.30	Organ Recital (no details of programme)
07.07.69	10.30	Organ Recital (no details of programme)
22.10.69	17.45	Organ Recital Bach: Prelude and Fugue in A (s 536) Franck: Pastorale Liszt: Evocation a la Chapelle Sixtine
05.06.70	17.45	Organ Recital Mozart: Fantasia in F minor (K 608) Preludes on hymn tunes: Charles Wood St Mary's Vaughan Williams Rhosymedre Parry St Thomas
09.09.70	16.00	Choral Evensong
16.09.70	16.00	Choral Evensong
30.03.71	09.50	Organ Recital Mozart Fantasia in F minor (k 608); Preludes on hymn tunes: Charles Wood St Mary's Vaughan Williams Rhosymedre Parry St Thomas
05.05.71	11.55	Organ Recital Bach Prelude and Fugue in D major (s 532); Bach Chorale Prelude on Ach bleib' bei uns, Herr Jesu Christ (s 649); Boellmann Suite gothique
20.08.71	10.45	Organ Recital from St John's RC Cathedral Portsmouth Bach Toccata and Fugue in D minor (The Dorian); Bach Fugue in G (The Jig): Bach Chorale Preludes: Liebster Jesu, wir sind hier (s 6331; Nun danket alle Got! (s 657): Roger-Ducasse Pastorale in F
31.12.71	09.45	'Sound of Stone' with Bournemouth Brass Ensemble & Julian Smith (Baritone)

02.05.72	11.35	Organ Recital Bach Prelude and Fugue in A (BWV 536); Widor Scherzo (Symphony No 4, in F minor); Reger Fantasia and Fugue on BACH, Op 46
14.03.73	11.05	Vierne Symphony No 3 from The Colston Hall, Bristol
29.03.74	11.45	Organ & Voices (BBC West Of England Singers) Bach Prelude and Fugue in D major Gigout Scherzo; Toccata
16.10.74	09.35	Music for Organ Bach Fantasia and Fugue in G minor (bwv 542); Stanley Voluntary in Bonnet Elfes: Caprice Héroïque Weitz Stella Maris (Symphony No 1)
25.06.75	09.45	Music for Organ Bach Fugue a la Gigue (BWV 5771, Chorale Prelude on Ach bleib bei uns. Herr Jesu Christ (BWV 649); Vierne Allegro, Scherzo and Final (Symphony 2)
15.09.76	09.40	Music for Organ Bach Prelude and Fugue in c minor (bwv 546); Franck Prelude, Fugue and Variation; Leo Sowerby Pageant
03.08.77	09.50	Music for Organ Vierne Cortege (Book 1); Arabesque (Book 2); Carillon (24 Pieces in Free Style); Widor Scherzo (Symphony No 4); Allegro (Symphony No 6)
01.03.79	09.05	This Week's Composer: Frank Bridge to which GOT contributed 'First Book of Organ Pieces'

Radio Four

| 10.01.68 | 16.00 | Choral Evensong |
| 05.10.69 | 10.30 | Morning Service |

BBC TV

| 11.08.63 | 10.30 | Choral Mattins |

BBC ONE Television

01.10.67	18.45	Harvest Festival
12.11.67	18.55	Songs of Praise
11.04.71	10.30	Sung Eucharist for Easter Day

List of broadcasts by Geoffrey Tristram on the BBC according to BBC Genome Website
all from Christchurch Priory unless otherwise stated
ORGANISED CHRONOLOGICALLY
(HS=Home Service, LT=Light, N3 =Network 3, R3=
Radio 3, R4 = Radio 4, TV =Television)

08.10.47 HS	18.30	Organ (no other details of this 15 min programme on Home Service West)
24.02.48 HS	22.15	Organ (no other details of this 15 min programme on Home Service West)
24.09.48 HS	22.15	Organ (no other details of this 30 min programme on Home Service West)
21.12.49 HS	22.40	Organ (no other details of this 20 min programme on Home Service West)
19.11.50 HS	09.30	Morning service (Choral Mattins)
15.06.51 HS	19.30	Festival of Arts with BBC West of England Singers
04.04.52 HS	22.00	Organ & Cello Recital with Lillian Warmington
20.04.52 HS	16.00	Choral Evensong
22.03.53 HS	16.00	Choral Evensong
22.03.53 LT	20.30	Community hymn singing mass choirs conducted by GOT
07.06.53 HS	22.00	Organ & Baritone Recital with Frederick Harvey
21.10.53 HS	22.00	Organ & Baritone Recital with Henry Cummings
23.05.54 HS	19.45	Evening Service (Act of Praise & Intercession')
06.06.54 HS	22.15	Organ & Baritone Recital with Henry Cummings
13.02.55 HS	22.15	Organ & Violin with Raymond Mosley
10.08.55 HS	16.00	Choral Evensong
17.08.55 HS	16.00	Choral Evensong
01.01.56 HS	22.35	Organ Recital (25 mins for end of New Year's Day – no details of programme)
04.01.56 HS	16.00	Choral Evensong
24.02.56 HS	19.45	'Faith in the West' with GOT Interlude
28.03.57 HS	19.00	with Southampton Singers
16.06.57 HS	10.00	with Poole Grammar School Choir 'Anthology of Readings and Music for Trinity Sunday'

04.09.57 HS	16.00	Choral Evensong
18.10.57 HS	19.00	with Southampton Singers
29.01.59 HS	22.15	Organ
12.08.59 HS	16.00	Choral Evensong
05.08.59 HS	16.00	Choral Evensong
31.08.59 N3	19.00	Organ Recital Mendelssohn Prelude & fugue in G; Rheinberger : Monologue in D Flat; Karg-Elert :Chorale Improvisation Jesu geh voran; Francis Jackson: Fanfare, Procession, Pageant,
05.05.60 N3	18.10	Organ Recital from Portsmouth Guildhall (no details of programme
03.08.60 HS	16.00	Choral Evensong
28.12.60 HS	16.00	Choral Evensong
23.08.61 HS	16.00	Choral Evensong
27.12.61 HS	09.10	Sung Eucharist
13.09.62 N3	18.30	Organ Recital Scherzo Symphonique. Guilmant
04.11.62 N3	18.30	Organ Recital from The Colston Hall, Bristol (no details of programme)
26.05.63 N3	14.40	Organ Recital from The Colston Hall, Bristol (no details of programme)
11.08.63 TV	10.30	Choral Mattins
15.09.63 N3	14.40	Organ Recital (no details of programme)
16.01.64 N3	14.00	Organ Recital (no details of programme)
16.08.64 HS	09.45	Choral Mattins
12.01.65 HS	21.00	With Bournemouth Brass Ensemble
15.06.65 HS	21.00	With Bournemouth Brass Ensemble
27.09.65 N3	11.20	Organ Recital (no details of programme)
10.11.65 HS	16.00	Choral Evensong
06.01.66 N3	18.00	Organ Recital (no details of programme)
10.10.66 N3	15.00	Organ Recital (no details of programme)
04.01.67 HS	16.00	Choral Evensong
30.03.67 N3	10.15	Organ Recital (no details of programme)
01.05.67 N3	17.55	Organ Recital (no details of programme)
01.10.67 TV	18.45	Harvest Festival
12.11.67 TV	18.55	Songs of Praise

29.11.67 N3	10.45	Organ Recital from The Colston Hall, Bristol (no details of programme)
10.01.68 R4	1600	Choral Evensong
01.05.68 R3	10.20	Organ Recital (no details of programme)
16.10.68 R3	10.30	Organ Recital (no details of programme)
07.07.69 R3	10.30	Organ Recital (no details of programme)
22.10.69 R3	17.45	Organ Recital Bach: Prelude and Fugue in A (s 536) Franck: Pastorale Liszt: Evocation a la Chapelle Sixtine

Late 60s-early 70s several programmes for Southern Television including being judge on 'Carols for Children', and recordings with his school choir and others for two competitions: 'Carols for Christmas' and 'Hymns for all Occasions'.

05.06.70 R3	17.45	Organ Recital Mozart: Fantasia in F minor (K 608) Preludes on hymn tunes: Charles Wood St Mary's Vaughan Williams Rhosymedre Parry St Thomas
09.09.70 R3	16.00	Choral Evensong
16.09.70 R3	16.00	Choral Evensong
30.03.71 R3	09.50	Organ Recital Mozart Fantasia in F minor (k 608); Preludes on hymn tunes: Charles Wood St Mary's Vaughan Williams Rhosymedre Parry St Thomas
11.04.71 TV	10.30	Sung Eucharist for Easter Day
05.05.71 R3	11.55	Organ Recital Bach Prelude and Fugue in D major (s 532); Bach Chorale Prelude on Ach bleib' bei uns, Herr Jesu Christ (s 649); Boellmann Suite gothique
20.08.71 R3	10.45	Organ Recital from St John's RC Cathedral Portsmouth Bach Toccata and Fugue in D minor (The Dorian); Bach Fugue in G (The Jig): Bach Chorale Preludes: Liebster Jesu, wir sind hier (s 6331; Nun danket alle Got! (s 657): Roger-Ducasse Pastorale in F
31.12.71 R3	09.45	'Sound of Stone' with Bournemouth Brass Ensemble & Julian Smith (Baritone)
02.05.72 R3	11.35	Organ Recital Bach Prelude and Fugue in A (BWV 536); Widor Scherzo (Symphony No 4, in F minor); Reger Fantasia and Fugue on BACH, Op 46

14.03.73 R3	11.05	Vierne Symphony No 3 from The Colston Hall, Bristol
29.03.74 R3	11.45	Organ & Voices (BBC West Of England Singers) Bach Prelude and Fugue in D major Gigout Scherzo; Toccata ON MAKIN ORGAN onwards
16.10.74 R3	0935	Music for Organ Bach Fantasia and Fugue in G minor (bwv 542); Stanley Voluntary in Bonnet Elfes: Caprice Héroïque Weitz Stella Maris (Symphony No 1)
25.06.75 R3	09.45	Music for Organ Bach Fugue a la Gigue (BWV 5771, Chorale Prelude on Ach bleib bei uns. Herr Jesu Christ (BWV 649); Vierne Allegro, Scherzo and Final (Symphony 2)
15.09.76 R3	09.40	Music for Organ Bach Prelude and Fugue in c minor (bwv 546); Franck Prelude, Fugue and Variation; Leo Sowerby Pageant
03.08.77 R3	09.50	Music for Organ Vierne Cortege (Book 1); Arabesque (Book 2); Carillon (24 Pieces in Free Style); Widor Scherzo (Symphony No 4); Allegro (Symphony No 6)
01.03.79 R3	09.05	This Week's Composer: Frank Bridge to which GOT contributed 'First Book of Organ Pieces'

APPENDIX J

DISCOGRAPHY

(From Christchurch Priory unless otherwise stated)
Compiled by Michael Tristram

Blue EP (Ryemuse) 1964

Widor	Toccata from 5th Symphony
Festing	Largo, Allegro, Aria & Variations

Red EP (Ryemuse) 1964

Whitlock	Folk Tune
Bach	Toccata & Fugue in D minor

Yellow LP (Ryemuse) 1965

Dubois	Toccata
Saint-Saëns	Fantasie
Alain	Litanies
Yon	Humoresque
Karg-Elert	'Ein Feste Burg'
Dubois	Fiat Lux
Gigout	Toccata
Franck	Prelude, Fugue & Variations

Ryemuse 1965 'Music for the Quiet Hours' with Raymond Mosley (Violin):

Kreisler	Praeludium & Allegro
Crowther	Gweedore Brae
Svendsen	Romance
Bach	Air on a G String
Elgar	Chanson de Matin
Tartini/Kreisler	Variations on a Theme of Corelli
Grieg	Last Spring
Tchaikovsky	Melodie

Wieniawski   slow movement 2nd Violin Concerto

This was re-released in **1970** by **Rediffusion 'The World's Best Loved Classics'** (pink) same programme

Rediffusion 1971 accompanying Bournemouth Municipal Choir:

Liszt	Missa Choralis

Grosvenor ?1971 Organ Music from Lakeland (Compton-Makin)

Bach	Fugue in E Flat ('St Anne')
Roger-Ducasse	Pastorale
Bach	Toccata in D minor ('Dorian')
Franck	Prelude, Fugue & Variations
Vierne	Carillon

Grosvenor ? 1973 accompanying the Priory Choir

Schubert	Mass in C
Griffin	Surely the Lord is in this place
Franck	Chorale in A Minor

Vista LP 1977

Stanford	Postlude in D minor
Bridge	First Book of Organ Pieces:

i) Allegretto, ii) Allegro comodo, iii) Allegro marziale

Whitlock	Salix (from Plymouth Suite)
Parry	Chorale Prelude on 'St Thomas'
Vierne	3rd Symphony

Allegro maestoso, Cantilène, Intermezzo, Adagio, Final.

Stanford	Postlude in D minor

CD VIF Records 1994 The Historic Pipe Organ of Christchurch Priory
containing all the pieces on the yellow 1965 LP + 1972 recital

Langlais	Incantation pour un jour saint
Stanford	Postlude in D minor

APPENDIX K

List of pieces on the CD or SoundCloud
Compiled by Michael Tristram

Piece	Composer	Date of live Performance at Priory	Length of each Piece Mins/secs
Fanfare	Francis Jackson (1917-2022)	16.09.71	1.14
Toccata in F	J S Bach (1685-1750)	03/11.71	8.09
Chorale Prelude 'Ach bleib bei us, Jesus Christ'	J S Bach (1685-1750)	18.07.62	3.16
Tuba Tune	Norman Cocker (1889 – 1953)	19.09.62	4.54
A Maggot from 3rd Organ Concerto)	Thomas Arne (1710-1978)	26.08.70	2.27
Fantasia in F minor	W A Mozart (1756-1791)	11.07.62	12.20
Lied (Symphony No 2)	Louis Vierne (1870-1937)	26.08.70	5.57
Pièce Héroique	César Franck (1822-1890)	12.08.70	8.16
Toccata for the flutes	John Stanley (1712-1786)	12.08.70	2.30

Allegro maestoso (Sonata No 1 in G)	Edward Elgar (1857-1934)	26.08.70	8.56
Sketch III written for piano with pedals	Robert Schumann (1810-1856)	12.09.62	2.54
Carillon de Westminster	Louis Vierne (1870-1937)	16.09.71	8.10
Aria	Flor Peeters (1903-1986)	11.07.62	3.36
Toccata 'Tu es Petra'	Henri Mulet (1878-1967)	30.09.70	4.44

Use this QR Code to gain access to the Recordings via SoundCloud

https://soundcloud.com/ted-ohare/sets/geoffrey-tristram

INDEX

A

All Saints' Church 25, 68

B

Bands 32, 33, 41, 46, 47, 48

Benson, Garth 28, 150, 159, 183

Bernard, Brother xvii, 181

Blandford, Jeremy xvii, 64, 146, 168, 190

Bournemouth xiii, 32, 33, 39, 46, 47, 48, 49, 50, 52, 53, 54, 60, 83, 85, 91, 128, 142, 148, 151, 167, 182, 189

  Symphony Orchestra 4, 33, 46, 49, 151

Bridlington Priory 120

Bristol, St Mary Redcliffe 28

British Broadcasting Corporation (BBC) xi, 25, 46, 62, 65, 72, 74, 131, 143, 150, 172

  Concert Orchestra 46

  Symphony Orchestra 4, 33, 46, 49, 151

Broad, John xvii, 92, 152

C

Cambridge University 4

Campbell, Daniel xviii, 33, 130, 140, 143, 146

Charleton-Burden, Norman 33

Choirboys 56, 61, 63, 64, 76, 85, 88, 160, 186

Christchurch Priory v, xi, xiii, xix, 25, 27, 32, 44, 55, 58, 62, 67, 68, 72, 74, 75, 84, 88, 89, 90, 93, 96, 98, 122, 126, 129, 131, 135, 142, 151, 155, 156, 183, 186, 189

  Bells xiii, 91, 185

  Heating system 130, 133

Coffin, John xviii, 37

Collier, Paul 89

Colston Hall, Bristol 140, 148

Compton-Edwards Organs 131

Compton-Makin Organs 131

Cook, Columba xviii, 41, 51, 87

Cordell, David xviii, 50

Council for the Care of Churches 135

Cunningham, G.D. 13, 14, 18, 26, 145, 146, 147, 148

D

Daughtry, Dr E.O. 4, 6, 16, 19

Dawson, John 132

Degens and Rippin (organ-builders) 146

Dinenage, Fred xviii, 45, 177

Doncaster Parish Church 22

E

Eagle, R.F. 122, 125, 126

Electronic organs 40, 131, 132, 139

F

Forsyth-Grant, Maurice 127, 128
Fox, Douglas 70, 71, 159

G

Germani, Fernando 140
Gerveshi, Christine xviii, 49
Gilbert and Sullivan Society
  (Bournemouth) xiii, 32, 33, 39,
  46, 47, 48, 49, 50, 52, 53, 54,
  60, 83, 85, 91, 128, 142, 148,
  151, 167, 182, 189
Ginn Brothers (organ-builders) 117
Glyndebourne 181, 182
Groves, Sir Charles 151, 152
Guest, Douglas 6

H

Hands, Gordon 6, 20, 167, 187
Hands, Richard xvii, xviii, 22, 65, 86,
  87, 88, 120, 139, 145, 149, 164
Helman, Harold 67
Hereford Cathedral 122, 159
Hicks, Miss V.E. 30
Holy Trinity, Bournemouth 128
Howell, Geoffrey xviii, 27, 142

J

John Compton Organ Company 65,
  66, 120, 131

K

Knight, Cyril 53
Kynaston, Nicolas xviii, 139, 158

L

Lawton-Barrett, Kevin xviii, 51
Lindley, Dr Simon xviii, 151
Ling, Laurence J. 33
Lipscombe, Nick xviii, 52
Long, Kenneth R. 28

M

Massey, Dr Roy xi, xvii, 122, 139, 159
Mitchell, Cecil 35
Morgan, Geoffrey xviii, 132, 135,
  136, 140, 142, 143, 145, 147,
  148, 149
Morgan, Gillian xviii, 75
Mosley, Raymond 150

N

Nicholson (organ-builders) 73, 130,
  135, 138
Norris, Tim xviii, 40, 43, 46, 130,
  133, 186, 189

O

O'Luby, Ray xix, 42
Orbell, Ian xix, 32
Oxford University 20, 75, 132, 175

P

Palace Court Theatre,
  Bournemouth 53
Pantlin, Lilian 27
Poole Grammar School 33, 34, 35, 37,
  39, 53
Powell, Terry xix, 50
Price, Reverend R.P. 60, 61, 62, 63,
  64, 65, 67, 68, 69, 70, 84

R

Reading School xvii, 4, 6, 7, 187, 188
Reading Town Hall 4, 140
Price, Reverend R.P. 59
Ringwood Grammar School 31, 32
Royal Academy of Music 13, 46
Royal College of Organists (RCO)
xxvii, xxviii, 6, 7, 10
Royal Festival Hall 140, 151, 152, 170

S

Saunders, Dr Percy 22
Savidge, Kenneth 35, 36
Shail, Reverend Frederick 183
Shearlock, The Very Reverend David
xix, 86, 130, 132, 146, 154
Skeet, Rayner xix, 90
Smith, Ken 160, 161
Southampton Guildhall 122
Southbourne High School 30
Southern Television 43, 45, 46
St John's, Boscombe 128
St Joseph's College Chapel, Birkfield,
Ipswich 128
St Mary's, Reading 4, 16, 18, 19
St Michael's Southampton 122
Stourbridge 1, 3, 4
    Odeon Cinema 3
St Peter's School, Bournemouth 39, 40,
41, 42, 43, 46, 47, 48, 49, 50,
51, 52, 85, 177, 189
Strange, Revd Canon Peter xix, 42, 79
Stuart, Vivian 55, 62

T

Taylor, J.I. (John Compton
director) 65
Technique 13, 14, 18, 57, 145
Choral xi, xv, xxvii, 17, 25, 29, 30,
35, 38, 44, 57, 58, 59, 62,
64, 68, 70, 75, 76, 85, 86,
90, 92, 97, 98, 169, 190
Organ xi, xiii, xiv, xvii, xxvii,
xxviii, 3, 4, 6, 7, 16, 17, 18,
19, 21, 22, 25, 27, 28, 30,
40, 41, 43, 51, 52, 55, 57,
58, 62, 63, 64, 65, 66, 67,
68, 69, 75, 76, 83, 84, 85,
87, 88, 90, 91, 92, 94, 117,
118, 119, 120, 121, 122,
124, 125, 126, 127, 128,
129, 130, 131, 132, 134,
135, 136, 139, 140, 142,
143, 145, 146, 147, 148,
149, 150, 151, 152, 158, 170,
176, 179, 183, 184, 185,
187, 189, 191
Thalben-Ball, Dr George 14, 19, 139,
147, 149
Trevor-Morgan, Reverend Basil 183
Trinity College, Dublin 4, 29
Tristram, Carolyn v, xiv, 38, 42, 48,
68, 158, 159, 160, 161, 162, 163,
168, 169, 170, 171, 179, 180,
182, 184, 190
Tristram, Geoffrey Oliver v, 1
Broadcasting 25, 36, 62, 143
Character 35, 49, 53, 57, 143,
159, 190
'Church Hatch' v, xi, xiii, xiv, 47,
59, 85, 87, 91, 125, 139,
155, 157, 158, 160, 161, 162,
163, 164, 171, 174, 175, 186

Cinema 3, 18, 124

Compositions 6, 17, 19, 64, 82, 84, 145, 147, 148, 164

Conducting 41

Early life 1

Easter Responsory 84

Education 4, 33, 48, 170, 171, 189

Estate agent 14, 15, 25, 30

Family xi, xv, 1, 4, 42, 54, 82, 83, 85, 94, 97, 146, 158, 159, 160, 167, 168, 169, 175, 176, 190

Forbears 1

Foreign students 160, 172, 176, 177

Funeral 59, 181, 183

Heart attacks xv, 79, 163, 181, 182

Illness v, 1, 16

Improvisation 86, 92, 132

Marriage 14, 59, 96

Mass xiv, xvii, 42, 43, 51, 82, 84, 98, 99, 184, 185

Memorial prize 188

Model railways 37, 85, 170

Musical 13, 28, 33, 34, 35, 37, 45, 47, 48, 50, 51, 52, 53, 55, 58, 67, 68, 82, 83, 96, 121, 122, 147, 184, 186, 189, 190

Obituaries 190

Onyx (pet dog) 159, 160

Organist and Choirmaster posts 22, 58

Organs xi, xiii, xiv, xvii, xxvii, xxviii, 3, 4, 6, 7, 16, 17, 18, 19, 21, 22, 25, 27, 28, 30, 40, 41, 43, 51, 52, 55, 57, 58, 62, 63, 64, 65, 66, 67, 68, 69, 75, 76, 83, 84, 85, 87, 88, 90, 91, 92, 94, 117, 118, 119, 120, 121, 122, 124, 125, 126, 127, 128, 129, 130, 131, 132, 134, 135, 136, 139, 140, 142, 143, 145, 146, 147, 148, 149, 150, 151, 152, 158, 170, 176, 179, 183, 184, 185, 187, 189, 191

Parents xiii, xxix, 1, 27, 56, 64, 92, 94, 96, 142, 172, 186

Patsy (family dog) 175, 182

Perfectionism 57

Practice 13, 30, 53, 55, 76, 85, 91, 139, 185

Praise 22, 29, 34, 35, 42, 70, 72, 74, 76, 175

Recitalist xi, xiii, xiv, xxi, xxvii, 16, 22, 26, 68, 132, 139, 147, 148, 151, 158, 190

Recordings xiv, xxvii, 25, 43, 44, 50, 54, 63, 68, 83, 132, 133, 143, 145, 150, 172, 173, 177, 185

Repertoire xiii, xxi, 18, 25, 64, 95, 98, 147, 148, 152

Reputation 16, 79, 82, 83, 84, 139, 152

Reviews xiv, xvii, xxvii, 17, 18, 34, 53, 67, 145

Royalties 150

Salary 22

Scholarship 13, 20, 171, 175, 186

Students xvii, 6, 14, 27, 30, 32, 33, 37, 39, 40, 42, 44, 48, 49, 50, 52, 90, 91, 95, 160, 162, 163, 172, 173, 176, 177, 189

Teaching xxviii, 30, 32, 37, 38, 39, 43, 68, 91, 96, 97, 170

Tours xxvii, 42, 98, 170, 189

Yacht Club 159

Tristram, Michael xiv, 39, 40, 42, 83, 84, 87, 130, 135, 158, 160, 162, 163, 164, 167, 169, 172, 173, 175, 176, 177, 182, 184, 186

Tristram, Rene (Irene) xxi, 20, 25, 54, 155, 158, 159, 160, 162, 163, 167, 175, 181, 184, 187

Twynham County Secondary School 33, 37, 38

W

Wakefield Cathedral 22

Wastie, David 186

Weddings 21, 27, 59, 85, 86, 87, 93, 96, 168, 170

Westminster Cathedral 6, 139, 158

Whitchurch Parish Church 22

Williams, Reverend Anthony 28

Willis, Henry (organ-builder) 4, 16, 19, 117, 121, 122, 146, 159

Winchester Cathedral 64

Worship 63, 68, 70, 72, 86, 122, 183

Wright, Dennis ('Bob') 85

Wymondham Abbey xxvii, 33

Y

Yorke, Canon Leslie 73, 75, 82

York Minster 98, 152, 153

Printed in the United States
by Baker & Taylor Publisher Services

Printed in the United States
by Baker & Taylor Publisher Services